P9-EGC-362

RED STAR

Soviet History, Politics, Society, and Thought

James Michael Holquist and
Alexander Rabinowitch,
general editors

ADVISORY BOARD

Katerina Clark

Stephen F. Cohen

Murray Feshbach

Loren Graham

Gail W. Lapidus

Moshe Lewin

Sidney Monas

S. Frederick Starr

РУКОПИСЬ ЛЕОНИДА

RED STAR

The First Bolshevik Utopia

Alexander Bogdanov

RED STAR

ENGINEER MENNI

A MARTIAN
STRANDED ON EARTH

EDITED BY
Loren R. Graham and Richard Stites

TRANSLATED BY
Charles Rougle

INDIANA UNIVERSITY PRESS • BLOOMINGTON

Copyright © 1984 by Indiana University Press

All rights reserved

No part of this book may be reproduced or utilized in any form
or by any means, electronic or mechanical, including photocopying
and recording, or by any information storage and retrieval system,
without permission in writing from the publisher. The Association
of American University Presses' Resolution on Permissions constitutes
the only exception to this prohibition.

Manufactured in the United States of America

Library of Congress Cataloging in Publication Data

Bogdanov, A. (Aleksandr), 1873–1928.
  Red star.

  (Soviet history, politics, society, and thought)
  Contents: Red star—Engineer Menni—Martian
stranded on Earth.
    1. Bogdanov, A. (Aleksandr), 1873–1928—Translations,
English. I. Graham, Loren R. II. Stites, Richard.
III. Rougle, Charles, 1946–   IV. Title. V. Series.
PG3467.M29A27   1984   897.1'33   83-48637
ISBN 0-253-17350-7
ISBN 0-253-20317-1 (pbk.)
1 2 3 4 5 88 87 86 85 84

CONTENTS

Preface

The first edition of *Red Star* appeared in St. Petersburg in 1908. It was reissued in Petrograd and in Moscow in 1918, and again in Moscow in 1922. A stage version was produced by Proletcult theater in 1920. In 1928, after Bogdanov's death, it was published as a supplement to *Around the World.* It was not again reissued in the Soviet Union for almost fifty years, until 1979, when it was anthologized in a slightly expurgated version in the collection *The Eternal Sun: Russian Social Utopia and Science Fiction.* It appeared in a German translation in 1923, and this was reprinted in 1972. An Esperanto edition came out in Leipzig in 1929, celebrating, no doubt, the Esperantists' admiration of unilingual utopias. The first English translation recently appeared in *Pre-Revolutionary Russian Science Fiction: An Anthology* (1982), edited by Leland Fetzer. There were at least six editions of *Engineer Menni* between 1913 and 1923, and it was reissued also by *Around the World* in 1929. The present translations are of the original 1908 and 1913 editions. Chronologically, *Engineer Menni* comes first as a historical novel about the social revolution on Mars long before Leonid's voyage of 1905–06. We have placed *Red Star* first, however, because it was written first and because this order makes for better reading. As a writer, Bogdanov was no master of style, and so we have given preference to clarity over literalness of translation, without omitting or violating anything essential. For the Martian place names, we have used the standard classical terminology still employed by astronomers (and used by Bogdanov in Russian translation). The illustrations for *Red Star* are taken from the 1923 Moscow edition.

The editors and translator wish to thank the following people for reading and commenting on our work: in Philadelphia, Mark Adams; in New York, Abraham Ascher and Kenneth Jensen; in Leeds, Moira Donald; in Washington, D.C., Murray Feshbach; in Helsinki, Ben Hellman, Eugene Holman, Pekka Pesonen, and Ilmari Susiluoto; in Turku, Kurt Johansson; in Berkeley, Louise McReynolds; in Freiburg, Thomas Markowsky; in Montreal, Darko Suvin. Charles Rougle and Richard Stites thank each other for what Bogdanov would have called our "com-

radely exchange of labor" in Helsinki in the summer of 1982. Loren
Graham and Richard Stites thank each other for joining together our once
independent projects. We all thank Janet Rabinowitch of Indiana University Press for her stubborn faith in our work.

RED STAR

FANTASY AND REVOLUTION
Alexander Bogdanov and the Origins of Bolshevik Science Fiction

Richard Stites

"Blood is being shed [down there] for the sake of a better future," says the Martian to the hero of *Red Star* as they are ascending to Mars. "But in order to wage the struggle we must *know* that future." The blood he speaks of was the blood of workers shot down in the streets of St. Petersburg, of revolutionaries put against the wall of prison courtyards, of insurgent sailors and soldiers, of Jewish victims of pogroms in the Russian Revolution of 1905. And by "that better future" he means not the immediate outcome of the revolution but the radiant future of socialism that will dawn on earth after revolution has triumphed everywhere. In order to inspect the coming socialist order, the hero—a Bolshevik activist named Leonid—has accepted the invitation of a Martian visitor to fly with him and his crew to Mars.

In this manner Alexander Bogdanov, a major prophet of the Bolshevik movement and one of its most versatile writers and thinkers, begins his utopian science fiction novel *Red Star,* first published in 1908. The red star is Mars; but it is also the dream set to paper of the kind of society that could emerge on Earth after the dual victory of the scientific-technical revolution and the social revolution. Bogdanov, a professional revolutionary, was one of those people, peculiar to revolutionary societies of our century, who moved easily back and forth between the barricade and the study table, the prison cell and the laboratory. He was a physician and a man of science; and he was the first in Russian fiction to combine a technical utopia, grounded in the latest scientific theories of the time, with the ideas of revolutionary Marxism. This was the central theme of both *Red Star* and his other novel, *Engineer Menni.*

Bogdanov's revolutionary Martian fantasy grew out of his personal

1

experiences as a Marxist during the Revolution of 1905, the popularity of
science fiction in Russia around the turn of the century, and his still
developing theory of tectology, the science of systems thinking and organization. Bogdanov was born in Tula in 1873 to an educated family,
studied science and psychology in Moscow and Kharkov, and received a
medical degree in 1899. By that time he had also become a Populist and
then a Marxist. On the surface, Bogdanov's path from medicine to revolution appears typical of radical Russians of that age in that so many of
them—Mark Natanson, Fëdor Dan, Vera Figner, among others—had begun their love affair with "the people" by learning how to cure their
physical illnesses. Unlike most of them, Bogdanov did not abandon science for revolution: rather, he deepened and extended his study of physi-
ology, technology, and natural science and combined them with his own
version of Marxian sociology. An early member of the Marxist Russian
Social Democratic Party—the matrix of Bolshevism and Menshevism—
Bogdanov worked as an underground agent, fomenting agitation and dis-
seminating propaganda among workers, students, and educated society in
Moscow as well as in provincial towns far distant from the two capitals. In
terms of on-the-spot experience, he was one of the best informed of the
Social Democrat leaders about actual life and labor conditions in Russian
cities. As a physician he was also keenly aware of the social misery of poor
people in the burgeoning factory centers of industrializing Russia. His
repugnance for the contemporary city reveals itself in his loving description of the utopian factory settlements of *Red Star* and the dreadful working conditions in *Engineer Menni*. Numerous arrests and terms in exile
punctuated his revolutionary career, and these experiences—often called
the university education of radicals—threw him into contact with like-
minded young thinkers and rebels such as Anatol Lunacharsky, future
Bolshevik Commissar of Education and Culture, Fëdor Bazarov, a well-
known economist, and I. I. Skvortsov-Stepanov, publicist, economist, and
writer on atheism.

     When the newly formed Russian Marxist party split into Bolsheviks
and Mensheviks in 1903, Bogdanov—like the hero of *Red Star*—chose
the more impetuous and revolutionary current of Bolshevism headed by
Lenin. Bogdanov was among the original Bolsheviks (not yet a separate
party), one of those "twenty-two," with Lenin as the central figure, who
fashioned in Switzerland early in 1904 a group dedicated to disciplined
revolutionary action. In the stormy years of war and revolution from 1904
to 1907, Lenin and Bogdanov were close associates, with Lenin mostly in
emigration and Bogdanov inside Russia organizing and directing the
underground network of party cells and organizations. In 1905 the social
unrest that had been brewing since the 1890s exploded in a revolution
that swept over the vast expanse of the Russian land. In an unprecedented display of revolutionary energy, workers, peasants, soldiers,

sailors, intellectuals, teachers, students, schoolchildren, priests, actresses, musicians, and people of every rank of society revolted; they demonstrated, shouted down their former masters, fought, struck, boycotted, burned out manor houses, and in every imaginable way disrupted society. In the midst of this ferment, Tsar Nicholas II issued a constitution and created a parliament. Then the authorities struck out with vengeful fury to punish the insurgents and restore order to the beleaguered empire. Martial law, drumhead trials and shootings, brutal punitive expeditions, and murderous repression of urban uprisings crushed the radical wing of the revolution and drowned it in blood.

Bogdanov, like thousands of other revolutionaries, was seized with the spirit of insurgence, heroism, and hope. He saw what superior military technology could do against insufficiently armed and organized revolutionary forces. And yet the revolutionary élan generated by the recent events was so highly developed that even in the summer of 1907, when the tide was visibly and rapidly ebbing, Bogdanov was still hoping for a resumption of action that would turn the tide again. This led him to a tactical quarrel with Lenin, who was convinced that the revolution was over. And it led Bogdanov to write *Red Star*—a novel of revolutionary optimism set in a far-distant utopia.

The spectacle of fire and devastation in the 1905 revolution formed the backdrop for Bogdanov's story. The revolution is the scene of the opening and the closing chapters, and it also underlies the fantasy world of Mars. The voyage itself and the accompanying technological explanations, though striking in predictive detail, were not wholly original. "Mars, gleaming red and hateful," had been the object of fascination to astronomers since antiquity. But the man most responsible for generating public speculation about life on Mars for almost a century was Giovanni Schiaparelli, whose observations in the late 1870s and early 1880s from a Milan observatory led him to use the word *canali* to indicate the straight lines he detected on the surface of the planet. The word, normally meaning channels or natural waterways, was quickly mistranslated as "canals," suggesting massive engineering projects, a huge labor force, and advanced minds (it had recently taken ten years to dig a hundred miles of the Suez Canal). The specter of human life on Mars was fleshed out by the American astronomer Percival Lowell, who claimed to have identified four hundred canals by 1900. His *Mars and Its Canals* (1906), with its depiction of a complex network of man-made waterways, great engineers, and a struggle against a dying environment, may have been a direct inspiration for Bogdanov.

The first novel to capitalize on Schiaparelli's "canals" was Percy Gregg's *Across the Zodiac*, which appeared in London in 1880, complete with "apergy"—an antigravity substance—huge canals, an engineer hero, advanced humans, and orange vegetation with red foliage, all discovered by human astronauts. More ambitious and plausible was Kurd Lasswitz's *Auf zwei Planeten* (1897), which brought large-eyed Martians to Earth. In an elaborate plot, Martians and Earthmen, Martian militarists and pacifists, are locked in friction. The issues are finally resolved in favor of democracy and peace. (A generation of German scientists was raised on this novel, although it was banned by the Nazis in the 1930s for its exaltation of internationalism and antimilitarism.) In 1897–98 also appeared the much more famous *War of the Worlds* by H. G. Wells, a writer who enjoyed enormous popularity in Russia at the time. Bogdanov in 1908 may have drawn from all of these, updating them with the latest speculation in science and technology, including the writings of the Russian rocketry pioneer Konstantin Tsiolkovsky. What Bogdanov added was a communist utopia on Mars.

But there was also a rich native tradition of utopian science fiction to draw from. From about 1890 to the eve of the Revolution of 1917, at least twenty Russian tales of utopian societies, fantastic voyages, and interstellar space travel appeared. Some of these were blatant copies of the numerous Western science fiction novels that were widely circulated and serialized in translation in the same period. Others drew on native Russian utopian dreams of the nineteenth century, such as Vladimir Odoevsky's *The Year 4338* (1840), Nicholas Chernyshevsky's *What is to Be Done?* (1863), and Vladimir Taneev's *The Communist State of the Future* (1879). Still others were antisocialist tracts written in the form of "warnings" of the danger of utopian collectivism, materialism, and a dehumanizing high technology—predecessors of the famous anticommunist dystopias of the mid-twentieth century: Eugene Zamyatin's *We* (1920), Aldous Huxley's *Brave New World* (1931), and George Orwell's *1984* (1948). In addition to these, scientific and popular science journals of the period were full of stories and speculations about rocketry, space travel, alien life, and new forms of energy and fuel. There is hardly anything in the technology of Leonid's voyage to Mars that did not appear either in scientific writings or in the science fiction of the period before 1907.

The industrialization of Russia in the 1890s and the accompanying growth of technology, transport, and urbanization opened up broad vistas for utopian speculation. A whole series of European and American utopias appeared in Russian translation between 1890 and 1905: the works of August Bebel, Friedrich Engels, Karl Kautsky, Atlanticus, and Lili Braun, with their exaltation of electricity, communal apartment living, and the technologizing of everyday life, captured the imagination of Russian socialists who were looking for the ultimate purpose of revolution to inspire themselves and their followers—a dream of a golden future where men and women could work, study, and love in total freedom, harmony, and community, liberated from the backwardness, poverty, and greed which had always tormented humanity. In this sense, utopia was seen by Bogdanov (through the eyes of his hero) as a weapon in the arsenal of revolution: a snapshot of man's future that would dazzle the eye of the worker and inspire him more deeply than could the arid words of party programs.

Studies of reading habits in tsarist Russia have shown that the urban lower classes were far more interested in adventure tales than in polemical propaganda. Bogdanov, who had close connections with workers, knew this. And socialist writers had no monopoly on futuristic fantasy. In 1895 the engineer V. N. Chikolev wrote an "electric tale" of a coming world transformed by technology, particularly electricity, that could provide everything human life needed, including musical concerts. L. B. Afanasev's *Journey to Mars* (1901), on the other hand, was a warning against industrialization per se, whether capitalist or socialist. Using Martian society as a vehicle, the author related how the appearance of cities, roads, and factories turned the simple, primitive, trusting, rural Martians (read the peasants of Russia) into greedy, competitive, cannibalistic brutes and egoists—into what Afanasev called "the nervous society." More devastating yet was N. Fëdorov's *An Evening in the Year 2217* (1906), with numbered citizens, monstrous conformity, abolition of marriage and family, sex by appointment, and a lifeless socialist urban milieu of glass and stone—a virtual prototype for Zamyatin's *We*.

Bogdanov, in constructing his utopia on Mars, was not indifferent to the dangers of collectivism and high technology projected by some of the anti-utopian fantasies of the late tsarist epoch. He may well have had some of the dark warnings in mind as he set out to describe, through Leonid's narrative, the "self-adjusting" and socially just world on Mars. Indeed, he was acutely aware of the dreadful consequences of a premature revolution in a backward society. But a deep-seated belief in the rational power of "systems" prevented him from descending into the depths of social pessimism or cosmic fear—a feeling that enveloped many thinkers after the failure of the 1905 revolution.

Bogdanov's systems thinking, still developing when he wrote *Red Star*, eventually blossomed into a full-scale theory which he called "tectology." The term, borrowed from Ernst Haeckel, denoted a study of the regulatory processes and the organization of all systems, a "general natural science." As a physician and a political ideologist, Bogdanov was struck by the systemic analogies between living organisms and societies, between scientific and social organizations and processes. His main goal was to suggest a super-science of organization that would permit regulative mechanisms to preserve stability and prevent cataclysmic change in any of life's major processes—including the production and distribution of goods. As a Marxist he believed this to be possible only under a system of collective labor and collectivized means of production; but he also believed that Marx had to be updated by means of contemporary scientific and organizational discoveries. The complex theory of organization that he devised and revised in the 1910s, tectology, has often been cited as an early version of cybernetics or systems thinking. Thus one of the functions of *Red Star,* with its highly elaborate Martian system of feedback, information control and retrieval, statistics, protocomputers, regulation, and "moving equilibrium," was to lay out the author's first thoughts on the theory that has won him so much attention in recent years, both in the Soviet Union and in the world at large.

Bogdanov combined his Marxist convictions, his revolutionary experiences of 1905, and his facility for technological projection in his fantasy of life on Mars in the early twentieth century. Failed revolutions and even enforced isolation, as in a counterrevolutionary prison cell, have often produced free flights of fantasy. Nicholas Chernyshevsky wrote the famous utopian "Dream of Vera Pavlovna" in *What is to Be Done?* while languishing in the Peter Paul Fortress. The terrorist Nicholas Kibalchich designed a flying machine in 1881 while awaiting his execution (a crater on the Moon now bears his name). Nicholas Morozov, a long-time inhabitant of the Schlüsselburg Fortress prison, wrote in 1910 a lighthearted account of a voyage to the moon describing the joy of flight experienced by himself and his fellow astronauts—all former political convicts. The revolutionary euphoria that had seized so many thinkers and writers in the years 1905–07 and had produced so many apocalyptic visions and assorted dreams of an imminent New Jerusalem also permeated the spirit of Bogdanov and endowed his social vision with a sense of immediacy and hope. A rank-and-file Bolshevik of the period recalled that he and his comrades read Bogdanov's novel with enormous enthusiasm and saw it as a sign of renewed and triumphant revolutionary upheaval. What they overlooked at the time, as he later admitted, was the novel's principal theme: the organization of society in the socialist future. Yet the high drama of the work lies precisely in the wonderfully contrived juxtaposition of a unified, harmonious, serene, and rational life on Mars with the chaotic, barbarous, and self-destructive struggles of the peoples and social classes of twentieth-century Earth.

The vegetation on Bogdanov's Mars (as on Wells's) is red, and the hero calls it socialist vegetation. This is one of the few playful devices in the novel. For the most part *Red Star* is a straightforward science fiction utopia. Leonid, the protagonist, is a Bolshevik at the time of the 1905 Revolution caught up in political work and a dying romance. A mysterious comrade from the south of Russia reveals himself as a Martian, explains his mission on Earth, and invites Leonid to Mars. The episodes of the Revolution and the voyages are the frame of the story; at its center is the description of Martian society. The irony, an almost invariable feature of science fiction utopias, is particularly sharp in the contrast between a Russia devoured by "problems" and a Mars where such problems have long since vanished.

In Russia, for example, three major problems that beset society and state were the peasant question, the national question, and the labor question. But on Mars there were no peasants. Farming had been industrialized, and rustic life—which Marx had called idiotic—no longer existed. Nor were there any nationalities. Mars, with a population smaller than Earth's, had an ethnically homogeneous race with a single language (another utopian dream, by the way, made popular in Russia at that time by the Esperantists). Workers or laborers existed, of course: but since everyone was a worker who produced according to capacity and consumed according to desire, there was no "labor question" as such. Bogdanov also addressed on Mars the vexing question of the opposition and contradiction between city and countryside—a big problem of Russian social history up to Stalinist times. Unlike More, Campanella, and Morelli, Bogdanov does not aspire to destroy the countryside. Unlike Rousseau, Ruskin, and Morris, he does not aspire to destroy the city. He creates a whole new kind of arrangement that is neither country nor city, though retaining elements of both.

On Bogdanov's Mars there is no state and no politics, although there are clothes made of synthetic material, three-dimensional movies, and a death ray. People are quartered in various kinds of urban and semiurban planned settlements, such as the Great City of Machines or the Children's Colony. Voluntary labor alternates with leisure and culture, and the drama of life is provided by the never-ending struggle with the natural environment—not with other people. The climax of the story occurs when someone tries to alter this Martian scenario.

The systematization of the productive process is the main focus of the hero's interest. Factories are operated by electrical power and fully automated. "Moving equilibrium" is maintained by data retrieval machinery in all enterprises. Data on stockpiles and inventories, production rates, and labor needs according to specialty are channeled into a Central Institute of Statistics, which collates and computes the information and sends it where it is needed. Since consumption is unlimited, all work is voluntary and unpaid. Short workdays and the rotation of jobs reduce the menace of alienation and psychic enslavement to the machine. Bogdanov, though he certainly revered machines, feared and hated the system of capitalist production that made human beings appendages to machinery. He thus not only fought against the so-called Taylor System of industrial labor but also against the Bolshevik "Taylorists"—particularly Alexei Gastev, the greatest proponent of man-the-machine mentality. Planning, productivity, labor discipline, and recruitment—all problems of developed industry outlined in the novel—became issues of heated debate among Soviet planners of the 1920s and 1930s. No wonder that Bogdanov's novel was sometimes invoked at the dawn of the First Five-Year Plan by economic chieftains and planners.

"SCIENTIFIC SOCIALISM"

      Equality and collectivism are the social values held in highest esteem by Martians. Even on the voyage out, the captain's role as commander is deemphasized and he is ranked along with the rest of the crew as a specialist. Rules and regulations are minimal and are based upon science, not on philosophical or religious moral values. Coercive, authoritarian, categorical "norms" were as repugnant to the author as they had been to Nietzsche, whom Bogdanov had once admired. Equality expressed itself on Mars in many ways: the absence of gender in names, unisex clothing, and the businesslike intercourse among people, free of superfluous greetings and empty politeness—reminiscent of the Russian nihilists of the 1860s. There are people of superior talent on Mars, but they are afforded no special prizes or recognition in life or after death. The monuments on Mars are erected to commemorate historic events, as products of collective wills, and not to heroes. After the Russian Revolution of 1917, a kindred surge toward anonymity, egalitarianism, collective creativity, and iconoclasm burst forth for some time before it was repudiated by the authorities, who soon began to set up live heroes, stone statues, and cultic idols of the Revolution. Bogdanov's ultimate gesture of fraternal solidarity on Mars was the "comradely exchange of life" in which mutual blood transfusions were employed to prolong life.

      Bogdanov clung to his vision of collective creativity after the Revolution of 1917. In a reply to Gastev written in 1919, he said that in proletarian cooperation, comradely recognition of competence would replace authority and force in the workplace and that leadership roles would be rotated according to the task and the talent:

> The proletarian collective is distinguished and defined by a special organizational bond, known as *comradely cooperation.* This is a kind of cooperation in which the roles of organizing and fulfilling are not divided but are combined among the general mass of workers, so that there is no authority by force or unreasoning subordination but a common will which decides, and a participation of each in the fulfillment of the common task.*

      From his central premises about collectivism, anti-individualism, and a wide arena for personal choice, Bogdanov's depiction of other features of Martian life flow neatly and consistently. The scenes in the Children's Colony, where upbringing is collective, in the hospital, where suicide rooms are available, and in the Museum of Art, where the themes of facing death and the dignity of labor are celebrated—all these are extensions of Bogdanov's social philosophy. They also reflect debates then current among the intelligentsia about childrearing, family, and educa-

---

*Quoted in Kendall Bailes, "Alexei Gastev and the Soviet Controversy over Taylorism, 1918–24," *Soviet Studies,* 29/3 (July 1977), 380.

tion, about suicide, which ran rampant after the collapse of the revolution of 1905, and about the meaning and function of art.

But the recurrent discussion of sex and love requires more than a passing comment. Debate on the "sexual question" reached a crescendo in Russia at the very moment when *Red Star* was published. Love, marriage, divorce, birth control, abortion, prostitution, and sexuality were hotly discussed in the media, especially in the years between Leo Tolstoy's *Kreutzer Sonata* (1889) and Michael Artsybashev's *Sanin* (1908). Outraged society took issue particularly with sexual "decadence" as illustrated in *Sanin;* and the many nuances between "comradely union," free love, and promiscuity were canvassed endlessly in the press and in popular brochures. The accompanying wave of suicides in 1907 and 1908 led cultural critics of the time to link sensualism and suicide as forms of self-destruction and escapism born of the recently failed revolution and the upsurge of repression. Among socialists in Russia the debate on sex was especially painful and ambivalent because socialism generally inscribed high moral behavior as well as personal liberation on its banner. In 1908 a socialist woman physician, A. P. Omelchenko, linked *Red Star* and *Sanin* in a book attacking free love and upholding the family.

How did Bogdanov treat the sexual issue under communism? Leonid in fact does resemble Sanin, the vulgar amoralist of Artsybashev's creation. Both are in love with life and sneer at the notion of moral duty. But there the similarity ends. Sanin is a wild libertine and seducer who scorns all values and all causes. Leonid, on the other hand, finds personal expression in the proletarian cause and, though he believes that polygamy is more life-enriching than monogamy, he does not practice it until he arrives on Mars. There his shallow Nietzscheanism undergoes a series of shocks. Leonid's advanced and conventionally radical ideas on sex seem old-fashioned indeed on a planet where the words "liaison," "affair," "romance," and "marriage" have the same meaning. Bogdanov, like his contemporary and fellow Marxist Alexandra Kollontai—who shared many of Bogdanov's ideas on collectivism and antiauthoritarianism—was groping experimentally toward a reasonable and yet warmhearted solution to the question that has plagued so many dreamers and social reformers throughout the ages: how to reconcile personal freedom with the need for long-time loyalties, commitments, and emotional stability. Dr. Omelchenko, gently chiding her fellow socialist, Bogdanov, proclaimed that the family, not free love, would be the social base of the new socialist order because it did not violate the spirit of collective life and labor but rather enhanced it. Not surprisingly, a recent Soviet edition of Bogdanov's novel saw fit to omit Leonid's ruminations on marriage and sex.

After the survey of society, mandatory in almost all utopias, Leonid is permitted to enter into an emerging drama, one that threatens to pit planet against planet, man against man. Bogdanov extricates his hero and returns him to the explosive urban battlefields and barricades of Moscow as the Revolution of 1905 nears its climax.

The circumstances under which *Engineer Menni* was written in 1912 were very different from those of 1907. Bogdanov's dream of an imminent upsurge of the proletarian offensive in Russia was ill-founded. By 1908 the reaction was in full swing and tsarist authorities were in full command of the situation. Many members of the intelligentsia and of educated society at large fell into a mood of postrevolutionary despondency and withdrawal. Mysticism, the occult, and even what was then considered pornography came into vogue. Social daydreamers now sought salvation in personal liberation and predictions of a revolution of the spirit. Some former revolutionary thinkers turned to religion—and even to conservatism and nationalism. Those who clung to revolutionary political tactics and programs were either banished to the fringes of the Russian state or forced into emigration. Bogdanov was among the latter. The expatriate world of Russian revolutionaries—Geneva, London, Paris, Stuttgart, Capri—was a world of disappointed men and women who lashed one another with bitter recriminations and ideological squabbles. One of these differences of opinion was the break between Bogdanov and Lenin.

At the end of *Red Star,* Bogdanov makes fleeting reference to the Old Man of the Mountain, an invaluable, hardheaded, but somewhat conservative and inflexible revolutionary leader. Bogdanov was clearly referring to his comrade Lenin. The two men fell out over philosophical and tactical questions. The philosophical controversy had begun to emerge years earlier when Bogdanov embraced the epistemological theories of Ernst Mach, the Austrian scientist who denied the existence of a material world independent of the observer. To Mach the world was only organized perception and nothing more. Bogdanov's acceptance of "empiriomonism," as this latest version of a very ancient idea was called, evoked an assault from George Plekhanov, the father of Russian Marxism, who wounded Bogdanov to the quick by addressing him in print as "Gospodin" (mister) instead of as "comrade." Lenin kept his own hostility to Machism muted for some time, until, in 1908, he could no longer contain it and wrote the famous massive polemic *Materialism and Empiriocriticism.* This was after the appearance of *Red Star.* Lenin mentioned the novel only once, briefly and obliquely, in an ironic comment about Lowell's *Mars and Its Canals.*

The philosophical duel merged with the political fight, of more recent duration. This latter was based upon Bogdanov's insistence on the possibility of mounting a new armed uprising in 1907 and 1908. Because of this he diverted party funds into revolutionary partisan operations and vigorously opposed Bolshevik participation in the new parliament. The break which ensued was, in the last analysis, caused by a fundamental difference between an increasingly rigid and ideologically authoritarian Lenin and a Bogdanov whose encyclopedic knowledge of the sciences and whose personal proclivities toward revolutionary action could not be reconciled to the views of a self-appointed and self-righteous leader. Bogdanov recalled years later in his autobiography that the barracks and prisonlike atmosphere of his school had taught him as a schoolboy "to fear and to hate those who coerce and to flaunt authority."

Bogdanov spent the years 1908–1914 in Western Europe. He and his associates retreated to Italy, to the island of Capri, where Gorky had been living since 1906, and founded a party school for workers. Bogdanov, Lunacharsky, Gorky, Bazarov, and Skvortsov-Stepanov, now estranged from Lenin's party, taught there, as did non-Bolsheviks Trotsky, Pokrovsky, and Menzhinsky. All of these men would hold important posts in Soviet life after the revolution, at least for a while. Bogdanov continued to develop his system of tectology; Gorky and Lunacharsky engaged in what was called "god-building"—the attempt to forge a religion out of socialism. And all of them tried to create the basis for a new proletarian culture. By the time of the composition of *Engineer Menni* in 1912, most of Bogdanov's friends had drifted back into the Bolshevik party. Bogdanov abandoned active political work in 1911 and devoted his time exclusively to the organizational science and proletarian culture. *Menni* was one of the fruits of this decision.

Engineer Menni combines the then-current speculation about the natural history of Mars with a plausible story of canal construction and class struggle. It is a historical novel about economic development, political change, and revolutionary labor movements on Mars in the seventeenth century—anticipating the events of Bogdanov's time by three hundred years. The structure of the history is straightforward Marxism, schematic in places but cleverly contrived. By placing the class struggle in "nowhere" (utopia), Bogdanov universalizes the Marxist scheme of history, suggesting that something like it would happen "everywhere." To dramatize the process, Bogdanov provides fictitious characters who represent various aspirations of struggling forces in the painful process of Martian modernization. These are not brilliant portraits, but they are far from being simple pasteboard figures speaking political platitudes. Menni, the chief protagonist, is a sympathetic person, upright and decent, but one who happens to be on the wrong side of the barricades in the fight between progress and conservatism. In his rigid logic and rugged individualism, he resembles in many ways the Nietzschean and Darwinian characters in some of Ayn Rand's novels (her formative years were spent in revolutionary Russia). Bogdanov's technological premise was taken from Schiaparelli and Lowell. The latter's theory of man-made canals for irrigation was long opposed even in his time and was definitely disproved in the 1960s and 1970s by the Mariner and Viking missions.

Mars and Marx,* the red planet and the red philosopher, are thus combined to provide the historical explanation of the communist society described in *Red Star.*

Engineer Menni is a novel about socialists and labor leaders, capitalist villains and blind aristocrats—but it is especially a novel about engineers, a profession that has played an enormously important role in Russian and Soviet development in the last ninety years and is only recently being studied by serious scholars. Despite Bogdanov's desire to play down the hero and the individual of great talent, technological heroes dominate this book: Menni, the engineer of genius, master of planning and efficiency, and his son Netti, who, like Bogdanov himself, devotes his later life to an encyclopedic study of work and an all-embracing science of organization. It was precisely this celebration of technocratic power, of the technical intelligentsia, and of self-correcting systems and moving equilibria based on science, and the corresponding downplaying of proletarian energy, party authority, and class struggle, that caused orthodox Bolsheviks to look askance at the author—a man who lived before his time.

In the scene depicting a workers' meeting, Bogdanov discloses some of the elements of his theory of "proletarian culture." Like the Bolsheviks with whom he had just parted company, Bogdanov (through the voice of Netti) teaches a doctrine of sacrifice of the few in the present time for the welfare of the many not yet born; unlike them, he also insists upon fairness in all human relations, including the treatment of enemies. Bogdanov believed in the inherent egalitarianism of all workers (who address each other as "brothers"), but also was painfully aware that the intelligentsia and the more politically and socially aware workers, while able to represent the aspirations of an entire class as a species, rise above the proletariat and become detached from them. The problem of the elite who *know* and the masses who are constrained to *believe* is poignantly illustrated in the moving lament of the bewildered worker at the meeting. Bogdanov's answer—again voiced by Netti—is the creation of a unified science of organization that will link all the sciences, currently fragmented, to the processes of labor and life. And in the debate between Menni and Netti, father and son, the author presents his own sociology of ideas and feelings and an original gloss on the Marxian philosophy of history.

How were these novels received in Russia? The moderate Populist journal *Russian Wealth* dismissed *Red Star* as trendy, derivative, and unmoving. Neither wing of Russian Social Democracy reviewed it. On the other hand, a Bolshevik reviewer of 1918 recalled, as we have seen,

---

*Xarma, the Martian socialist philosopher in the story.

how inspiring the novel was to rank-and-file party workers even after the revolution had subsided. After the Bolshevik Revolution of 1917, *Red Star* became very popular and was reprinted at least five times inside the Soviet Union, including once as a supplement to a very widely read popular science magazine, *Around the World.* "The first utopia embellished with proletarian pathos," as one critic has called it, was well received in Party circles after the Revolution. A writer in *Messenger of Life,* a journal for proletarian culture, announced that Bogdanov's utopian vision contained scientific laws and features of life already discernible in the revolutionary Russia of 1918.

The most incisive review of *Red Star* was written by Lunacharsky just as it came out. He praised the poetry and prophecy of innovation and the scientific insight of Bogdanov's futurology, defending the author from literary purists who might object to his pedestrian style. Bogdanov's art was in his contrasting of the "crystal atmosphere of rationality that reigns on Mars," its lack of drama, color, and passion, with the stormy scenes of Earth's contemporary life. Lunacharsky saw the brutally analytical speech of Sterni, the would-be destroyer of Earthlings, as the high point of the novel.

Bogdanov's predictions of 1908, put into the mouth of Sterni, are eloquent indeed. Like the American socialist Jack London, whose *Iron Heel* was written in the same year, Bogdanov warns of the coming time when capitalists and ruling classes would use the latest technology to persecute and provoke the proletariat into a premature uprising which the provocateurs would then crush. On the militaristic *revanchisme* of the day Sterni says:

> Patriotic fervor intensifies and becomes extremely acute after military defeats, especially when the victors seize a part of the loser's territory. The patriotism of the vanquished then takes the form of an intense and prolonged hatred of the victors, and revenge becomes the ideal of not just the worst groups—the upper or ruling classes—but of the entire people, including the best elements, the toiling masses.

Bogdanov also perceived the growth of what Lenin would call "social patriotism" in 1914, the desire of European Marxist Social Democrats, in defiance of their allegiance to internationalism, to fight off and defeat the national enemy. Socialists, says Sterni, in reference to a Terrestrial-Martian war, "would start a bitter and ruthless war against us [Martian liberators], because they would never be able to reconcile themselves to the killing of millions of their own kind to whom they are bound by a multitude of often very intimate ties." The most striking of all these passages, one that must have jolted both Lunacharsky and Bogdanov in later years, referred to the possibility of a revolution and the establishment of a few islands of socialism surrounded by a hostile capitalist sea.

These would be beleaguered by the capitalist states. "It is difficult to foresee the outcome of these conflicts," says Sterni, "but even in those instances where socialism prevails and triumphs, its character will be perverted deeply and for a long time to come by years of encirclement, unavoidable terror and militarism, and the barbarian patriotism that is their inevitable consequence. This socialism will be a far cry from our own."

Engineer Menni attracted less attention than had *Red Star*, coming as it did in 1913, when hopes for revolution were not high. The Populist journal *Testaments* was very negative and considered it dry, schematic, and contrived. Lenin wrote to Gorky in 1913: "Just read his *Engineer Menni*. Another case of Machism and idealism, but obscured so that neither the workers nor the silly editors at *Pravda* understood it." The Bolshevik reviewer of 1918 referred to above recalled that the mood of skepticism and pessimism was so deep among his people when *Menni* came out that they could not apprehend its extravagant picture of the socialist victory on Mars. But he also suggested that Menni's dream of bringing proletarian culture to the masses was now within reach of the new regime. In later years both *Red Star* and *Menni* were criticized for placing too much emphasis upon the "progressive" technocracy—that is, the engineers—and not enough upon the creative role of the proletariat. Yet contemporary Soviet critics recognize Bogdanov as the authentic founder of Soviet science fiction. He was, in the words of one historian of the genre, the "first writer of Russian science fiction to combine a well written technological utopia with scientific Marxist views on communism and the idea of social revolution."*

Bogdanov's works pointed the way to an enormous blossoming of revolutionary science fiction in the 1920s, a period that saw the publication of about two hundred works of this kind, most of them dealing with the two main themes of Bogdanov's work: capitalist hells, militarism, frightful weapons, greed, and exploitation leading to catastrophe; and communist heavens adorned with life-easing technology and complete social justice. Eugene Zamyatin's *We* (1920), called by Ursula LeGuin the greatest of all science fiction novels, was, in its pervasive imitative irony, an emphatic repudiation of Bogdanov's utopia—its technology and its rationalism, as well as its version of socialism. Yakov Okunev, a popular Soviet science fiction writer of the 1920s, borrowed *Red Star*'s computerized society for his *The Coming World* (1923). Alexis Tolstoy's once famous *Aelita* (made into a classic silent film) again featured two planets, Earth and Mars, and two revolutions, though with a political premise about Mars opposite to that of Bogdanov's. One writer, Innokenty

---

*A. F. Britikov, *Russkii Sovetskii nauchno-fantasticheskii roman* (Leningrad: Nauka, 1970), 55.

Zhukov, even incorporated Bogdanov's title into his fantastic tale: *Voyage of the Red Star Detachment to the Land of Marvels* (1924). The "land of marvels" is Earth in the year 1957, after a communist revolution has transformed it into a unified planet resembling that of Bogdanov's Mars. Examples of Bogdanov's influence on the golden age of Soviet science fiction are legion. Soviet critics proclaim it, in spite of residual hostility to Bogdanov as a thinker. It is no exaggeration to say, as the foremost Western authority on Soviet science fiction, Darko Suvin, has said, that Bogdanov was the progenitor of this genre in Soviet literature.

By the time he finished *Engineer Menni* in 1913, Bogdanov had abandoned the active political struggle and was devoting himself to research and theorizing on a wide range of subjects, scientific, philosophical, and cultural. During World War I—whose horrors he had foreseen—he returned to Russia and served as a military physician at the front. After the Bolsheviks came to power he threw himself into the Proletkult, the proletarian culture movement that he had helped to found before the Revolution, and established thousands of cells and studios all over Soviet Russia and issued a huge number of publications with enormous circulations. Bogdanov did not rejoin the Communist (formerly Bolshevik) Party but held several high posts in academic and economic institutions. After 1921, with the dismantling of the independent Proletkult movement at the behest of Lenin, Bogdanov devoted himself fully to scientific work and experimentation. In 1926 he founded the Institute for Blood Transfusion as a way to realize his dream, first described in *Red Star*, of performing the "comradely exchange of life." He gave his own life in this cause, so characteristic of the utopian experiments generated by the Revolution: in 1928, while carrying out a transfusion on himself, he died.

Bogdanov's works circulated in hundreds of thousands of copies in the 1920s, including several editions of *Red Star* and *Engineer Menni* in huge printings. Though he ceased to wield political or philosophical influence, Bogdanov nonetheless remained a major figure in the intellectual landscape of the early Soviet years. Nicholas Bukharin, still a prominent communist political leader and a disciple of Bogdanov, wrote his obituary in *Pravda*, stressing Bogdanov's personal courage and revolutionary boldness in giving his life "as a victim" and praising his intellectual breadth and influence. Bukharin called *Red Star* "one of the best socialist 'utopias.'" When the novels were reissued after the author's death, discussion of them came into vogue once again as the Soviet Union entered that fatal and frenetic period of its history known as the Pyatiletka (Five-Year Plan), the Great Break, or the Revolution from Above. During the debates and reports at the outset of the Five-Year Plan, G. M. Krzhizhanovsky, an engineer and one of the architects of the plan, made oblique reference to Bogdanov's great canal projects on Mars. In 1929, the famous city planner L. M. Sabsovich likened the plan to "the great projects" of *Red Star.* Indeed the atmosphere had become filled with revolutionary utopianism once again, with its frantic energy and wild dreams of the refashioning of cities, of Earth, and of mankind. But this last burst of utopia soon gave way to a massive despotism undreamed of even in the most extravagant fantasies of Alexander Bogdanov.

RED STAR

A Utopia

Contents

To my colleague
THE AUTHOR

Prologue

Letter from Dr. Werner to Mirsky

Dear Comrade Mirsky,

I am sending you Leonid's notes. He wanted them published, and you, as a man of letters, can arrange that matter better than I. He himself has gone into hiding. I am leaving the clinic to try and trace him. I think I shall probably find him in the mountains, where the situation has lately become critical. By exposing himself to the dangers there he is evidently indirectly trying to commit suicide. He is obviously still unstable mentally, although he impressed me as being near complete recovery. I shall inform you the moment I learn of anything.

My warmest regards,

N. Werner

24 July 190? (illegible: 8 or 9)

LEONID'S MANUSCRIPT

PART I

1. The Break

It was early in that great upheaval* which continues to shake our country and which, I think, is now approaching its inevitable, fateful conclusion.

The public consciousness was so deeply impressed by the events of the first bloody days that everyone expected a quick and victorious end to the struggle. It seemed as though the worst had already occurred, that nothing more terrible could possibly happen. No one had realized how tenacious were the bony hands of the corpse that had crushed and still crushes the living in its convulsive embrace.

The excitement of battle quickly spread throughout the masses. Souls opened selflessly to welcome the future as the present dissolved in a rosy mist and the past receded somewhere into the distance and disappeared. All human relationships became unstable and fragile. During these days something happened that radically altered the course of my life and separated me from the rising tide of the people's struggle.

Although I was but 27, I was numbered among the "old" party workers. I had six years of service behind me, the only interruption being a year of prison. I had sensed the approaching storm earlier than many, and I greeted it more calmly than they when it came. I was forced to work much more than previously, but I did not abandon either my scientific pursuits or my literary endeavors. I was particularly interested in the structure of matter and made my living by writing for two children's magazines. And then I was in love . . . or so it seemed to me.

Her party name was Anna Nikolaevna. She supported another, more moderate current in our party,† which fact I attributed to the mildness of

---

*The Russian Revolution of 1905.
†The Russian Social Democratic Workers' Party, founded in 1898, split in 1903 into Bolsheviks and Mensheviks. The "more moderate current" referred to here was Menshevism.

her character and the general political muddle. Although she was my senior, I considered her a not yet fully developed person. There I was mistaken.

Very soon after we became intimate, the consequences of the difference in our personalities began to appear painfully obvious to us both. We gradually became aware of a profound ideological discrepancy in our attitudes toward both the revolution and our own relationship. She had entered the revolution under the banner of duty and sacrifice, while I had joined it under the banner of my own free will. She joined the great movement of the proletariat because she found satisfaction in its supreme morality, whereas all such considerations were alien to me. I simply loved life and wanted it to flourish as fully as possible, and I was therefore attracted to the current which represented the main historical path leading to such prosperity. To Anna Nikolaevna, proletarian ethics were sacred in and of themselves, whereas I considered them a useful appurtenance necessary to the working class in its struggle, but transitory, like the struggle and the system which generated it. According to Anna Nikolaevna, in socialist society the class ethics of the proletariat would necessarily become the universal moral code, while I believed that the proletariat was already moving toward the destruction of all morals and that the comradely feeling uniting people in labor, joy, and suffering would not develop fully until it had cast off the fetishistic husk of morality. These disagreements of ours often gave rise to evidently irreconcilable interpretations of political and social facts.

Our views on our own relationship differed even more sharply. She thought that love implied certain obligations—concessions, sacrifices, and, above all, fidelity for the duration of the union. In actual fact I had no intention whatever of entering into other liaisons, but I was unable to recognize fidelity as an obligation. I even believed that polygamy was in principle superior to monogamy, since it provided for both a richer private life and a greater variety of genetic combinations. In my opinion, it was only the contradictions of the bourgeois order which for the time being made polygamy either simply unfeasible or merely the privilege of the exploiters and parasites, who were all befouled by their own decadent psychology. Here too the future would bring a radical transformation. Anna Nikolaevna deeply resented such views, in which she perceived an attempt to mask a coarsely sensual outlook with intellectual phrases.

None of these disagreements had given me any reason to think of ending our relationship, but then an external factor entered our lives that contributed to such a rupture. At about this time, a young man bearing the unusual code name Menni arrived in the capital. He had with him certain information and messages from the South which indicated that he enjoyed the full confidence of our comrades there. After completing his assignment he decided to stay on for a while in the city. He began dropping in on us rather often and was obviously interested in getting to know me better.

Menni was original in a number of respects, beginning with his appearance. His eyes were so completely masked by a pair of very dark glasses that I did not even know their color. His head was disproportionately large, and although he was handsome, his face was strikingly immobile and lifeless, entirely out of keeping with his soft, expressive voice and well-built, youthfully supple figure. His speech was free and elegant, and his remarks were always pregnant with meaning. He had a broad education and was evidently an engineer by profession.

In conversation Menni constantly tended to reduce all individual practical questions to their general ideological foundations. When he visited us, somehow it seemed that the differences in character and opinions between my wife and myself always emerged so clearly and vividly that we became painfully aware of just how irreconcilable they really were. Menni's general outlook was evidently similar to my own. His remarks were always formulated gently and tactfully, but they always cut straight to the point. He was so skillful at relating the political disagreements between Anna Nikolaevna and myself to the basic discrepancy between our outlooks that these differences appeared to be psychologically inevitable, and we lost all hope of influencing each other or finding any common ground. Anna Nikolaevna regarded Menni with a mixture of hate and lively interest, while my attitude was one of great respect and vague distrust. I sensed that he had some sort of goal, but I was unable to put my finger on it.

During January (it was already the end of January), the leaders of both party currents were preparing to discuss organizing a mass demonstration which would probably result in an armed conflict. The evening before the planned meeting, Menni visited us and raised the question whether the party leaders themselves should participate in the demonstration in the event that it was decided upon. Anna Nikolaevna declared that anyone who voted for the demonstration was morally obliged to march at its head. I considered that no such obligation existed, but that the participants should be such persons as might be necessary or useful. Since I had had some experience of similar matters, I included myself in that category. Menni went further, asserting that in view of the fact that an armed clash with the troops was evidently unavoidable, the presence of street agitators and combat organizers was a must, whereas political leaders were quite out of place and people who were weak or jittery might even be downright harmful. Anna Nikolaevna was insulted by these arguments, taking them to be aimed specifically at her. She broke off the conversation and went to her room. Menni left soon after.

The following day I was obliged to get up early and leave without seeing Anna Nikolaevna, and I did not return until evening. The demonstration was voted down both by our committee and, I was told, by the executive collective of the other current. I was satisfied with the decision, because I knew that we were quite unprepared for an armed conflict and I considered such an action a useless waste of energy. I thought that the decision would mollify Anna Nikolaevna after the conversation of the day before, but when I arrived home I found a note from her on the table:

> I'm leaving. The better I understand myself and you the clearer it seems to me that we have chosen different paths and have both made a mistake. I think we had best not see each other any more. Farewell.

Exhausted, with a feeling of emptiness in my head and a chill in my heart, I wandered the streets for a long time. When I returned home I found an unexpected guest waiting for me. Menni was sitting at my table writing a note.

2. The Invitation

"I must speak to you on a certain very serious and rather curious matter," said Menni.

I had no objections, so I sat down and prepared to listen.

"I have read your brochure on electrons and matter," he began. "I have been studying this problem for several years myself, and I think that many of the ideas in your brochure are correct."

I gave a silent nod of appreciation. "In your study," he continued, "you make one observation that I think is especially interesting. You express the hypothesis that the electrical theory of matter, since it necessarily represents the force of gravity in the form of an attraction and repulsion deriving from a play of electric forces, should eventually enable us to discover a different gravitational principle. In other words, we should be able to obtain a type of matter such that it is repelled rather than attracted by Earth, the sun, and other known celestial bodies. By way of comparison you refer to the diamagnetic repulsion of bodies and the repulsion of parallel currents of different sets. All of this is mentioned in passing, but I have the impression that you yourself attach more importance to it than you wished to disclose."

"You are right," I replied, "and I think that it is along these lines that man is going to solve the problems of free movement in the atmosphere and interplanetary travel. Whether or not my idea is in itself correct, however, it will lead to nothing until we have developed an accurate theory of matter and gravity. If another type of matter exists, then it is obviously impossible simply to find it, as the force of repulsion has long since eliminated it from the entire solar system. Or, more likely, it was

LEONID WANTS TO FREE HIMSELF FROM THE WEIGHT OF GRAVITATION

never included in the composition of the system in its initial nebular stage of development. Thus this type of matter must first be constructed theoretically and then actually be reproduced. At present we lack the data necessary for such an operation, so that all we can do now is begin to envisage the problem itself."

"Nevertheless, the problem has already been solved," said Menni.

I looked at him in amazement. His face was as frozen as ever, but something in the tone of his voice told me I was not dealing with a charlatan. "Perhaps he is mad," flashed through my mind.

"I have no need to deceive you," he answered my thought, "and I am quite aware of what I am saying. Hear me out patiently, and then, if you are still unconvinced, I shall give you the proof."

And he told me the following.

"The great discovery we are talking about was not made by any one individual. It is the achievement of an entire scientific society that has been in existence for quite some time now and has been working along these lines for many years. Until now the society has been a secret, and I am not at liberty to give you the particulars of its origin and history until you and I have come to an agreement on the main issue.

"Our society is far ahead of the academic world in many important scientific questions. We knew about radioactive elements and their decay long before Curie and Ramsay, and our analysis of the structure of matter has come much further than theirs. We foresaw the possible existence of elements that are repelled by the planetary bodies and subsequently succeeded in synthesizing this minus-matter, as we briefly designate it.

"After that it was easy to develop and implement technical applications for the discovery—first, flying machines for movement within the atmosphere, and then vehicles for travel to other planets."

Menni's tone was calm and persuasive, but his story seemed too strange and improbable to believe. "And you were able to do all this in secret?" I interrupted.

"Yes, because we considered secrecy to be of the utmost importance. We decided that it would be very dangerous to publish our findings so long as most countries are ruled by reactionary governments. You, as a Russian revolutionary, would be the first to agree. Look how your Asiatic government uses European means of communication and destruction to oppress and eradicate all the most vigorous and progressive elements in the country. Or take the government of a certain semifeudal, semiconstitutional country whose throne is occupied by a warmongering, jabbering blockhead in the power of a pack of known swindlers—is it much better? How much are even the two philistine republics of Europe worth? It is clear that if our flying machines were to become known, the governments would first of all try to get a monopoly on them and use them to enhance the power and might of the upper classes. That is something we most decidedly do not want, and we shall therefore retain the monopoly for ourselves and wait for more favorable circumstances."

"Have you actually succeeded in reaching other planets?" I asked.

"Yes, the two closest, the telluric planets Venus and Mars. Of course I am not counting the moon, which is dead. At this very moment we are exploring them in detail. We have all the necessary technical resources— what we lack is people, strong, reliable people. By the authority vested in me by my comrades, I am inviting you to join our ranks. Naturally, you would have all the rights and obligations of any other member."

He paused to wait for my answer. I did not know what to think.

"Proof!" I said. "You promised to show me the proof."

Menni took from his pocket a glass bottle containing a metallic liquid, which I took to be mercury. Strangely, however, this liquid, which filled not more than a third of the container, was not at the bottom of the bottle but in its upper part from just below the neck right up to the cork. Menni turned the bottle upside down and the liquid flowed upward to the bottom. He released the phial, and it hung suspended in midair. This was incredible, but there could be no doubt that it was really true.

"This is an ordinary glass phial," Menni explained, "but it contains a liquid which is repelled by the bodies of the solar system. Just enough liquid has been poured in to counterbalance the weight of the bottle, so that they are weightless taken together. We construct all our flying machines on the same principle. They are made of ordinary materials, but they have a reservoir filled with the appropriate quantity of this minus-matter. All that remains is to give this entire weightless system the proper speed. The flying machines intended for use in Earth's atmosphere have simple electric motors and wings. Such craft are of course unsuited for interplanetary travel, where we employ an entirely different system, with which I shall familiarize you in more detail later."

There was no longer any room for doubt.

"What restraints does your society place upon its members, besides, that is, the obligation to keep its existence a secret?"

"Actually, hardly any at all. Neither the private lives nor the public activities of our comrades are circumscribed in any way, so long as the activity of the society as a whole is not jeopardized. Upon joining, however, each new member is required to perform some important task for the society. This binds him more closely to the organization and also affords us an opportunity to observe his talents and initiative in action."

"In other words, I will also be assigned such a mission?"

"Yes."

"What, exactly?"

"You are to participate in the expedition leaving tomorrow for Mars in our etheroneph."

"How long will this expedition take?"

Menni shows Leonid antimatter as he tries to convince him to
come with him

"We do not know. The round trip will require at least five months. Of
course, there is always the possibility we may never return."

"I understand, but that is not the point. What will become of my
revolutionary work? You are obviously a Social Democrat yourself, so you
must understand my problem."

"Make your choice. We think that you should pause in your work to
complete your training. The mission cannot be postponed. If you refuse
to accept it now you will not be given another chance."

I thought for a moment. Now that the broad masses had entered
upon the scene, the absence of any one party worker was of little conse-

quence to the cause as a whole. Besides, I would only be away temporarily, and, when I returned, my new connections, knowledge, and skills would make me considerably more useful. I made up my mind.

"When am I to start?"

"Immediately, with me."

"Can you give me two hours to notify my comrades? They will have to replace me tomorrow in the district."

"That matter has almost been taken care of already. Andrei arrived today, fleeing from the South. I told him that you might be leaving, and he is prepared to take your place. While waiting for you I wrote him a letter with detailed instructions, just in case. We can drop it off to him on our way."

There was nothing more to discuss. I quickly destroyed my personal papers, wrote a note to my landlady, and began dressing. Menni was ready already.

"Well then, let's go. From this moment on, I am your prisoner."

"You are my comrade!" answered Menni.

3. Night

Menni's apartment took up the entire fifth floor of a large building that towered above the little houses of one of the suburbs of the capital.*
No one was there to greet us. The rooms through which we proceeded were empty, and in the glaring light of the electric light bulbs this bareness seemed even more gloomy and unnatural. Menni stopped in the third room.

"Here," he said, pointing at the door to the fourth room, "is the flying boat that will presently take us to the etheroneph. First, however, I shall have to undergo a slight transformation. It would be difficult to pilot the gondola in this mask."

He unbuttoned his collar and removed his glasses and an incredibly realistic mask, which, until this moment, I and everyone else had taken to be his face. I was astonished by the sight that greeted me. His eyes were monstrously huge, much larger than any human eyes. The pupils were disproportionately large, which made his gaze almost frightening. Due to the unnatural size of the eyes, the upper part of his face and head was unusually broad. The lower half of the face, on the other hand, was relatively narrow, and he lacked any sign of a beard or mustasche. All in all, his appearance was highly original, deformed even, but not to the point that it could be called grotesque.

"You see what nature has endowed me with," said Menni. "You can

---

*St. Petersburg

understand that I must wear a mask if only to avoid frightening people, not to mention the demands of underground political work. You shall simply have to get used to my ugliness, however, as you will be obliged to spend quite a lot of time with me."

He opened the door to the next room and turned on the light. It was a spacious hall, in the middle of which stood a small, rather broad boat of metal and glass. The sides and bottom of the fore were of glass bound in steel. This transparent hull was some two centimeters thick and appeared to be very sturdy. Above the sides of the bow were two flat crystal plates joined at a sharp angle which were meant to cut through the air and shield the passengers from the wind at high speeds. The engine was in the middle part of the boat and was connected to a three-bladed propeller half a meter across in the stern. The front of the boat and the engine were covered by a thin lamellar awning fastened to the metal binding of the glass hull and a number of light steel columns. The entire craft was like some finely fashioned toy.

Menni invited me to sit down on the side bench in the gondola, switched off the lights, and opened the enormous window of the room. He took a seat in the fore near the engine and threw out several sacks of ballast lying on the floor of the boat. He grasped the engine lever. The boat rocked, slowly rose, and quietly slipped through the open window.

I sat riveted to the spot, not daring to move. The noise of the propeller became more distinct. The winter air streamed in under the awning, pleasantly cooling my burning face but unable to penetrate my warm clothing. Thousands of stars twinkled and shimmered above us, while through the transparent floor of the gondola I could see the black dots of the houses growing smaller. The bright spots of the electric lights of the capital receded into the distance and the snowy plain shone a dull, bluish white far below us. I felt dizzy. At first the sensation was slight and almost pleasant, but as it grew stronger I was forced to close my eyes to get rid of it.

The rush of air became sharper, and the sound of the propeller and the whistle of the wind grew louder and louder. Obviously, our speed was increasing. Among these noises I began to distinguish an even, unbroken, delicate silvery sound produced by the vibrations of the glass hull slicing through the air. I was filled by this strange music; my thoughts became confused and vanished, leaving only a sensation of natural, free, easy movement forward and ever forward into endless space.

"Four kilometers a minute," said Menni, and I opened my eyes.

"Is it much farther?" I asked.

"About an hour's flying time. We will be landing on a frozen lake."

We were at an altitude of several hundred meters. The gondola flew in a perfectly even horizontal trajectory, neither rising nor descending. I was able to see better as my eyes became used to the dark. We had entered the land of lakes and granite crags.* These rocks showed black in the spots that were free of snow. Small villages were nestled here and there among them.

Behind us to the left the snowy field of the frozen gulf stretched into the distance, while off to our right lay the plain of an enormous lake. It was in this lifeless winter landscape that I was about to cut my ties with the ancient Earth. Suddenly I suspected—no, I was seized by absolute certainty—that this break would be forever.

The gondola slowly descended between the rocks toward a small inlet of a mountain lake and stopped before a structure looming dark against the snow. I could not see any doors or windows. A part of the metal cover of the structure slowly moved to one side, and our craft sailed into the black opening. It closed again, and electric lights went on around us, illuminating a large, elongated, unfurnished room. A pile of bags filled with ballast lay on the floor.

Menni moored the gondola to columns especially designed for the purpose and opened one of the side doors of the room. We entered a long, dimly lit corridor flanked on both sides by what appeared to be cabins. Menni led me to one of them and said:

"Here is your cabin. Get settled down, I am going to the engine room. I will see you tomorrow morning."

I was glad to be left alone. I was beginning to feel weary from the excitement caused by the strange events of the evening. I did not touch the supper prepared for me on the table but turned out the light and lay down on the bed. My thoughts were in an absurd jumble, leaping unpredictably from subject to subject. I stubbornly tried to force myself to sleep, but I lay awake for a long time. Finally my mind became blurred as dimly flickering images began to throng before my eyes. Everything around me receded into the distance and my brain was overpowered by oppressive visions.

I had a series of dreams which ended in a terrible nightmare. I was standing on the brink of an enormous black abyss. Stars shone at the bottom, and Menni was irresistibly dragging me down into it, telling me that there was no reason to fear the force of gravity and that in a few hundred thousand years we would reach the nearest star. I moaned in my final agonizing struggle and awoke.

My room was flooded with a soft blue light. Sitting beside me on the bed and bending over me was . . . Menni? Yes, Menni, but he was different somehow . . . strange, shadowy. He seemed to be much smaller, and his eyes did not stand out so sharply. His expression was tender and

---

*A literary reference to Finland.

Importance
of dreams

kind, not cold and implacable like a moment ago on the edge of the precipice.

"You are so good . . ." I said, vaguely sensing the change.

He smiled and put his hand on my forehead. It was a small, soft hand. I closed my eyes again, and with the absurd thought that I must kiss this hand I sank into a quiet, blissful sleep.

4. The Explanation

When I awoke and turned on the light my watch showed ten o'clock. When I had finished my toilet I pressed a button, and a moment later Menni entered the room.

"Are we leaving soon?" I asked.

"In an hour," replied Menni.

"Were you in here last night, or was I only dreaming?"

"No, you were not dreaming. It wasn't I, however, but our young doctor, Netti. You were sleeping restlessly, and Netti used the blue light and suggestion to calm you down."

"Is he your brother?"

"No," replied Menni with a smile.

"You have not told me your nationality yet. Do all of your comrades look like you?"

"Yes," answered Menni.

"In other words, you lied to me," I declared sharply. "This is no scientific society. It is something else."

"Yes," Menni answered calmly. "We are all inhabitants of another planet, representatives of another humanity. We are Martians."

"Why did you deceive me?"

"Would you have listened to me if I had told you the truth straight-away? I did not have time to convince you. It was necessary to distort the truth for the sake of plausibility. Without this transitional stage you would have been severely shaken. But about the main point, the trip ahead of us, I told you the truth."

"So I am your prisoner after all?"

"No, you are still free to go. You have an hour in which to make your decision. If you refuse, we will take you back and postpone the journey, because there is no point in our returning alone."

"Just why do you need me?"

"You are to serve as a living link between the human races of Earth and Mars by familiarizing yourself with our way of life and acquainting the Martians with yours. For as long as you yourself wish, you are to be the representative of your planet in our world."

"Are you telling me the whole truth now?"

"The whole truth—if, that is, you are equal to the task."

"In that case I shall have to try. I am staying with you."

"Is that your final decision?" asked Menni.

"Yes, unless your last explanation is also some sort of . . . transitional stage."

"Well then, let's go," said Menni, ignoring my caustic remark. "I must go to give the final instructions to the mechanic now. I'll return in a moment, and we can watch the etheroneph take off together."

He left, and I fell to pondering. Actually, our explanation was not quite complete. One rather serious question remained, but I was unable to bring myself to ask it. Had Menni knowingly contributed to my rupture with Anna Nikolaevna? It seemed to me that he had. He probably thought that she was in the way. Perhaps he was right. At any rate, he could only hasten the break, not cause it. Even doing that much, of course, was a case of insolent interference in my private business. Now that I was tied to Menni I would have to repress my hostility toward him, however, so there was no use in bringing up the past. It would be best not to think of the matter at all. Otherwise, the new turn things had taken did not astonish me too greatly. Sleep had refreshed me, and after all that had happened the night before I was no longer easily surprised by anything. All that remained was to work out a plan for further action.

I obviously had to orient myself in my new situation as quickly and thoroughly as possible. The best procedure would be to start with what was near at hand and proceed step by step to things that were more distant. Closest to me just then were the etheroneph, its passengers, and the takeoff. Mars was still a long way off—two months at the very least, according to what Menni had told me the day before.

I had already managed to take note of the external form of the etheroneph the previous evening. It was almost spherical, being flattened at the lower end rather like Columbus's egg. Such a shape, of course, provided for the greatest volume with the least amount of materials and the smallest cooling surface. The etheroneph was evidently made mostly of aluminum and glass. Menni would show and explain to me the interior structure of the craft and would also introduce me to the other "monsters," as I mentally called my new comrades.

When Menni returned he took me to meet the other Martians, who were all gathered in a side room with an enormous crystal window half the length of one wall. Real sunlight was very pleasant after the ghostly light of the electric lamps. There were about twenty Martians, and my first impression was that they all looked exactly alike. The absence of beards, mustaches, and wrinkles on their faces almost erased even the age differences among them. I unconsciously kept my eyes on Menni in order not to lose him in this strange company. Soon, however, I was able to recognize my nocturnal visitor, Netti, who was distinguished from the rest by his youth and liveliness, and the broad-shouldered giant Sterni, with his strikingly cold, almost sinister expression. Only Menni and Netti spoke Russian with me, while Sterni and three or four others spoke French and the others English and German. Among themselves they evidently used their native language, a tongue I had never heard before. It was sonorous and pleasing to the ear, and I noted with satisfaction that it did not seem to be particularly difficult to pronounce.

5. Takeoff

Interesting though the "monsters" were, most of my attention was on the approaching solemn moment of takeoff. I gazed intently at the snowy surface before us and at the sheer granite cliff rising above it. I expected at any moment to feel a sharp jolt and then watch everything shrink as we rapidly pulled away from it, but nothing of the sort happened. A slow, noiseless movement gradually began to separate us from the snowy field. For some seconds the rise was almost imperceptible.

"Acceleration two centimeters," said Menni.

I understood what that meant. The first second we would move only one centimeter, the second three, the third five, the fourth seven, and so on, as our speed steadily increased in arithmetical progression. In a minute we would reach the speed of a man walking, in fifteen minutes, that of an express train, and so on. We were moving according to the law of falling bodies, except that we were falling upward and five hundred times slower than ordinary heavy bodies falling near the surface of the Earth.

The plate-glass window extended from the floor, with which it formed an obtuse angle, and conformed to the spherical hull of the etheroneph, of which it was a part. Thus by bending forward we could also see what was directly below us.

The Earth was receding faster and faster, and the horizon became increasingly broader. The dark spots of the rocks and villages shrank, and the outline of the lake stood out as on a map. The sky darkened, and the blue band of the open sea now occupied the entire western half of the horizon. I was already able to discern the brightest stars in the midday sunlight.

A very slow revolving movement of the etheroneph on its vertical axis afforded us a view of the entire space around us. The horizon seemed to rise together with us, while Earth below resembled a huge concave saucer with embossed designs. The contours of their relief became progressively shallower, and soon the entire landscape looked like a map that was drawn with sharp lines in the middle and blurred toward the edges, over which there hovered a semitransparent, bluish fog. The sky had now become quite black. Countless stars, even the tiniest ones, shone with a tranquil, unblinking light in defiance of the bright sun, which was beginning to become uncomfortably hot.

"Tell me, Menni, this acceleration of two centimeters at which we are now moving—will it continue throughout the journey?"

"Yes," he replied, "except that when we are about halfway its direction will be reversed, so that second by second our velocity will decrease rather than increase along the same gradient. Thus although the maximum speed of the etheroneph will be approximately 50 kilometers a second and its average velocity about 25 kilometers, by the time we arrive it will be as low as it was at takeoff, and we will land on the surface of Mars with no jolt or bump whatever. Were it not for these tremendous variations in velocity we would be unable to reach either Earth or Venus, because even though they are relatively close—60 and 100 million kilometers respectively—at the speed of, say, your trains it would take us centuries rather than months to cover the distance. As for the 'cannon shot' method I have read about in your science fiction novels, it is of course simply a joke, because according to the laws of mechanics there is practically no difference between being hit by the shot and being inside the projectile at the moment it is fired."

"But how do you manage to achieve such an even deceleration and acceleration?"

"The motive power of the etheroneph is provided by a certain radioactive substance which we can obtain in great quantities. We have discovered a method of accelerating its decay by hundreds of thousands of times. This is done in the engine by means of certain fairly simple electrochemical processes which release an enormous amount of energy. As you know, the particles of decaying atoms fly apart at a speed tens of thousands of times greater than that of an artillery shell. When these particles are allowed to issue from the etheroneph in only one direction, that is, through a passage whose walls they cannot penetrate, the entire craft is propelled in the opposite direction. Thus it is the same principle that operates in a recoiling rifle or artillery piece. You can easily calculate that in accordance with the well-known law of kinetic energy, a tiny fraction of a milligram of such particles per second is quite sufficient to give our etheroneph its evenly accelerated movement."

As we were talking the other Martians disappeared from the room. Menni suggested we go to his cabin and have breakfast. His quarters were along the outer hull of the etheroneph and had a large crystal window. We resumed our conversation. I knew that I would be experiencing new and strange sensations as my body became weightless, and I asked Menni about it.

"Yes," said Menni, "the sun continues to attract us, but here its force is negligible. The force of Earth will also become imperceptible by tomorrow or the day after. Only the steady acceleration of the etheroneph will allow us to retain 1/400 to 1/500 of our previous weight. It is difficult to get used to this at first, even though the change occurs very gradually. As you

[handwritten margin note: CRUDE ATOMIC POWER]

become weightless, you will lose your former agility and make a great many clumsy movements. You are going to find flying through the air a most dubious pleasure. As for the palpitations of the heart, the dizziness, and even the nausea that are bound to occur, Netti will be able to give you some relief. It will be difficult to cope with water and other liquids, as they will slip out of their containers at the slightest bump and scatter about in huge spherical drops. However, we have taken great pains to eliminate these inconveniences. Furniture and dishes are fastened down, liquids are kept in corked containers, and everywhere in the ship there are handgrips and straps to keep you from bouncing off into the air should you make a sudden movement. Don't worry, you will have plenty of time to get used to it."

We had been traveling about two hours, and my decrease in weight was already quite perceptible, although the sensation was still very pleasant. All I could feel was my body becoming lighter and my movements freer. We had already left Earth's atmosphere, but this was of no concern to us, since our hermetically sealed craft naturally had an adequate supply of oxygen. The visible portion of Earth's surface now very definitely resembled a map. Its scale was distorted, however, being smaller at the middle and larger toward the horizon. Here and there it was covered with white patches of clouds. To the south, beyond the Mediterranean, the north of Africa and Arabia were clearly visible through a blue haze. The area beyond Scandinavia to the north faded away in a wasteland of ice and snow; only the cliffs of Spitzbergen still stood out as a black spot. In the east, beyond the greenish brown band of the Urals, which was dotted with patches of snow, there again began an expanse of solid white occasionally shot with a greenish hue, a faint reminder of the vast coniferous forest of Siberia. Beyond the clear contours of central Europe to the west the shores of England and France were lost in the clouds. I was unable to look at this gigantic panorama for very long, for the mere thought of the terrifying depth of the abyss below almost made me faint. I renewed my conversation with Menni.

"You are the captain of this ship, are you not?"

Menni nodded and said:

"But that does not imply that I have what you call the power of command. I just happen to have the most experience in piloting the etheroneph, and my instructions are observed in the same way that I observe Sterni's astronomical calculations, or in the way we all follow Netti's medical advice so as not to jeopardize our health or fitness for work."

"How old is this Doctor Netti, anyway? He seems awfully young to me."

"I forget, 16 or 17," Menni answered with a smile.

That was about what I thought, but I could not help being surprised at such early erudition.

"A doctor already at that age!" I exclaimed in spite of myself.

"A competent and experienced one at that," Menni added.

I did not realize at the time (and Menni intentionally neglected to mention the fact) that the Martian year is almost twice as long as ours. Mars completes a revolution around the sun in 686 of our days, so that Netti's age of 16 was equivalent to about 30 Earth years.

6. The Etheroneph

After breakfast Menni took me on a tour of our ship. First we went to the engine room, which occupied the entire lowest floor of the etheroneph at its flattened bottom. It consisted of five rooms, with one in the center and four others arranged around it, all of them separated by partitions. The huge engine stood in the middle of the center room. Round glass windows were set in the floor on all four sides around it. One was pure cyrstal, while three were of different colored glass. They were all about three centimeters thick and marvelously transparent, though at that moment we could only see a small part of Earth's surface through them.

The main part of the engine was a vertical metal cylinder three meters high and a half meter in diameter. Menni explained that it was made of osmium, a very refractory precious metal resembling platinum. It was in this cylinder that the decomposition of the radioactive material took place. Its red-hot, 20-centimeter thick walls gave an indication of the enormous energy being released in the process. It was not very warm in the room, however, for the cylinder was encased in 40 centimeters of a transparent material that provided excellent insulation from the heat. The etheroneph was evenly heated by warm air conducted through pipes running off in all directions from the top of this case. The other parts of the engine attached to the cylinder—electric coils, accumulators, dials, and so on—were arranged in perfect order around it, and a system of mirrors enabled the mechanic to see all of them at once without leaving his seat.

Of the side compartments, one was the astronomy room. To the right and left of it were the water and oxygen chambers, while on the opposite side was the calculations room. The floor and outer wall of the astronomy room were of pure, geometrically ground crystal. They were so transparent that as I happened to glance straight down while following Menni along the suspended footbridges, I was seized by a distressing fit of giddiness and forced to close my eyes, for I saw absolutely nothing between us and the abyss below. I tried instead to look to one side at the instruments arranged on the intricate supports which extended down from the ceiling and the inner wall of the room between the bridges. The main telescope was about two meters long, but its lens was disproportionately large, as was apparently its optical power.

"We use only diamond lenses," said Menni. "They provide the broadest field of vision."

"What is the ordinary power of this telescope?" I asked.

"Its direct-vision magnification is about 600," Menni replied, "but when that is insufficient we take a photograph and examine it under a microscope, which raises the power to 60,000 or more. The operation only takes about a minute."

Menni invited me to sit down and look at the planet we had left behind us. He aimed the telescope.

"We are about 2,000 kilometers away right now," he said. "Do you recognize what you see before you?"

I immediately recognized the harbor of a Scandinavian capital I had passed through a number of times on party business. The ships anchored in the roads presented a fascinating sight. With a single twist of a knob on the side of the telescope, Menni replaced the eyepiece with a camera. A few seconds later he removed it and inserted the entire device in an apparatus to one side which proved to be a microscope.

"We develop and print the image right here in the microscope without touching it with our hands," he explained.

After a few simple operations, which took some 30 seconds, he turned the eyepiece of the microscope over to me. One of the familiar steamships of the Northern Company stood out with amazing sharpness, as if it were only a few dozen paces away. The picture seemed three-dimensional in the transmitted light, and the colors were all quite natural. Standing on the bridge was the gray-haired captain with whom I had chatted a number of times while traveling on the ship. A sailor setting a large box on the deck was frozen in his pose, as was a passenger showing him something with his hand. And to think that all this was 2,000 kilometers away!

A young Martian, one of Sterni's assistants, entered the room to measure the exact distance the etheroneph had covered. Not wishing to disturb him in his work, we went on to the water chamber, which contained a huge reservoir of water and several large apparatuses for purifying it. A multitude of pipes carried the water from the tank to all parts of the etheroneph.

Next came the calculations room, which was crammed with strange machines bristling with dials and needles. Sterni was working at the largest device, out of which flowed a long tape that evidently showed the result of his calculations. The signs on the tape and dials, however, were all strange to me. I did not want to disturb Sterni or even speak to him.

We quickly went on to the last side compartment, the oxygen chamber, which contained supplies of oxygen in the form of 25 tons of potassium chlorate, from which up to 10,000 cubic meters of oxygen could be separated. Such a quantity was sufficient for several voyages like ours. Equipment for breaking down the potassium chlorate was also kept here. Other supplies included barites and caustic potash for the absorption of carbon dioxide and stores of sulfuric anhydride used to absorb excessive moisture and volatile leucomaine, a poison far more dangerous than carbon dioxide that is produced in the body and exhaled into the air. Doctor Netti was in charge of the room.

We returned to the central engine room and then ascended in a small elevator directly to the top story of the etheroneph. The middle room there housed a second observatory, identical with the one below except that the instruments were larger and its ceiling rather than floor was of crystal. From this observatory we could see the other half of the celestial sphere and our destination, Mars, which glowed a dull red off to one side of the zenith. Menni trained the telescope on it, and I could distinguish clearly the contours of the continents and the seas and canal networks, which I recognized from the maps of Schiaparelli. Menni photographed the planet, and soon we had a detailed picture of it under the microscope. It meant nothing to me without Menni's explanations, however, for the spots that were cities, forests, and lakes were distinguished from one another by details which I found elusive and incomprehensible.

"How far off is it?" I asked.

"We are relatively close at the moment—about 100 million kilometers."

"But why isn't Mars at the zenith of the dome? Does this mean that we are flying off to one side rather than directly toward it?"

"Yes, and we have no other choice. Due to the force of inertia, as we left Earth we retained the speed of its movement around the sun—30 kilometers a second. The speed of Mars is only 24 kilometers, so that if we were to fly perpendicularly between the two orbits we would strike the surface of Mars with the remaining lateral velocity of 6 kilometers a second. That would be most uncomfortable, so we must take a curvilinear trajectory in order to counterbalance the excessive lateral velocity."

"In that case, how long is our total journey?"

"Approximately 160 million kilometers, which is going to take at least two and one-half months."

Had I not been a mathematician, these figures would have left me unmoved. As it was, however, they evoked in me a sensation that reminded me of my nightmare, and I hastened to leave the astronomy room.

The six side compartments of the upper section surrounding the observatory in a ring had no windows, and their ceiling, which was part of the spherical hull of the craft, sloped all the way down to the floor. Near the ceiling were two large reservoirs of minus-matter, whose repulsive force was calculated to neutralize the weight of the entire etheroneph. The intermediate second and third stories were occupied by conference rooms, laboratories at the disposal of individual members of the expedition, their cabins, bathrooms, libraries, a gymnasium, and so on. Netti's room was next to mine.

7. The People

My loss of weight was now more perceptible, and the growing sensation of lightness, accompanied by an element of uncertainty and a vague uneasiness, had ceased to be pleasant. I went to my cabin and lay down on the cot. I lay there quietly engrossed in thought for a couple of hours, and before I knew it I had dozed off. When I awoke, Netti was sitting at the table in my room. Arising from the bed with an unintentionally abrupt movement, I was flung upward and hit my head on the ceiling.

"When you only weigh 20 pounds you have to be a little more careful," Netti remarked, with a good-natured, philosophical air.

The specific reason he had come to my cabin was to tell me what to do in the event my weightlessness should make me feel seasick. I was in fact already experiencing such symptoms. There was a special signal button in my room connected to a buzzer in his room so that I could always call for him if I again needed his help.

I took advantage of this opportunity to talk with the young doctor. In spite of his great erudition, he was a good-natured and likeable young fellow, and for some reason I felt involuntarily attracted to him. I asked him why, of all the Martians on the etheroneph, only he and Menni spoke my native language.

"It is quite simple," he explained. "When we were searching for someone Menni chose himself and me to go to your country, where we spent over a year before we accomplished our mission by finding you."

"So the others were 'searching for someone' in other countries?"

"Of course, among all the major peoples of the world. But, just as Menni expected, we found him first in your country. The pulse of life throbs stronger there, and, more than anywhere else, people are forced to look to the future. When we found our man we notified the others, they returned from their assignments, and here we are on our way."

"What exactly do you mean when you say that you were 'searching for someone' and that you 'found your man'? I understand that you wanted an individual suited to a certain role, and Menni explained to me just what it is. I am very flattered to observe that you have chosen me, but I would like to know why you think I am so deserving of the honor."

"I can tell you in the most general terms. The person we were looking for represented an ideal combination of sound physical health, flexibility, a capacity for intellectual labor, few or no personal attachments on Earth, and as little individualism as possible. Our physiologists and psychologists reasoned that the transition from the eternally discordant conditions of your society to what you would call the socialism of our system would be a difficult ordeal. The person chosen for the mission, therefore, would have to be well qualified psychologically and physically, and Menni felt you were better suited than the others."

"And Menni's opinion was good enough for the rest of you?"

"Yes, for we have complete confidence in his judgment. He has an exceptionally powerful and lucid intellect and is very seldom mistaken. He has more experience than any of us in dealing with Earthlings. In fact, it was he who first established such relations."

"Who developed the means of communicating with other planets?"

"That was the work of many people. Minus-matter was obtained as early as several decades ago. At first, however, we could produce only insignificant quantities of it, so the efforts of a great many factory teams were required to find and develop the means of manufacturing it on a large scale. After that it was necessary to perfect techniques for obtaining and decomposing the radioactive substances used as fuel for the etheroneph, and that also demanded enormous research. Furthermore, there were a great many difficulties connected with the conditions of the interplanetary environment. We had to find ways of protecting ourselves both from the terrible cold and from the sun, for in space there is no atmospheric envelope to filter its scorching rays. Computing the course also proved to be fraught with unforeseen difficulties and errors. A number of earlier expeditions to Earth were completely annihilated. It was Menni who finally managed to organize the first successful voyage. And now, using his methods, we even succeeded in reaching Venus recently."

"In that case, Menni must be a truly great man," I said.

"Yes, if that is what it pleases you to call someone who has indisputably done a great deal of valuable work."

"That is not what I meant. Even quite ordinary people, the executors, can make valuable contributions. But Menni is obviously in an entirely different category; he is a genius, a creator, a pioneer leading mankind forward."

"I find your expressions rather vague and even incorrect. Every worker is a creator, but what does the creating is mankind and nature. After all, Menni had at his disposal the experience amassed by preceding generations and contemporary researchers, and he based each step of his work on that experience. Nature provided him with the raw materials and germs of his ideas, and the struggle between man and nature furnished the necessary stimuli. A man is an individual person, but his work is impersonal. Sooner or later he will die and take his joys and suffering with him. His accomplishments are his lasting contribution to life, and life will go on developing forever. In this respect there is no difference between workers. The only inequality is a quantitative one determined by how much they have experienced and how much they leave behind them."

"But surely the *name* of a man like Menni will outlive him and remain in human memory when the names of countless others have disappeared without a trace?"

"A person's name is preserved as long as those who knew and lived with him are still alive. But mankind needs no dead symbols of an individual once he is no more. Our science and our art preserve impersonally the collective accomplishments of all. The ballast of names from the past is useless to the memory of man."

"Perhaps you are right, but our sense of reality rebels against such logic. To us the names of the leaders of thought and action are living symbols which are indispensable to our science, our art, and our entire social life. In the struggle of forces and ideas it often happens that a name on a banner means more than an abstract slogan. And the names of geniuses are not mere ballast in our memory."

"That is because the common cause of mankind is not yet really a common cause among you. It has become so splintered in the illusions generated by the struggle among men that it seems to belong to individual persons rather than to mankind as a whole. It used to be as difficult for me to understand your point of view as it is for you to comprehend ours."

"Well then, for better or worse, none of our party is immortal. The mortals here, on the other hand, must belong to an elite, do they not? They must be among those who have 'done a great deal of valuable work,' as you put it?"

"In a way, yes. Menni chose his comrades from among thousands of applicants."

"After him I suppose the most outstanding would be Sterni?"

"Yes, if you really must insist on measuring and comparing people. Sterni is a prominent scientist, though of quite a different type than Menni. Mathematicians of his caliber are very rare indeed. He discovered a number of errors in the calculations upon which all the previous expeditions to Earth were based and proved that certain of these mistakes in themselves were sufficient to doom the enterprises. He developed new methods of making these calculations, and thus far his findings have proved accurate."

"That is just how I imagined him on the basis of my first impressions and what Menni has told me. And yet I cannot understand why the sight of him inspires me with a certain alarm, a vague uneasiness, a kind of unmotivated antipathy. Would you happen to have an explanation for this, doctor?"

"You see, Sterni has a very powerful but cold and mainly analytical intellect. He tears everything apart, logically and implacably, and his conclusions are sometimes one-sided, sometimes extremely severe, because an analysis of the parts of something, after all, yields not the whole, but something less than the whole. You know that wherever there is life the whole is greater than the sum of its parts, just as a living human body is more than just its combined organs. Consequently, Sterni is less capable than many of entering into the moods and thoughts of other people. He will always willingly help you with anything you yourself bring to him, but he will never guess your needs for you. Another inhibiting factor here, of course, is that he is almost always entirely engrossed in his work, for his head is constantly full of some difficult problem or other. In this respect he is quite unlike Menni, who is always aware of everything around him and has more than once been able to explain even to me what it is I want, what is troubling me, what my mind and feelings are groping for."

"In that case I should imagine that Sterni's attitude toward us contradictory and inadequate Earthlings must be rather hostile."

"Hostile . . . no. That emotion is alien to him. But I do think he is more skeptical than he need be. He had been in France only six months when he telegraphed Menni that there was no point in searching there. Perhaps he was partly right, because Letta, who was with him, did not find a suitable candidate either. But his descriptions of the people he saw there are much more severe than Letta's, and of course they are also much more one-sided, even though they do not contain anything that is actually incorrect."

"Who is this Letta you mentioned? For some reason I do not remember him."

"A chemist, one of Menni's assistants. He is an elderly man, the oldest among us here. You will find it easy to make his acquaintance, and it would be useful to you to do so. He has a gentle temperament and is an excellent judge of human nature, although he is not a psychologist like Menni. Drop in and see him sometime in his laboratory. He will be happy to see you and can show you many interesting things."

At that moment I remembered that we were far away from Earth, and I wanted to take a look at it. We went to a big window in one of the side rooms.

"Won't we have to pass close to the moon?" I asked on the way.

"No, unfortunately the moon is far off to one side. I should also like to take a closer look at it, because it appeared so strange to me from Earth. Huge, slow, mysteriously serene, it does not resemble at all our two little moons, which dash across the sky and constantly change their faces like lively, capricious children. On the other hand, of course, your moon is much brighter and its light is most pleasant. Your sun is also brighter than

Looking back at Earth

ours, and in this respect you are much more fortunate than we. Your world is twice as bright, which is why you do not need eyes with large pupils like ours to catch the feeble rays of our day and night."

We sat down by the window. Earth shone far off in the distance like a giant sickle. All that could be distinguished on it were the contours of the western part of America, the northeast of Asia, a dull patch which was part of the Pacific, and the white spot of the Arctic Ocean. The entire Atlantic and the Old World lay shrouded in darkness. The only reason I could guess they were there at all was that the invisible part of Earth eclipsed the stars, leaving a stretch of empty black sky. Our oblique trajectory and the rotation of Earth on its axis were responsible for this change of view.

As I gazed I felt sad that I could not see my native land, where there was so much life, such a struggle and such intense suffering, where only yesterday I was still in the ranks of my comrades, and where now some-one else had probably taken my place. Doubt began to arise from deep within me.

"Back there blood is being spilled," I said, "yet here stands yester-day's revolutionary in the role of a calm observer."

"Blood is being shed for the sake of a better future," replied Netti. "But in order to wage the struggle one must *know* that future. And it is for the sake of such knowledge that you are here."

In an involuntary burst of emotion I squeezed his tiny, almost child-ish hand.

8. New Friends

Earth receded further and further into the distance, and, as if it waned thin from the pain of parting, it shrank to a moonlike sickle accom-panied by the now very small crescent of the real moon. By now my fellow passengers and I were all becoming fantastic acrobats, able to fly without wings and make ourselves comfortable in any position, with our heads toward the floor or the ceiling or the wall—it made practically no difference which. Gradually I got to know my new comrades and felt more at ease with them.

Already on the second day after our departure (we continued to use this time measure, although for us, of course, there no longer existed either days or nights), I took the initiative myself and changed into Mar-tian dress in order not to stand out so sharply from the others. True, I liked the attire for its own sake: simple, comfortable, without any superfluous conventional items such as ties or cuffs, it afforded the wearer the maximum freedom of movement. The individual parts of the costume were joined together by small clasps in such a way that the entire suit was a single whole, yet if need be one could easily unfasten and take off, say, one or both sleeves or the entire blouse. The manners of my fellow passengers resembled their dress, being marked by the same simplicity and absence of anything superfluous or conventional. They never greeted one another, never said goodbye or thank you, never dragged out a con-versation just to be polite if its immediate goal had already been reached. At the same time they were very patient when it came to giving explana-tions, painstakingly adapting themselves to the level of their interlocutor and entering into his psychology, however little it might resemble their own.

Naturally, from the very first days aboard I set about learning their language. Everyone, but in particular Netti, was most willing to teach me. The language is a very original one, and despite the great simplicity of its grammar and rules of derivation, there are certain peculiar features which I found difficult to master. Its rules have no exceptions whatever, nor are there any limitations such as the masculine, feminine, and neuter genders. At the same time, however, the names of all objects and qualities are declined according to their temporal status. I simply could not get this into my head.

"Tell me, what is the point of having such forms?" I asked Netti.

"I am surprised you should ask such a question, considering that you understand the much less logical morphology of your languages. When you name something you are careful to designate whether you consider it masculine or feminine, which is not very important and even rather odd in the case of inanimate objects. The difference between objects or persons which exist and those which no longer exist or have yet to come into being is far more significant. The word for 'house' in Russian is masculine and that for 'boat' feminine, whereas in French it is the other way round, but the essence of the matter does not change a jot for that. Yet when you speak of a house which has already burned down or a house which you are still planning to build, you use the word in the same form you employ to designate the house in which you are living. Is there in nature a greater difference than that between a man who is alive and a man who has died—between that which is and that which is not? You need whole words and phrases to express this distinction. Is it not better to indicate it simply by adding a single letter to the same word?"

At any rate, Netti was satisfied with my memory. His teaching methods were superb, and I made rapid progress. This helped me to make friends with the Martians, and I began traveling about the etheroneph with increased confidence, dropping in to the rooms and laboratories of my fellow passengers and interrogating them about everything that interested me.

Sterni's assistant, a young astronomer by the name of Enno, was among my new acquaintances. He was a lively, good-natured sort of fellow, like Netti, not much more than a boy. He showed me a great many interesting things, and he was obviously carried away not so much by the measurements and formulas themselves (although in that field he was a real expert) as by the beauty of what he observed. I felt quite at ease with this young astronomer-poet, and my natural desire to acquaint myself with my new environment constantly gave me occasion to visit Enno and his telescopes.

Once he showed me a picture of the tiny planet Erot under maximum magnification. A segment of its orbit passes through that of Earth and Mars, while the remainder lies beyond Mars and continues into the region of the asteroids. Although Erot was 150 million kilometers away at the time, the photograph of its little disc under the microscope had as much detail as our maps of the moon. Like the moon, of course, the planet is lifeless. On another occasion Enno photographed a swarm of meteors passing only a few million kilometers away. Naturally, the picture showed only an indistinct nebula. It was then that Enno told me that on one of the earlier expeditions to Earth an etheroneph had been destroyed by such a swarm. The astronomers on Mars following the craft in the largest of their telescopes saw its electric lights go out, and the etheroneph vanished forever into space.

"The ship probably collided with several of these small bodies, which, due to the great difference in their respective speeds, must have pierced all its walls. The air in the craft escaped into space, and the cold of the interplanetary environment froze solid the already lifeless bodies of the voyagers. Even now the etheroneph is flying on in orbit like a comet. It has left the solar system forever, and it is impossible to say where the journey of this terrible corpse-laden ship will finally end."

As I heard Enno say this, the cold of the ethereal wastes seemed to pierce my heart as well. I had a vivid mental picture of our bright little island in the middle of an endless dead ocean. Plunging along at a dizzying speed, we were utterly alone and completely surrounded by a black vacuum. Enno guessed what I was feeling.

"Menni is a reliable helmsman," he said, "and Sterni never makes a mistake. As for death . . . I am sure you have seen it close up sometime in your life. Death, after all, is only that and nothing more."

The hour would come when I would recall these words as I struggled with the agonizing pain in my heart.

I was attracted to the chemist Letta not only by the extraordinary gentleness and sensitivity of character Netti had told me about, but also by his enormous knowledge of the scientific field that interested me most, namely the structure of matter. Only Menni was more competent than Letta in this area, but I sought Menni's assistance as little as possible, realizing that his time meant too much to both science and the expedition for me to presume to disturb him. The elderly, good-natured Letta, however, tolerated my ignorance with such inexhaustible patience and explained the rudiments of the subject to me with such courtesy and even evident relish that I felt quite at ease with him.

Letta began giving me an entire course on the theory of the structure of matter, illustrating it with a number of experiments on the decomposition and synthesis of its elements. He was forced, however, to limit himself to a verbal description of many relevant experiments, because certain of them involved a risk of explosion. On one occasion Menni happened to enter the laboratory during a lecture. Letta was just concluding a description of a very interesting experiment and was now preparing to perform it.

"Be careful," Menni warned him. "I remember that once this experiment almost ended in disaster. The slightest contamination of the substance you are decomposing, and even a weak electric charge can detonate it during heating."

Letta was ready to abandon the experiment, but Menni, unfailingly attentive and thoughtful toward me, offered to assist him by checking the preparations, and in fact we obtained splendid results.

The following day we were to carry out some experiments on the same substance. It seemed to me that this time Letta took it from a different jar than the one he had used the day before. He had already set the retort in the electric bath when it occurred to me to mention the fact. He became alarmed and went straight to the cabinet containing the reagents, leaving the bath and the retort on a little table next to the wall, which was also the hull of the etheroneph. I went along with him. Suddenly there came a deafening crash, and we were both flung violently against the door of the cabinet. This was followed by an earsplitting whistle and howl and metallic clatter. An irresistible force, like a hurricane, propelled me backward toward the outer wall. Letta and I both automatically grabbed hold of a sturdy strap attached to the cabinet and hung there horizontally, held in that position by a powerful rush of air.

"Hang on!" he shouted, and I could barely hear his voice above the roar of the storm. A sharp cold pierced my body.

Letta quickly glanced around him. His face was frighteningly pale, but his confused expression suddenly changed to one of lucidity and firm resolve. He uttered only two words—I could not make them out, but I guessed that he was saying goodbye forever—and he released his grip. There was a muffled thump and the howl of the hurricane ceased. I felt that I could let go, and glanced behind me. There was not a trace left of the table. Letta stood stock still with his back pressed tightly to the wall. His eyes were wide open, and his entire face was frozen. With a single bound I reached the door and opened it. I was repulsed by a burst of warm air. A moment later Menni entered the room and went straight to Letta. In a few seconds the room was full of people. Netti pushed everyone aside and rushed to Letta. The others surrounded us in alarmed silence.

"Letta is dead," said Menni. "An explosion during a chemical experiment punctured the wall of the etheroneph and Letta plugged the breach with his body. The air pressure exploded his lungs and paralyzed his heart. Death was instantaneous. Letta saved the life of our guest, for otherwise the death of both would have been inevitable."

Netti burst into a muffled sob.

9. The Past

Netti did not leave his cabin for several days after the accident, and in Sterni's eyes I began to notice an expression that was at times downright hostile. There was no denying that an outstanding scientist had perished on my account, and Sterni's mathematical mind could not help but compare the value of the life that had been lost with the worth of the one that had been spared. Menni remained as even-tempered and calm as ever, even doubling his attention and concern for me. Enno and all the others did the same.

I began an intensive study of the Martian language, and at the first convenient opportunity I asked Menni to give me a book on the history of their peoples. Menni thought that that was a good idea and brought me a handbook in which the history of Mars was presented in a popular form for Martian children. With Netti's help I began reading and translating the work. I was astonished by the grace with which the anonymous author used illustrations to enliven and concretize general concepts and theories which were at first glance extremely abstract. This skill enabled him to present his materials in a geometrically harmonious system and with a logical consistency that no Earthly popularizer would think of using in a book intended for children.

The first chapter was thoroughly philosophical in nature and was devoted to the idea of the Universe as a single all-inclusive and self-determining Whole. This section reminded me of the writings of the worker-philosopher who first expounded the principles of the proletarian philosophy of nature in a simple and naïve form.* In the next chapter the discussion went back to the immensely remote period before the forms of life familiar to us had yet arisen in the Universe and chaos and indeterminacy reigned supreme in boundless space. The author told how the first amorphous accumulations of elusively delicate and chemically indeterminate matter began to separate in this environment. These accumulations served as the embryos of the vast starry worlds of the stellar nebulas. They included the 20 million suns of our own Milky Way, ours being one of the smallest.

From there the book proceeded to an account of the process by which matter, as it became more concentrated and entered into more stable combinations, was transformed into the chemical elements. Parallel to this the primary, amorphous accumulations decomposed, giving rise to the gaseous solar and planetary nebulas, many thousands of which may be observed today with the aid of a telescope. The history of the development of these nebulas and the process by which suns and planets crystallized from them has been treated in a like manner by our Kant-Laplace theory of the origin of the Universe, but here it was clearer and presented in greater detail.

"Tell me, Menni," I asked, "do you really find it advisable to start children off with these exceedingly general and abstract ideas, these pallid pictures of the world so far removed from their concrete everyday life? Is that not filling their little brains with empty, almost exclusively verbal images?"

"The point is that we never begin studying from books," replied

---

*The author is undoubtedly referring to August Bebel (1840–1913), one of the leaders of German Social Democracy.

Menni. "The child draws his information from firsthand observations of nature and real intercourse with other people. Before he even attempts to read such a book he has already been on numerous excursions and seen various pictures of nature. He knows a great many types of plants and animals, is acquainted with the use of the telescope, the microscope, photographs, the phonograph, and has listened to many stories told to him by older children, educators, and other adults about things that are distant in time or space. Books like this one are merely intended to consolidate and reinforce his knowledge, filling in gaps in the process and suggesting to him further avenues of study. Obviously, the idea of the Whole must constantly and above all be brought out as distinctly as possible; the notion must run from beginning to end if it is not to be lost in a welter of detail. The creation of the whole man must begin in the child."

This was all quite new to me, but I did not attempt to question Menni any further. I would in any event soon become acquainted at first hand with Martian children and the system by which they were brought up. I returned to my book.

The subject of the following chapters concerned the geological history of Mars. Although the discussion was presented in very condensed form, it abounded in comparisons with the histories of Earth and Venus. Despite the significant parallels that existed among the three planets, the basic difference lay in the fact that Mars was almost twice as old as Earth and nearly four times the age of Venus. There were exact figures of these ages and I remember them well, but I shall refrain from citing them here lest I irritate scientists on Earth, to whom they would come as quite a surprise.

Next came the history of life from its very beginnings. There was a description of the first compounds, complex cyanic derivatives, which, although they were not yet real living matter, possessed many of its qualities. This was followed by a description of the geological conditions under which these chemical compounds arose. It was explained why it was these substances, rather than other, more stable but less flexible compounds, which were preserved and accumulated. Step by step the author traced the process whereby these chemical embryos of life became more complicated and differentiated, until they finally formed real living cells and initiated the "reign of the Protista." Life continued to develop along the evolutionary ladder or common genealogical tree of all living beings, from the Protista to the highest plants on the one side and to man on the other. There were also of course a number of side branches. In this evolution from the most primitive cells to man, the first and final links in the Martian chain differed only insignificantly from their Earthly counterparts, whereas the discrepancy in the intermediate stages was much greater. I found this to be most curious.

"As far as I know," Netti told me, "this problem has not been given special attention. After all, as recently as twenty years ago we did not even know what the highest animals on Earth were like, and we were very surprised ourselves to discover that humans there resemble us so closely. The number of higher types that can attain the fullest degree of development is evidently limited. Even on planets as similar as ours and under nearly identical conditions, nature was able to evolve this maximum of life in only one way."

"Also," Menni remarked, "the highest type, the one which masters the planet, is the one which most fully reflects the entire sum of its conditions. The intermediate stages, on the other hand, are capable of embracing only a part of their environment. Consequently, their reflection of these conditions is also only partial and one-sided. Thus given the enormous similarity between the respective sets of conditions as a whole, the highest types will coincide to a greater degree than will the intermediate ones, whose very one-sidedness allows them to develop greater variations."

I recalled that while I was yet a university student the same notion of the limited number of possible higher types had occurred to me in quite a different context. Octopuses, marine Cephalopoda that represent the highest organisms of an entire branch of evolution, have eyes which are unusually similar to those of the animals on our branch, the vertebrates. Yet the origin and development of the eyes of the vertebrates are completely different—so different that even the order of the corresponding layers of tissue in the optic apparatus of the mollusks is exactly opposite ours.

As to historical times and the first phases of human life on Mars, here there were also many similarities to Earth. The forms of tribal life were the same on both planets, individual communities detached themselves in the same way, and the same exchange of commodities led to the establishment of very similar intercommunal ties. Beyond that, however, a distinction began to emerge, although it concerned the style and character of the development more than its basic direction. The course of history on Mars was in certain respects gentler and simpler than that on Earth. Naturally there were wars between different tribes and peoples, and there was also a class struggle. However, the wars played a relatively minor role in Martian history and ceased altogether rather early, while the class struggle resulted in far fewer and much less violent clashes of brute force than on Earth. None of this was stated in so many words in the book I was reading, but it was evident to me from the entire context. Slavery was entirely unknown on Mars. There was very little militarism in their feudalism, while their capitalism surmounted the division into nation-states at a very early stage and produced nothing comparable to our modern armies.

I was forced to seek the explanation of these facts on my own. The

Martians, even Menni, had only begun to study the history of mankind on
Earth and had not yet made a comparative investigation of our respective
pasts. I recalled one of my earlier conversations with Menni as I was
preparing to study the language spoken by my fellow passengers. I in-
quired whether it was the most widespread of the languages on Mars.
Menni explained that it was the only literary and spoken language of all
Martians.

"At one time," he added, "peoples from different countries on Mars
could not understand each other either. Long ago, however, several centuries before the socialist revolution, all the various dialects drew closer
to one another and merged in a single common language. This occurred
freely and spontaneously. No one tried to bring it about or even gave it
much thought. Certain local pecularities survived for quite some time, so
there existed something akin to individual dialects, but these were fairly
comprehensible to everyone. The development of literature finally eliminated them as well."

"I can only find one explanation for this phenomenon," I said. "From
the very beginning, communication among people on your planet must
have been much broader, easier, and more intimate than it was on
Earth."

"That is quite correct," replied Menni. "Mars lacks your vast oceans
and impassable mountain ranges. Our seas are not large, nor do they at
any point completely separate continents from one another. Except for
certain individual peaks, our mountains are not high. The entire surface
area of our planet is only one-fourth that of Earth; at the same time the
force of gravity is two and one-half times less, making our bodies so light
that we can move about quite rapidly even without man-made means of
transportation. We can run at the same speed that you ride on horseback,
and it does not tire us the more. Nature has erected far fewer walls and
barriers between our peoples than she has between yours."

This, then, was the main factor that had prevented Martian humanity
from splitting into different nations and races, and such unity in turn
inhibited the development of militarism, wars, and systems of mass destruction. Due to its inherent contradictions, capitalism probably still
would have evolved all these distinguishing characteristics of advanced
civilization, but even the development of capitalism followed a unique
course which created new conditions for the political unification of all the
tribes and peoples of Mars. In agriculture, for example, the small peasants were crowded out at a very early stage by large-scale capitalist farming, and the land was totally nationalized soon after. The reason for this
development lay in the increasing aridity of the soil, which the smallholders were unable to remedy. The crust of the planet soaked up the
surface water and did not yield it up again. This was a continuation of the
natural process by which the once existing oceans on Mars shrank to

become relatively small inland seas. The same process of absorption has also begun on Earth, but there it has not yet progressed very far. On Mars, which is twice as old as Earth, the situation had already become critical a thousand years ago, since as the oceans shrank there was naturally a parallel decrease in cloud cover and precipitation, which meant in turn that the rivers and streams also began to dry up. Artificial irrigation became a necessity in most places. What could independent small farmers do in such a situation?

In some instances they were simply ruined, and their land fell to the large regional holders with enough capital to finance irrigation. In other cases the peasants formed large cooperative associations and pooled their assets in the interest of the common cause. Sooner or later, however, these associations were bound to suffer a lack of pecuniary resources. The deficiency seemed only temporary at first, but as soon as the first loans were concluded with the powerful capitalists the cooperatives rapidly began to deteriorate. High rates of interest on the loans increased outlays, it then became necessary to seek new loans, and so it went. The associations fell under the economic control of their creditors, who eventually ruined them and took over the holdings of hundreds and thousands of peasants in a single sweep.

Thus all cultivated land was transferred to a few thousand powerful agricultural capitalists. In the interior of the continents, however, there still remained vast deserts which the individual capitalists could not afford to irrigate. When the by then thoroughly democratic state was forced to involve itself in the project in order to absorb the growing surplus of the proletariat and aid the remnants of the dying peasantry, it turned out that even it did not possess the kind of resources necessary to build the gigantic canals. The capitalist syndicates wanted to take charge of the enterprise, but the entire people rose in protest, realizing that this would give the syndicates complete control over the state. After a long struggle in which the agricultural capitalists put up desperate resistance, a progressive tax on profits from the land was introduced. The revenues obtained through this tax went into a fund to finance the enormous project of building the canals. The power of the landlords was broken, and soon the land was nationalized. The last remnants of the small peasantry disappeared in the process, because in its own interests the state leased land only to the big capitalists, and the agricultural concerns became vaster than ever. Thus the famous canals served as a powerful stimulus to economic development at the same time as they firmly reinforced the political unity of all mankind.

When I finished reading all this I could not refrain from telling Menni how surprised I was at the fact that human hands had built water routes so gigantic that they could even be seen from Earth with our weak telescopes.

"That is not altogether correct," said Menni. "The canals are indeed immense, but they are not dozens of kilometers wide, as they would in fact have to be for your astronomers to be able to see them. What they see are the broad bands of forest we have planted along the canals in order to maintain an even level of humidity in the air and prevent the water from evaporating too rapidly. Some of your scientists seem to have guessed as much."

The epoch of the digging of the canals was a time of great prosperity in all areas of industry and a period of profound calm in the class struggle. The demand for labor was tremendous, and unemployment disappeared. But when the Great Project was finished, bringing to completion the capitalist colonization of the former wastelands, an industrial crisis soon broke out which disrupted the "social peace." The result was a social revolution, but once again the course of events was relatively peaceful. Strikes were the workers' main weapon, while the rare uprisings that occurred were restricted to a few, almost exclusively agricultural regions. The owners retreated step by step before the inevitable, and even when the government fell into the hands of the workers' party, the vanquished did not attempt to assert their interests by force.

When the means of production were socialized, there was no compensation in the true sense of the word. At first, however, the capitalists were pensioned off. Many of them later played an important role in the organization of state-owned enterprises. It proved very difficult to distribute labor resources in accordance with the vocational training of the workers. Except for the capitalists on pension, for about a century there was an obligatory working day of six hours at first, which was successively shortened. Technical progress and the exact computation of available labor, however, finally helped to eliminate even these last vestiges of the old system.

I could not help feeling a certain envy as I viewed this picture of steady social evolution free from the fire and blood of our own history. I mentioned it to Netti as we were finishing the book.

"I don't know," he said thoughtfully, "but I think that you are wrong. True, the conflicts on Earth have been more acute than ours, and the natural environment has always shown a greater tendency to retaliate with death and destruction. But perhaps this is due to the fact that Earth is so much more richly endowed with natural resources and the life-giving energy of the sun. Look how much older our planet is, yet our humanity arose only a few tens of thousands of years before yours and is at present a mere two or three hundred years ahead of you in development. I tend to think of our two humanities as brothers. The elder one has a calm and balanced temperament, while the younger one is stormy and impetuous. The younger one is more wasteful with his resources, and prone to serious errors. His childhood was sickly and turbulent, and as he now approaches adolescence he often suffers from convulsive growing pains. But might he not become a greater and more powerful artist and creator than his elder brother? And in that case, will he not eventually be able to adorn our great Universe even better and more richly? I cannot be certain, but it seems to me that this is what may happen."

10. Arrival

Piloted by Menni's lucid intellect, the etheroneph continued toward its distant goal without further incidents. I had managed to adapt tolerably well to the conditions of a weightless existence and could already cope with the main difficulties of the Martian language by the time Menni announced that we had come halfway and attained maximum velocity, which now would begin decreasing. At the exact moment Menni had indicated, the etheroneph quickly and smoothly turned over. Earth, which long ago had shrunk from a large bright sickle to a little crescent and from a little crescent to a bright greenish star near the disc of the sun, now moved from the lower to the upper hemisphere of the black firmament, and the red star Mars that had been shining above our heads was now below us.

Dozens, hundreds of hours passed, and the red star became a bright little disc. Soon one could see two small stars, its satellites Deimos and Phobos, tiny, harmless little planets wholly undeserving of their ominous Greek names "Terror" and "Fear." The usually serious Martians became more lively and visited Enno's observatory more frequently to look at their native land. I looked too, but despite Enno's patient explanations I understood little of what I saw. The planet presented a strange sight indeed. The red patches were forests and meadows, while the darker ones were fields ready for harvesting. The cities appeared as bluish spots, and only water and snow were of a color familiar to me. The jovial Enno sometimes made me guess what it was I saw in the telescope, and he and Netti were greatly amused by my naïve mistakes. I repaid them by jokingly calling their planet the home of erudite owls and mixed-up colors.

The red disc grew steadily larger. Soon it was noticeably bigger than the circle of the sun and resembled an unlabeled astronomical map. The force of gravity also began to become perceptibly greater, and I found the sensation very pleasant indeed. Deimos and Phobos were transformed from bright points of light into tiny but distinctly marked little circles.

Fifteen or twenty hours later, Mars appeared spread out below us like a huge flat disc. I could see more with my naked eye than is found on any of our astronomical maps. Deimos glided across this map, while Phobos had disappeared from sight to the other side of the planet.

Everyone around me was happy. I alone could not overcome an uneasy, melancholy feeling of expectation. Closer and closer . . . No one

The approach of the space ship to Mars, with Leonid on board

could concentrate on work; everyone was gazing down at the world un-
folding below. It was their world; to me it was full of mysteries and
riddles. Only Menni was not with us. He was in the engine room, for the
last hours of the journey were the most risky, and he had to check the
distance and regulate our speed. Why was it that I—as fate would have it,
the Columbus of this world—felt no joy or pride or even the soothing
calm that should have come from the sight of the solid shore after a long
voyage across the Ocean of the Ethereal? The events of the future were
already casting their shadow on the present.

Only two hours to go. Soon we would be entering the atmosphere.
My head started throbbing so painfully that I could look no longer and
retired to my cabin. Netti came with me. He started talking to me—not
about the present but about the past, about distant Earth, there up
above.

"You must return when you have accomplished your mission," he
said, and to me his words sounded like a gentle reminder to be brave. I
lost track of time as we discussed the necessity of the assignment and its
many difficulties.

Netti looked at the chronometer. "We have arrived. Let's rejoin the
others!" he exclaimed.

The etheroneph came to a stop, the wide metal plates opened, and
fresh air rushed in. Above us was a clear blue green sky—around us, a
throng of people. Menni and Sterni disembarked first, carrying a transparent coffin containing the frozen body of their dead comrade, Letta.
The others followed after them. Netti and I left last. Together, hand in
hand, we made our way through a crowd of thousands, who all looked just
like Netti.

PART II

1. Menni's Apartment

During the first period of my stay I moved in with Menni in a factory
settlement—that is to say, a planned complex of industry and resi-
dences—whose physical center and economic base was a large chemical
laboratory located far below ground. The part of the settlement above
ground was spread through a park covering about ten square kilometers
and consisted of several hundred apartment buildings for the laboratory
workers, a large meeting hall, the Cooperative Depot, which was something on the order of a large department store, and the Communications
Center, which connects the settlement with the rest of the world. Menni

was the factory supervisor and lived not far from the community buildings right next to the main descent to the laboratory.

What first surprised me about nature on Mars, and the thing I found most difficult to get used to, was the red vegetation. The substance which gives it this color is similar in chemical composition to the chlorophyll of plants on Earth and performs a parallel function in their life processes, building tissues from the carbon dioxide in the air and the energy of the sun. Netti thoughtfully suggested that I wear protective glasses to prevent irritation of the eyes, but I refused.

"Red is the color of our socialist banner," I said, "so I shall simply have to get used to your socialist vegetation."

"In that case you must also recognize the presence of socialism in the plants on Earth," Menni remarked. "Their leaves also possess a red hue, but it is concealed by the stronger green color. If you were to don a pair of glasses which completely absorb the green waves of light but admit the red ones, you would see that your forests and fields are as red as ours."

I lack the time and space to describe the peculiar Martian flora and fauna, nor can I devote much attention to the atmosphere of the planet, which is pure and clear, relatively thin, but rich in oxygen. The sky is a deep, dark green, and the most prominent celestial bodies are the sun— much smaller than it appears on Earth—the two tiny moons, and two bright evening or morning stars, Venus and Earth. All of this was strange and foreign to me then and seems splendid and precious to me now as I look back upon it, but it is not essential to the purpose of my narrative. The people and their relationships are what concern me most, and they were the most fantastic and mysterious of all the wonders of this fairy-tale world.

Menni lived in a small two-story house that was indistinguishable architecturally from all the rest. The most original feature of this architecture was the transparent roof made of several huge sheets of blue glass. The bedroom and a parlor for receiving guests were located directly beneath it. Because of its soothing effect, the Martians prefer blue light during their leisure time. The color of the human face in this light does not strike them as gloomy. All of the work rooms—the study, Menni's home laboratory, the communications room—were on the ground floor, whose large windows freely admitted the restless red light reflected from the foliage of the trees in the park. This light made me uneasy and absentminded at first, but the Martians are used to it and find it has a stimulating effect on work.

Menni's study was full of books and writing implements, from ordinary pencils to a phonotype, a complex mechanism in which a phonograph recording of clearly enunciated speech activated the keys of a typewriter which accurately translated it into the written alphabet. Playing the phonogram did not erase it, so that one could use either it or the printed translation, whichever happened to be more convenient.

Above Menni's desk hung a portrait of a middle-aged Martian. He resembled Menni, although his almost sinister expression of grim energy and cold resolve was alien to Menni, whose face merely reflected a tranquil and resolute will. Menni told me the story of this man's life.

He was one of Menni's ancestors, a great engineer* who lived long before the social revolution, during the epoch of the Great Canals. It was he who planned, organized, and supervised that grandiose project. His first assistant envied his fame and power and launched a conspiracy against him. Several hundred thousand men were employed on the construction of one of the main canals, which passed through a swampy, disease-infested region. Thousands perished, and great discontent spread among the survivors. While the chief engineer was busy negotiating with the central government of Mars about pensions for the families of the dead and the incapacitated, his assistant was secretly rousing the dissatisfied workers against him, inciting them to strike and demand transfers to other regions. This was impossible, as it would have disrupted the entire plan of the Great Project, but he also urged them to call for the resignation of the chief engineer, which, of course, was quite feasible. When the latter learned of all this he summoned his assistant for an explanation and killed him on the spot. The engineer declined to defend himself at his trial, declaring that he considered his behavior just and necessary. He was sentenced to a long prison term.

Soon, however, it became obvious that none of his successors was capable of running the gigantic undertaking. Misunderstandings, embezzlement, and disorders followed. The entire mechanism of the project broke down; expenses increased by hundreds of millions, and the acute discontent of the workers threatened to end in open revolt. The central government hastenend to address an appeal to the chief engineer, offering to pardon him in full and reinstate him in his former position. He refused the pardon, but consented to head the project from prison. The inspectors he appointed quickly got to the bottom of things at the various construction sites. Thousands of engineers and contractors were put on trial. Wages were raised, the system by which the workers were supplied with food, clothing, and tools was reorganized from top to bottom, work plans were reviewed and revised. Order was soon fully restored, and once again the enormous mechanism began functioning rapidly and smoothly like an obedient tool in the hands of a real master.

The master, however, not only supervised the entire project but also planned its continuation in the years to come, grooming a certain

---

*Engineer Menni, the main character in the following novel.

energetic and talented engineer from a working-class background to be his successor. By the time his prison term had expired, everything had been so well prepared that the great master was confident the project could be safely entrusted to others. The very moment the prime minister of the central government arrived at the prison to release him, the engineer committed suicide. As Menni was telling me all this his face underwent a peculiar transformation, taking on an expression of inflexible severity that gave him a striking resemblance to his ancestor. I sensed that he understood and sympathized with this man who had died hundreds of years before he was born.

The communications room was at the center of the ground floor. It contained telephones attached to visual devices which transmitted an image of everything that passed in front of them at any distance. One of these apparatuses connected Menni's house with the Communications Center, which was in turn joined to all the cities of the planet. Other devices provided communication with the underground laboratory which Menni headed. These were in continuous function: several finely gridded screens showed a reduced image of illuminated rooms full of large metal machines and glass equipment attended by hundreds of workers. I asked Menni to take me on a tour of the laboratory.

"That would be ill-advised," he answered. "The substances handled there are unstable, and although we take considerable precautions, there is always a slight risk of explosion or of poisoning by invisible rays. You must not expose yourself to such dangers. Being the only one of your kind we have, you are irreplaceable."

Menni's home laboratory contained only the materials and equipment relevant to the research he was doing at a given moment. Near the ceiling of the corridor on the ground floor hung an aero-gondola that was always ready to take us wherever we might want to go.

"Where does Netti live?" I asked Menni.

"In a large city about two hour's flying time from here. A big engineering works employing tens of thousands of workers is located there, so Netti has ample material for medical research. We have another doctor at our enterprise."

"Surely I would be permitted to inspect that factory sometime?"

"Of course. There is nothing particularly dangerous there. We can visit it tomorrow if you like."

We decided to do so.

2. The Factory

We covered approximately 500 kilometers in two hours. That is the speed of a plummeting falcon, and so far not even our electric trains have been able to match it. Unfamiliar landscapes unfurled below us in rapid succession. At times we were overtaken by strange birds flying even faster than we. The blue roofs of houses and the giant yellow domes of buildings I did not recognize glittered in the sunlight. The rivers and canals flashed like ribbons of steel. My eyes lingered on them, for they were the same as on Earth. In the distance appeared a hugh city spread out around a small lake and transversed by a canal. The gondola slowed down and landed gently near a small and pretty house that proved to be Netti's. Netti was at home and glad to see us. He got into our gondola and we set off for the factory, which was located a few kilometers away on the other side of the lake.

It consisted of five huge buildings arranged in the form of a cross. They were all identically designed, each of them having a transparent glass vault supported by several dozen dark columns in a slightly elongated ellipse. The walls between the columns were made of alternating sheets of transparent and frosted glass. We stopped by the central building, also the largest, whose gates were about 10 meters wide and 12 meters high, filling the entire space between two columns. The ceiling of the first floor transected the gates at the middle. Several pairs of rails ran through the gates and disappeared into the interior of the building.

We ascended in the gondola to the upper half of the gates and, amid the deafening roar of the machines, flew directly into the second story. Actually, the floors of the factory were not stories as we understand them. At each level there were gigantic machines of a construction unfamiliar to me, surrounded by a network of suspended glass-parquet footbridges girded by beams of gridded steel. Interconnected by a multitude of stairways and elevators, these networks ascended toward the top of the factory in five progressively smaller tiers.

The factory was completely free from smoke, soot, odors, and fine dust. The machines, flooded in a light that illuminated everything yet was by no means harsh, operated steadily and methodically in the clean fresh air, cutting, sawing, planing, and drilling huge pieces of iron, aluminum, nickel, and copper. Levers rose and fell smoothly and evenly like giant steel hands. Huge platforms moved back and forth with automatic precision. The wheels and transmission belts seemed immobile. The soul of this formidable mechanism was not the crude force of fire and steam, but the fine yet even mightier power of electricity. When the ear had become somewhat accustomed to it, the noise of the machines began to seem almost melodious, except, that is, when the several-thousand-ton hammer would fall and everything would shudder from the thunderous blow.

Hundreds of workers moved confidently among the machines, their footsteps and voices drowned in a sea of sound. There was not a trace of tense anxiety on their faces, whose only expression was one of quiet concentration. They seem to be inquisitive, learned observers who had no real part in all that was going on around them. It was as if they simply

A Martian factory

found it interesting to watch how the enormous chunks of metal glided out beneath the transparent dome on moving platforms and fell into the steely embrace of dark monsters, where after a cruel game in which they were cracked open by powerful jaws, mauled by hard, heavy paws, and planed and drilled by sharp, flashing claws, small electric railway cars bore them off from the other side of the building in the form of elegant and finely fashioned machine parts whose purpose was a mystery to me. It seemed altogether natural that the steel monsters should not harm the small, big-eyed spectators strolling confidently among them: the giants simply scorned the frail humans as a quarry unworthy of their awesome might. To an outsider the threads connecting the delicate brains of the men with the indestructible organs of the machines were subtle and invisible.

When we finally emerged from the building, the engineer acting as our guide asked us whether we would rather go on immediately to the other buildings and auxiliary shops or take a rest. I voted for a break.

"Now I have seen the machines and the workers," I said, "but I have no idea whatever of how production is organized, and I wonder whether you could tell me something about that."

Instead of answering, the engineer took us to a small cubical building between the central factory and one of the corner edifices. There were three more such structures, all of them arranged in the same way. Their black walls were covered with rows of shiny white signs showing tables of production statistics. I knew the Martian language well enough to be able to decipher them. On the first of them, which was marked with the number one, was the following:

"The machine-building industry has a surplus of 968,757 man-hours daily, of which 11,325 hours are of skilled labor. The surplus at this factory is 753 hours, of which 29 hours are of skilled labor.

"There is no labor shortage in the following industries: agriculture, chemicals, excavations, mining," and so on, in a long alphabetical list of various branches of industry.

Table number two read:

"The clothing industry has a shortage of 392,685 man-hours daily, of which 21,380 hours require experienced repairmen for special machines and 7,852 hours require organization experts."

"The footwear industry lacks 79,360 hours, of which . . ." and so on.

"The Institute of Statistics—3,078 hours . . ." and so on.

There were similar figures on the third and fourth tables, which covered occupations such as preschool education, primary and secondary education, medicine in rural areas, and medicine in urban areas.

"Why is it that a surplus of labor is indicated with precision only for the machine-building industry, whereas it is the shortages everywhere else that are noted in such detail?" I asked.

"It is quite logical," replied Menni. "The tables are meant to affect the distribution of labor. If they are to do that, everyone must be able to see where there is a labor shortage and just how big it is. Assuming that an individual has the same or an approximately equal aptitude for two vocations, he can then choose the one with the greater shortage. As to labor surpluses, exact data on them need be indicated only where such a surplus actually exists, so that each worker in that branch can take into consideration both the size of the surplus and his own inclination to change vocations."

As we were talking I suddenly noticed that certain figures on the table had disappeared and been replaced by others. I asked what that meant.

"The figures change every hour," Menni explained. "In the course of an hour several thousand workers announce that they want to change jobs. The central statistical apparatus takes constant note of this, transmitting the data hourly to all branches of industry."

"But how does the central apparatus arrive at its figures on surpluses and shortages?"

"The Institute of Statistics has agencies everywhere which keep track of the flow of goods into and out of the stockpiles and monitor the productivity of all enterprises and the changes in their work forces. In that way it can be calculated what and how much must be produced for any given period and the number of man-hours required for the task. The Institute then computes the difference between the existing and the desired situation for each vocational area and communicates the result to all places of employment. Equilibrium is soon established by a stream of volunteers."

"But are there no restrictions on the consumption of goods?"

"None whatsoever. Everyone takes whatever he needs in whatever quantities he wants."

"Do you mean that you can do all this without money, documents certifying that a certain amount of labor has been performed, pledges to perform labor, or anything at all of that sort?"

"Nothing at all. There is never any shortage of voluntary labor—work is a natural need for the mature member of our society, and all overt or disguised compulsion is quite superfluous."

"But if consumption is entirely uncontrolled, there must be sharp fluctuations which upset all your statistical compilations."

"Not at all. A single individual may suddenly eat two or three times his normal portion of a given food or decide to change ten suits in ten days, but a society of billions of people is not subject to such fluctuations. In a population of that size deviations in any given direction are neutralized, and averages change very slowly and with the strictest continuity."

"In other words your statistics work almost automatically—they are calculations pure and simple?"

"No, not really, for there are great difficulties involved in the process. The Institute of Statistics must be alert to new inventions and changes in environmental conditions which may affect industry. The introduction of a new machine, for example, immediately requires a transfer of labor in the field in which it is employed, in the machine-building industry, and sometimes also in the production of materials for both branches. If a given ore is exhausted or if new mineral fields are discovered there will again be a transfer of labor in a number of industries—mining, railroad construction, and so on. All of these factors must be calculated from the very beginning, if not with absolute precision then at least with an adequate degree of approximation. And until firsthand data become available, that is no easy task."

"Considering such difficulties," I remarked, "I suppose you must constantly have a certain surplus labor reserve."

"Precisely, and this is the main strength of our system. Two hundred years ago, when collective labor just barely managed to satisfy the needs of society, statistics had to be very exact, and labor could not be distributed with complete freedom. There was an obligatory working day, and within those bounds it was not always or fully possible to take the vocational training of the workers into account. However, although each new invention caused statistical problems, it also contributed to solving the main difficulty, namely the transition to a system in which each individual is perfectly free to choose his own occupation. First the working day was shortened, and then, when a surplus arose in all branches, the obligation was dropped altogether. Note that the labor shortages indicated for the various industries are almost negligible, amounting to mere thousands, tens or hundreds of thousands of man-hours out of the millions and tens of millions of hours presently expended by those same industries."

"But shortages of labor do still exist," I objected. "Yet I suppose that they are covered by later surpluses, are they not?"

"Not only by later surpluses. In reality, necessary labor is computed by adding a certain quantity to the basic figures. In the most vital branches of industry—the production of food, clothing, buildings, machines, and so on—this margin can be as high as 5 percent, whereas in less important areas it is about 1.2 percent. Thus generally speaking, the figures in these tables indicating shortages express merely a relative deficiency, not an absolute one."

"How long is the average working day—at this factory, for example?"

"From an hour and a half to two and a half hours," replied the guide, "but there are those who work both more and less. Take, for example, the comrade operating the main hammer. He is so fascinated by his job that he refuses to be relieved during the entire six hours daily the factory is in production."

I mentally translated these figures from the Martian system of reckoning into our own. On Mars a day and night together are a little longer than on Earth and are divided into ten of their hours. This means that the average working day is from four to six Earth-hours, and the longest operational day is about fifteen hours, which is approximately the same as in our most intensely run enterprises.

"But isn't it harmful for that comrade at the hammer to work so much?" I asked.

"Not for the time being," Netti replied. "He can permit himself such a luxury for another six months or so. But of course I have warned him of the dangers to which his enthusiasm exposes him. One such risk is the possibility of a convulsive fit of madness that may irresistibly draw him under the hammer. Last year something like that happened at this very factory to another operator who was likewise fascinated by powerful sensations. It was only by a lucky chance that we managed to stop the hammer in time and avert the involuntary suicide. An appetite for strong sensations is in itself no disease, but it can easily become perverted if the nervous system is thrown ever so little off-balance by exhaustion, emotional disturbances, or an occasional illness. Of course I try to keep an eye on those workers who become overly engrossed in any sort of monotonous work."

"Shouldn't this man you mentioned have cut down his labor, considering that there is a surplus in the machine-building industry?"

"Of course not," Menni laughed. "Why should just he take it upon himself to restore the equilibrium? The statistics oblige no one to do that. Everyone takes these figures into consideration when making their own plans, but they cannot be guided by them alone. If you were to want to begin working at this factory you would probably find a job; the surplus figure in the central statistics would rise by one or two hours, and that would be that. The statistics continually affect *mass* transfers of labor, but each individual is free to do as he chooses."

We had time to rest up during our conversation, and everyone except Menni, who was forced to leave by a call from his laboratory, continued the excursion through the factory. I decided to spend the night at Netti's, as he promised to take me to the Children's Colony, where his mother was working as an educator.

3. The Children's Colony

There were some 15 to 20 thousand persons, almost all of them children or educators, living at the Children's Colony, which occupied the whole of one of the largest and best parts of the city. All major cities of the planet have such institutions, and in many cases they even comprise independent towns. The only places they are not generally found is in smaller communities such as Menni's "factory settlement."

Large two-story houses with the usual blue roofs were scattered among gardens with streams, ponds, fields for play and gymnastics, flower beds and plots of medicinal herbs, little houses for pets and birds. Everywhere were throngs of large-eyed children—of which sex it was impossible to tell, for boys and girls were dressed identically. True, it is difficult to distinguish even the adult Martian men from the women solely on the basis of their dress, as it is fundamentally the same and differs only slightly in style. The clothes of the men follow the form of the body more exactly than those of the women, which instead tend to conceal it. At any rate, the elderly person who greeted us as we descended from the gondola at the doors of one of the largest buildings was a woman, because Netti called her "Mama" as he embraced her. Later on, however, he simply said "Nella," addressing her by name as he would any other comrade.

Already informed as to the purpose of our visit, the Martian woman took us directly to her colony and led us on a thorough tour of it, beginning with the section for the youngest children, of which she was the superintendant, to the section for the oldest ones, who had already reached the first years of adolescence. Little "monsters" joined us on the way and followed along behind, their huge eyes observing with curiosity the man from another planet. They knew very well who I was, and by the time we had visited the last sections there was a whole crowd of them tagging along with us, even though most of the children in the colony had gone to play in the gardens early that morning.

In this particular part of the colony there were about three hundred children of different ages. I asked Nella why the age-groups were mixed, since separating them would considerably facilitate the assignment of tasks among the educators and simplify their work.

"Because such a system would not really be child-rearing," replied Nella. "If a child is to be trained to participate in society, he must live in society. Children acquire most of their knowledge of life from each other. Isolating the age-groups would mean creating a one-sided and narrow environment in which the development of the future man would be slow, sluggish, and monotonous. Age differences also make it easier to activate the children. The older children are our best helpers in caring for the little ones. No, not only do we deliberately mix children of all ages in our colonies, we also attempt to select personnel who differ greatly with respect to age and practical specialties."

"Yet I notice that in the sections the children are grouped according to age. This does not seem to agree with what you have just told me."

"The children are brought together in the sections only to sleep and eat. Here, of course, there is no reason to mix the different age groups. But when they play and study they are allowed to group themselves any way they want. Even when something such as the reading of a fictional or scientific work is presented to the children of one section, the auditorium is always filled by children from other sections. The children choose their own company, and they like to make friends with boys and girls of other ages and especially with adults."

"Nella," said one little boy, stepping out of the crowd, "Esta took my boat, the one I made myself. Take it away from her and give it back to me."

"Where is she?" Nella asked.

"She ran away to the pond to sail the boat on the water," explained the child.

"Well, I'm busy at the moment. Get one of the older children to go along with you and convince Esta to be nice to you. Or better yet, go alone and help her sail the boat. Small wonder that she likes it, if it is such a good one."

The child left, and Nella addressed the others:

"Listen, children, please leave us alone now. Our guest can hardly find it pleasant to have hundreds of children's eyes goggling at him. Just imagine, Elvi, that a whole crowd of foreigners like him were staring at you. What would you do?"

"I'd run away," bravely answered the nearest little boy she had named. And all the children immediately ran off laughing. We went out into the garden.

"Yes, well, there you can see that the legacy of the past is very powerful," said the educator with a smile. "Our communism seems to be complete; we almost never have to deny the children anything. Where could a sense of private ownership possibly come from? Yet a child will suddenly come along and start talking about 'my' boat, 'the one I made myself.' Such things happen very often, and sometimes they can even end in fights. There is no helping it; according to a universal law of life the development of the organism repeats in abbreviated form the development of the species. Analogously, the development of the individual repeats that of society. The process whereby most children in the intermediate and upper age-groups establish their self-identity often assumes such vaguely individualistic forms. The approach of sexual maturity at first intensifies that element even more. Not until adolescence is the social environment finally able to conquer the vestiges of the past."

"Do you acquaint the children with the past?" I asked.

"Of course, and they are very fond of hearing and discussing stories about bygone times. At first we give them fairy tales, beautiful and somewhat frightening fairy tales about another world that is distant and strange but whose pictures of struggle and violence awaken vague responses in the atavistic depths of the child's instincts. It is not until later, when the child has overcome the remnants of the past in himself, that he learns to grasp the temporal connection more clearly. The images and fairy tales then become real history for him and are transformed into living links in a living chain."

We strolled along the lanes of a spacious garden. From time to time we came upon groups of children playing, digging canals, working with handicrafts, building arbors, or simply talking animatedly among themselves. They all turned to look at me with curiosity, but none of them followed us. Evidently they had all been told not to. Most of the groups we met were of mixed ages, and there were one or two adults in many of them.

"There are quite a few educators in your colony," I remarked.

"Yes, especially if you count all the older children, which one really should do. But we have only three professionally trained educators here. Most of the other adults you see are mothers and fathers who are visiting us to be with their children, or young people interested in becoming educators."

"Do you mean that parents can move in here to live with their children?"

"Yes, of course, and some of the mothers stay on for several years. Most, however, come to visit for a week, two weeks, perhaps a month. Even fewer fathers live here. In our colony there are sixty separate rooms for parents and for children who want privacy, and as far as I can remember these rooms have always been quite sufficient."

"In other words, sometimes even the children would rather not live together with the collective."

"Yes, often the older children prefer to live separately. This is partly due to the vague individualism I was telling you about and partly, especially in the case of children with a strong aptitude for scientific pursuits, it simply reflects a desire to get away from everything that might distract or disturb them. After all, many adults also like to live alone. Most of them are people who are deeply engrossed in scientific research or artistic creation."

At this moment we noticed a child on the small field in front of us—I would say he was six or seven—who was chasing some sort of animal with a stick. We quickened our pace; the child did not see us. Just as we approached him he caught his quarry, an animal resembling a large frog, and dealt it a heavy blow with his stick. The creature slowly crawled off across the grass with a broken paw.

"Why did you do that, Aldo?" Nella asked him calmly.

"I couldn't catch it, it kept running away," explained the little boy.

"Do you know what you have done? You have broken the frog's leg and caused it pain. Give me the stick and I will show you what I mean."

The boy gave Nella the cane, and with a flick of her wrist she rapped him sharply on the hand.

"Does it hurt, Aldo?" Nella asked him in the same calm tone of voice.

"Yes! A lot! Naughty Nella!" he answered.

"You hit the frog even harder. I only bruised your hand, but you broke its leg. Not only is the frog in more pain than you, but now it cannot run and jump, it won't be able to find food and will die of hunger. Or else it won't be able to run away from the other mean animals, and they will eat it up. What do you think about that, Aldo?"

The boy stood in silence with tears of pain in his eyes, holding his bruised hand in the other. But he was thinking. After a moment he answered: "We have to fix its leg."

"Exactly," said Netti. "Come here and I will show you how."

They captured the animal, which had only managed to crawl a few paces. Netti took out his handkerchief and tore it into strips. Aldo followed his instructions and brought him some slivers of wood. Then both of them, with the gravity of children engrossed in something extremely important, set about bandaging the broken leg of the frog in a splint.

Soon Netti and I began thinking about going home.

"Incidentally," Nella suddenly remembered, "this evening you have a chance to see your old friend Enno. He is coming here to lecture to the older children on the planet Venus."

"I see. So he lives here in the city?" I asked.

"No, the observatory where he works is three hours from here. But he is very fond of children and has never forgotten old Nella, his former teacher. So he visits us often, and always has something interesting to tell the children."

That evening, of course, we returned to the Children's Colony at the appointed hour and proceeded to a large auditorium. All except the youngest children and a few dozen adults were already gathered there. Enno greeted me warmly.

"It almost seems as though I had you in mind when I chose the theme of my lecture," he joked. "You are saddened by the backwardness of your planet and the maliciousness of your humanity. I shall be talking about a planet where the highest forms of life at present are dinosaurs and flying lizards, whose manners are even worse than those of your bourgeoisie. Coal is not blazing in the furnaces of capitalism there, but is still growing in the form of gigantic forests. Shall we go hunting ichthyosauruses sometime? They are the local Rothschilds and Rockefellers—much gentler than the Earthly variety, of course, but then they are also far less cultivated. Life there is on a level of primary accumulation which your Marx neglects to mention in his *Capital*. Well, I notice Nella is frowning at my idle chatter, so I shall get on with my lecture."

Enno gave a fascinating account of the distant planet, its deep, storm-tossed oceans and towering mountains, its scorching sun and thick white clouds, terrible hurricanes and thunderstorms, grotesque monsters and majestic giant plants. He illustrated his lecture with moving pictures on a screen which took up an entire wall of the auditorium. Enno's voice was the only sound to be heard in the darkness; the audience was plunged into deep concentration. As he was describing the adventures of the first voyagers to Venus and telling how one of them had killed a giant lizard with a hand grenade, however, I witnessed an odd little scene which hardly anyone else noticed. Aldo, who had kept close to Nella the whole while, suddenly started crying.

"What's the matter?" she asked, bending over him.

"I feel sorry for the monster. He got hurt and died," the boy answered quietly.

Nella embraced him and began explaining something to him in a low voice, but it was some time before he calmed down.

Enno went on to tell about the incalculable natural resources of this splendid planet—giant waterfalls whose energy could be measured in hundreds of millions of horsepower, precious metals lying right at the surface in the mountains, enormously rich deposits of radium at a depth of just a few hundred meters, stores of energy that would last for hundreds of thousands of years. I did not yet speak the language well enough to be able to appreciate the beauty of Enno's descriptions, but I was as enthralled as the children by the pictures he painted. When he had finished and the lights went up, I even felt a little sad—like a child who has just heard the end of a beautiful fairy tale.

The lecture was followed by questions and objections from the audience. The questions were as varied as the listeners, concerning both details in the nature of Venus and the methods of conquering it. Someone asked how long it would take for human life to evolve on the planet, and what people would have to be like physically. The objections, mostly naïve but some of them fairly penetrating, were mainly aimed at Enno's conclusion that at present Venus was very inhospitable and that it would be a long time before her enormous riches could be exploited to any meaningful degree. The young optimists in the audience protested vigorously against these views, which, however, were shared by most Martian scientists. Enno pointed out a number of negative factors: the hot sun and the humid, bacteria-infested air, for example, made disease a constant threat, as all previous voyagers to Venus had discovered, while hurricanes and storms impeded work and were a danger to human life. The children thought it odd to retreat in the face of such obstacles—such a splendid planet simply had to be conquered. Thousands of doctors could be dispatched at once to combat the germs and diseases; as for the hurricanes and storms, engineers could build high walls and put up lightning rods. "Let nine out of ten die in the attempt," said a lad of twelve, "This is something worth dying for. Victory at any price!" And it was evident from his fiery gaze that he would not surrender even if he were to find himself among the doomed nine-tenths.

Enno gently and calmly demolished his opponents' flimsy arguments, but it was obvious that deep down he symphathized with them
and that his passionate youthful imagination entertained equally drastic
notions. His plans, of course, had been thought through more carefully,
but they were every bit as selfless. He himself had not yet been to Venus,
and it was evident from his enthusiasm that he was greatly fascinated by
her beauty and her perils.

When the talk was over, Enno left with me and Netti. He intended to
stay another day in the city and invited me to accompany him to the art
museum the following morning. Netti was busy, having been called to
another city to attend an important medical conference.

4. The Museum of Art

"I must say I never even imagined that you might have special
museums for works of art," I said to Enno on our way to the museum. "I
thought that sculpture and picture galleries were peculiar to capitalism,
with its ostentatious luxury and crass ambition to hoard treasures. I assumed that in a socialist order art would be found disseminated throughout society so as to enrich life everywhere."

"Quite correct," replied Enno. "Most of our works of art are intended
for the public buildings in which we decide matters of common interest,
study and do research, and spend our leisure time. We adorn our factories
and plants much less often. Powerful machines and their precise movements are aesthetically pleasing to us in and of themselves, and there are
very few works of art which would fully harmonize with them without
somehow weakening or dissipating their impact. Least decorated of all are
our homes, in which most of us spend very little time. As for our art
museums, they are scientific research institutes, schools at which we
study the development of art or, more precisely, the development of
mankind through artistic activity."

The museum was located on a little island, in the middle of a lake,
connected to the shore by a narrow bridge. The building itself, a rec-
tangular structure surrounded by a garden full of fountains and beds of
blue, white, black, and green flowers, was lavishly adorned outside and
flooded with light inside. It contained none of that jumbled accumulation
of statues and paintings that clutters the major museums of Earth. Several
hundred pictures depicted the evolution of the plastic arts from the first
primitive works of the prehistorical period to the technically perfect creations of the previous century. Throughout, one could sense the presence
of that living inner wholeness that people call "genius." Obviously, these
were the best works from all periods.

In order fully to understand the beauty of another world, one must
be intimately acquainted with life there, and in order to convey an idea of

Enno shows Leonid the Museum of Art on Mars

that beauty to others one must be an organic part of that life. For that reason I cannot possibly describe what I saw, but will limit myself to hints and fragmentary references to that which impressed me most strongly.

The basic motif of sculpture on both Earth and Mars is the marvelous human body. Most of the physical differences between us and them are not very great. If we disregard the considerable differences in the size of their eyes, and thus also to an extent the shape of their skulls, these distinctions are not greater than those between the various races on Earth. I am not well versed in anatomy and cannot give any accurate explanation of the divergencies, but I will note that my eye easily became accustomed to them and that they struck me almost immediately as original rather than ugly.

I noticed that men and women are more alike in build than is the

case among most races on Earth. The women have relatively broad shoulders, while the narrow pelvis and a certain tendency to plumpness in the
men make their muscles less prominent and tend to neutralize the physical differences between the sexes. This, however, is mainly true of the
most recent epoch, the era of free human evolution, for in the statues
dating from as late as the capitalist period the distinctions are much more
obvious. It is evidently the enslavement of women in the home and the
feverish struggle for survival on the part of the men which ultimately
account for the physical discrepancies between them.

I was constantly conscious—now clearly, now more vaguely—that I
was contemplating forms from an alien world, and this awareness somehow rendered my impressions strange and almost unreal. Even the beautiful female bodies depicted by the statues and paintings evoked in me an
obscure sensation that was quite unlike the admiring aesthetic attraction I
was accustomed to feeling. It resembled instead the vague premonitions
that troubled me long ago as I crossed the border between childhood and
adolescence.

The statues from the early periods were of a single color, as on Earth,
whereas the later ones were natural. This did not surprise me. I have
always thought that deviations from reality cannot be a necessary element
of art; they are even anti-aesthetic when they impoverish the viewer's
reception of the work. This is the case with uniformly colored sculpture,
as the concentrated idealization of life that constitutes the essence of art is
lessened rather than heightened by such a lack of realism.

Like our antique sculpture, the statues and pictures of the ancient
periods were infused with a majestic tranquillity, a serene harmony, an
absence of tension. In the intermediate, transitional epochs, elements of a
different order begin to appear: impulses, passions, an agitated drive
which is sometimes mellowed in the form of erotic or religious fantasies
but which sometimes bursts forth under the pressure of the enormous
strain generated by an imbalance between spiritual and corporeal forces.
In the socialist epoch the fundamental nature of art changed once again
into harmonious movement, a tranquil and confident manifestation of
strength, action free from morbid exertion, aspiration free from agitation,
vigorous activity imbued with an awareness of its well-proportioned unity
and invincible rationality.

If the ideal of feminine beauty expressed the infinite potential of love
in the ancient art of Earth, and if the ideal beauty of the Middle Ages and
Renaissance reflected the unquenchable thirst for mystical or romantic
love, then the ideal of this other world in advance of our own was Love
incarnate—pure, radiant, all-triumphant Love, serenely and proudly
aware of itself. Like the most ancient Martian works of art, the most
modern ones were characterized by extreme simplicity and thematic
unity. Their heroes were complex human beings with a rich and harmoni-

ous variety of experiences. The works chose to portray those moments of
the subject's existence when all of life was concentrated in a single emotion or aspiration. Favorite contemporary themes included the ecstasy of
creative thought, the ecstasy of love, and ecstatic delight in nature. Such
themes provided a profound insight into the soul of a great people who
had learned to live life in all its fullness and intensity and to accept death
consciously and with dignity.

The painting and sculpture section took up half the museum, while
the other half was devoted entirely to architecture. By architecture the
Martians mean not only buildings and great works of engineering but also
the artistic designing of furniture, tools, machines, and all other useful
objects and materials. The immense significance of this art in their lives
may be judged by the particular care and thoroughness with which this
collection was arranged. In the form of pictures, drawings, models, and
especially stereograms viewed in large steroscopes which reproduced
reality in the smallest detail, the exhibition contained examples of all
representative types of architecture, from the most primitive cave dwell-
ings, with their crudely embellished utensils, to luxurious apartment
buildings, decorated within by the best artists, to giant factories, with
their awesomely beautiful machines, to great canals, with their granite
embankments and suspension bridges. A special section was devoted to
the landscaping of gardens, fields, and parks. Although I was unaccustomed to the vegetation of the planet, I was often pleased by the combinations of colors and forms that had been created by the collective genius of
this large-eyed human race.

As on Earth, in the works of earlier periods elegance was often
achieved at the expense of comfort, and embellishments impaired dura-
bility and interfered with the utility of objects. I detected nothing of the
sort in the art of the contemporary period, either in the furniture, the
implements, or the buildings and other structures. I asked Enno whether
modern architecture permitted deviations from functional perfection for
the sake of beauty.

"Never," he replied. "That would be false beauty, artificiality rather
than art."

In presocialist times the Martians erected monuments to their great
people. Now they dedicate them only to important events, such as the
first attempt to reach Earth, which ended in the death of the explorers,
the eradication of a fatal epidemic, or the discovery of the process of
decomposing and synthesizing chemical elements. There were also
monuments on stereograms in the section devoted to graves and temples
(in the past the Martians had also had religion). One of the most recent
works in commemoration of a great individual was dedicated to the engineer Menni had told me about. The artist had succeeded in capturing the
spiritual power of a man who had led an army of labor to victory over

nature and proudly repudiated the cowardly judgment morality had
passed on his actions. When I paused in involuntary reflection before this
panoramic monument, Enno quietly recited some verses which expressed the essence of the spiritual tragedy of the hero.

"Who wrote that?" I asked.

"I did," replied Enno. "I wrote it for Menni."

I could not fully appreciate the inherent beauty of poetry in a language that was still foreign to me, but the idea in Enno's verses was lucid,
the rhythm was flowing, and the rhyme rich and sonorous. This suggested
a new train of thought.

"Ah," I said, "so your poetry still uses strict meter and rhyme?"

"Of course," said Enno, slightly surprised. "Do you mean that you
find it ugly?"

"Not at all," I explained. "It's just that it is commonly thought among
us that such form was generated by the tastes of the ruling classes of our
society, and that it reflects their fastidiousness and predilection for conventions which restrict the freedom of artistic expression. Whence the
conclusion that the poetry of the future, the poetry of the socialist epoch,
should abandon and forget such inhibiting rules."

"Nothing could be further from the truth," Enno retorted vigorously.
"Regular rhythmicality seems beautiful to us not at all because of any
liking for conventions, but because it is in profound harmony with the
rhythmical regularity of our processes of life and thought. As for rhyme,
which resolves a series of dissimilarities in uniform final chords, it is
intimately related to that vital bond between people which crowns their
inherent diversity with the unity of the delights of love, the unity that
comes from a rational goal in work, and the unity of feeling in a work of
art. Without rhythm there is no artistic form at all. If there is no rhythm of
sounds it is all the more essential that there be a rhythm of images or
ideas. And if rhyme really is of feudal provenance, then the same may be
said of many other good and beautiful things."

"But does not rhyme in fact restrict and obstruct the expression of
the poetic idea?"

"Well, what if it does? Such constraints, after all, arise from the goal
which the artist has freely chosen to set himself. They not only obstruct
but also perfect the expression of the poetic idea, and that is their only
raison d'être. The more complicated the goal, the more difficult the path
leading to it and, consequently, the more obstacles there are on the path.
If you want to build a beautiful building, just think how many rules of
technology and harmony are going to determine, that is, 'restrict' your
work. You are free to choose your goal, and that is the one and only
human freedom. Once you have chosen it, however, you have also
selected the means to attain it."

We went out into the garden to rest for a moment after all the new
impressions of the day. It was evening already, a clear and mild spring

evening. The flowers were beginning to furl up their blossoms and leaves for the night. All the plants on Mars share this feature, for it becomes very cold there after sunset. I resumed our conversation.

"Tell me, what sort of literature is most popular here?"

"The drama, especially tragedy, and nature poetry," replied Enno.

"What are the themes of your tragedy? Where in your happy, peaceful existence is there any material for it?"

"Happy? Peaceful? Where did you get that impression? True, peace reigns among men, but there cannot be peace with the natural elements. Even a victory over such a foe can pose a new threat. During the most recent period of our history we have intensified the exploitation of the planet tenfold, our population is growing, and our needs are increasing even faster. The danger of exhausting our natural resources and energy has repeatedly confronted various branches of our industry. Thus far we have overcome it without having to resort to what we regard to be the repugnant alternative of shortening the life span of present and coming generations, but at this very moment the struggle has become particularly acute."

"I could never have imagined that such dangers were possible, given the power of your technology and science. You said that such things have already happened?"

"Only seventy years ago, when our coal reserves were exhausted and the transition to hydroelectric power was still far from complete, we were forced to destroy a considerable portion of our beloved forests in order to give us time to redesign our machines. This disfigured the planet and worsened our climate for decades. Then, when we had recovered from that crisis, about twenty years ago it was discovered that our deposits of iron ore were nearly depleted. Intense research was begun on hard aluminum alloys, and a huge portion of our available technical resources was diverted to obtaining aluminum from the soil. Now our statisticians reckon that unless we succeed in developing synthetic proteins from inorganic matter, in thirty years we will be faced with a food shortage."

"What of other planets?" I objected. "Surely you can find something there to replenish the shortage."

"Where? Venus is obviously still inaccessible. Earth? Earth is inhabited, and it is otherwise uncertain how much we would be able to exploit her resources. Each trip there requires enormous energy, and according to what Menni told me recently about his latest research project, the Martian reserves of the radioactive substances necessary for such voyages are very modest. No, there are considerable difficulties everywhere, and the tighter our humanity closes ranks to conquer nature, the tighter the elements close theirs to avenge the victory."

"But wouldn't a simple reduction of the birth rate suffice to rectify the situation?"

"Check the birth rate? Why, that would be tantamount to capitulat-

ing to the elements. It would mean denying the unlimited growth of life
and would inevitably imply bringing it to a halt in the very near future.
We can triumph as long as we are on the offensive, but if we do not permit
our army to grow, we will be besieged on all sides by the elements, and
that will in turn weaken faith in our collective strength, in our great
common life. The meaning of each individual life will vanish together
with that faith, because the whole lives in each and every one of us, in
each tiny cell of the great organism, and each of us lives through the
whole. No! Curbing the birth rate is the last thing we would resort to, and
if it should happen in spite of us, it will herald the beginning of the end."

"Very well then, I understand that the tragedy of the whole always
exists for you, at least as a potential danger. So far, however, man has won,
and the collective has been able to shield the individual from this tragedy.
Even if the situation should become really dangerous, the gigantic exertions and suffering caused by the intense struggle will be distributed so
evenly among countless individuals that such hardships will not seriously
disturb their tranquil happiness. It seems to me that you have all you
need to ensure such happiness."

"Tranquil happiness! But how can the individual help being acutely
and profoundly aware of the shocks to the life of the whole in which his
beginning and end are immersed? Consider also that there are contradictions arising from the simple fact that the individual is so limited in
comparison to the whole; he is powerless fully to fuse with that whole and
can neither entirely dissolve himself in it nor embrace it with his consciousness. If such contradictions are beyond your understanding, it is
because in your world they are eclipsed by others which are more direct
and obvious. The struggle between classes, groups, and individuals pre-
cludes both the idea of the whole and the happiness and suffering implied
by the notion. I have seen your world, and I would not be able to tolerate
a fraction of the insanity in which your fellow creatures live. For that
reason I would not presume to decide which of us is closer to tranquil
happiness: the more perfectly ordered and harmonious life is, the more
painful are its inevitable dissonances."

"But tell me now, Enno, aren't you happy? You have your youth,
your science, your poetry, and doubtless you have love. What possible
experience of yours has been so severe as to make you speak so passionately about the tragedy of life?"

"How very nicely you put it," Enno said with a strange laugh. "You
do not know that at one time jolly old Enno had made up his mind to die.
And if Menni had been but a single day later in sending him an invitation
to travel to Earth, I am afraid your good-natured companion would not be
sitting here talking to you today. Just now, however, I cannot explain all of
this to you. You will see for yourself later that if there is any happiness
among us, then it is not the tranquil bliss you were talking about."

I hesitated to pursue this line of questioning any further. W
and returned to the museum. I was no longer able to examine the
systematically, however, for my attention strayed and I found it d
organize my thoughts. In the sculpture section I stopped in fi
statue depicting a beautiful young boy. His face reminded me of Netti,
but I was struck most deeply of all by the skill with which the artist had
managed to infuse incipient genius into the undeveloped body, the incomplete features, and the anxious, inquisitive gaze of the child. I stood
motionless before the statue for a long while, my mind blank to everything else. Enno's voice brought me out of my reverie.

"This is you," he said, pointing at the boy. "This is your world. It will
be a marvelous world, but it is still in its infancy. Look at the hazy dreams
and disturbing images troubling his mind. He is half asleep, but some day
he will awaken. I feel it, I sincerely believe in it!"

The joyous sensation these words evoked in me was mixed with a
strange regret: why was it not Netti who said that!

5. The Hospital

I returned home thoroughly exhausted. After two sleepless nights
and a whole day unable to work I decided to visit Netti once again, for I
did not feel like going to the unfamiliar doctor in the factory settlement.
Netti had been working since morning at the hospital, where I found him
examining patients. When he saw me in the waiting room he immediately
came over to me, gazed attentively into my face, took me by the hand and
led me off to a small separate room in which the soft blue light mingled
with the faint, pleasant odor of an unfamiliar perfume. Not a sound was to
be heard. He seated me comfortably in a deep armchair and said: "Try not
to think or worry about anything. Let me do that today. Relax, and I will
return shortly."

He left, and I did not think about anything, since I felt he had taken
all my thoughts and cares upon himself. It was very pleasant, and in a few
minutes I had dozed off. When I awoke Netti was standing in front of me
smiling.

"Do you feel better now?" he asked.

"I am quite well, and you are an amazing doctor!" I replied. "Attend
to your patients, and do not worry about me."

"The day's work is already done. If you like I will show you our
hospital," suggested Netti.

That interested me greatly, and we set off on a tour of the spacious,
beautiful building. Most of the Martian patients were there for surgery or
treatment for nervous disorders.

"Do you mean to say that the safety measures in your factories are
inadequate?" I asked Netti.

"There are practically no foolproof measures that would entirely rule out accidents. These patients, however, have come here from an area with a population of over two million. A few dozen victims from a region of that size is not so very many. Most of them are beginners who have not yet familiarized themselves with the machines they are operating. You know that people here like to switch from one area of production to another. Due to their own absentmindedness, specialists, scientists, and artists are especially accident-prone. They are constantly reflecting and pondering over other things, and then of course their attention lapses.

"What of those with nervous disorders? I suppose they are suffering from exhaustion?"

"No, there are no such patients here. There are special hospitals for them, since special facilities are needed to treat those who may harm themselves or others."

"In such cases do you also use coercion on the patients?"

"To the extent that it is absolutely necessary, of course."

"Now this is the second time I have encountered coercion in your world. The first was in the Children's Colony. Tell me, am I right in concluding that you have not wholly succeeded in eliminating these elements from your life but must knowingly permit them?"

"Yes, in the same sense that we permit illnesses and death. You might say that force is regarded as a bitter medicine. What rational being would decline to resort to violence in self-defense, for example?"

"You know, somehow this makes our two worlds seem much more alike."

"The main difference between them, however, does not at all lie in the fact that you have a great deal of violence and coercion and we have only a little. The chief distinction is that in your world both phenomena have been codified as laws and norms of justice and morality which dictate private and public behavior and are a constant source of oppression. Violence exists among us only as a symptom of disease or as the rational act of a rational being. In neither case does it either arise from or result in any privately or socially enforced laws or norms."

"But you also have rules which limit the freedom of your mentally ill and your children?"

"Yes, purely scientific rules on the care of the sick, and pedagogical rules. But of course even these technical regulations cannot foresee all the cases where force must be used, or its degree, or all the means of applying it. All such things depend on a combination of specific factors."

"In that case arbitrariness must be possible on the part of educators or those who care for the mentally ill."

"It depends what you mean by the word 'arbitrariness.' If you mean unnecessary, excessive violence, then it is possible only in the case of someone who is ill and needs treatment. A reasonable and conscious person is of course incapable of it."

We walked past the patients' wards, operation rooms, medicine storerooms, and the personnel quarters and ascended to the top floor. We entered a large, beautiful room whose transparent walls gave a view of the lake, the forest, and the distant mountains. It was furnished elegantly and luxuriously and adorned with statues and paintings of great aesthetic value.

"This is the room for the dying," said Netti.

"Do you bring everyone here to die?" I asked.

"We bring them or they come themselves," replied Netti.

"But are they still able to walk?" I asked with surprise.

"Those who are physically healthy can, of course."

I understood that he meant suicides.

"Do you mean that you put this room at their disposal for them to commit the act?"

"Yes, together with the means of assuring them a peaceful, painless death."

"There are no obstacles at all?"

"If the patient's mind is clear and he is really determined, what obstacles could there possibly be? A doctor, of course, first offers to talk with them. Some agree to do so, others do not."

"Are suicides common among you?"

"Yes, especially among old people. When the vital force becomes weak and blunted, many prefer not to wait for the natural end."

"What about younger people who are still strong and healthy?"

"Yes, even that happens, though not often. As far as I can recall there have been only two such instances at this hospital. In a third case we managed to discourage the attempt in time."

"Who were these unfortunate people, and what drove them to their deaths?"

"The first was my teacher, a remarkable doctor who made many scientific discoveries. He was extraordinarily sensitive to the suffering of others. This was what originally channeled his mind and energy into medicine, but it also proved his undoing. He could not bear what he saw. He concealed his state of mind so well that the disaster came as a complete surprise. It happened after a serious epidemic broke out in connection with the draining of an inlet of the sea, when millions of tons of fish were stranded and rotted. The illness was as painful as your cholera but even more dangerous, being fatal in nine out of ten cases. Due to this slight chance of recovery the doctors were unable even to comply with the requests of their patients for a quick and easy death. After all, a person in the throes of a severe fever cannot be considered to be in his

The room for the dying

right mind. My teacher worked dreadfully hard during the epidemic, and his research contributed to eradicating it fairly quickly. When that was done, however, he refused to live any longer."

"How old was he at the time?"

"About fifty of your years. For us that is still relatively young."

"And the second case?"

"A woman whose husband and child had died at the same time."

"And the third?"

"Only the comrade who survived it would be able to tell you about that."

"I see. But tell me something else," I said. "How do you Martians manage to preserve your youth so long? Is this a peculiarity of your race, the result of better living conditions, or is there some other explanation?"

"Race has nothing to do with it. Two hundred years ago our life expectancy was only half of what it is now. Better living conditions? Yes, that is a part of the answer, but only a part. The main factor is the method we use to *renew* life."

"What is that?"

"It is actually very simple, and although it will probably seem strange to you, your science already has the knowledge needed to apply this method. You know that in order to increase the viability of cells or organisms, nature constantly supplements one individual with another. Thus when the vitality of unicellular beings is impaired by a lack of variation in the environment, they fuse together, two becoming one; this is the only way they have of recovering the 'immortality' of their protoplasm, that is, their ability to procreate. The crossing of higher plants and animals does the same thing. In such cases as well vital elements of two different beings are united in order to obtain a more perfect embryo of a third one. Then of course, you are acquainted with blood serum transfusions and the way in which they transmit elements of vitality from one being to another. For example, they can increase resistance to different diseases. We go even further and perform *mutual blood transfusions* between human beings, whereby each individual receives from the other a number of elements which can raise his life expectancy. Such an exchange involves merely pumping the blood of one person into another and back again by means of devices which connect their respective circulatory systems. If all precautions are taken, it is a perfectly safe procedure. The blood of one person continues to live in the organism of the other, where it mixes with his own blood and thoroughly regenerates all his tissues."

"Are you able to rejuvenate old people by introducing young blood into their veins?"

"To an extent, yes, but not altogether, because there is more than just blood in the organism, and the body in its turn also has an effect upon the blood. That is why, for example, a young person will not age from the blood of an old one. The age and weakness in the blood are quickly overcome by the organism, which at the same time absorbs from it many elements which it lacks. The energy and flexibility of its vital functions also increase."

"But if this is all so simple, how is it that our medicine on Earth does not yet employ the method? If I am not mistaken, after all, blood transfusions have been known for hundreds of years."

"I don't know. Perhaps there are organic factors which render the method ineffective on Earthlings. Or perhaps it is merely due to your predominantly individualistic psychology, which isolates people from each other so completely that the thought of fusing them is almost incomprehensible to your scientists. Also, on Earth there are many common diseases which poison the blood—diseases of which even those who have them are often unaware or which they sometimes simply try to conceal. The blood transfusions presently performed by your medicine somehow smack of philanthropy: people who have a lot of blood give some of it to others who need it desperately due to, say, injuries. We, of course, do the same, but we do not stop there. Quite in keeping with the nature of our entire system, our regular comradely exchanges of life extend beyond the ideological dimension into the physiological one."

6. Hallucinations

The stormy torrent of impressions that engulfed me during my first few days on Mars gave me an idea of the enormous task confronting me. First of all, I had to comprehend this world and its immeasurably rich and original vital harmony. I then had to enter into it, not as a curious museum piece, but as a man among men, a worker among workers. Only then would I be able to accomplish my mission, only then would I be able to serve as the initial link of real mutual communication between our two worlds. As a socialist I stood on the border between them, like a split second of the present between the past and the future.

As I was leaving the hospital Netti told me not to be in such a hurry. It seemed to me he was wrong—hurry was exactly what I had to do. I had to throw all my strength and energy into the enterprise, because the responsibility on my shoulders was so terribly great! What colossal benefit our old, suffering humanity would derive from the living, vigorous influence of a higher, mightier, and more harmonious culture; how greatly this contact would accelerate its development and prosperity! And each moment I delayed my work might postpone that influence. No, there was no time for waiting or resting.

And I worked hard. I acquainted myself with the science and technology of the new world, I observed intensely its social life, I studied its literature. Yes, much of it was difficult. Their scientific methods bewil-

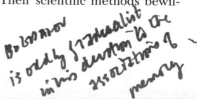

dered me. I learned them mechanically, and while I knew from experience that they could be applied easily, simply, and infallibly, I did not really understand them—I did not understand why they worked, I could not see their essence, their connection with real phenomena. I was like those mathematicians of the seventeenth century whose static thought was organically incapable of comprehending the living dynamism of infinitely small quantities.

I was struck by the intensely businesslike character of the Martian's public meetings. Whether they were dealing with scientific topics, questions relating to the organization of work, or even artistic problems, their reports and speeches were extremely concise and brief, their argumentation rigorous and precise. No one ever repeated himself or others. The resolutions of the gatherings were usually adopted unanimously and with incredible swiftness. If a meeting of experts in some field decided that it was necessary to organize a scientific undertaking, or if a conference of labor statisticians concluded that a new enterprise must be created, or if a gathering of the residents of the city wanted to decorate some building or other, new figures on the amount and types of labor that would be needed were immediately published by the Institute of Statistics, hundreds and thousands of new workers were flown in, and in a few days or weeks the whole project was completed and the workers had disappeared heaven knows where. All of this impressed me almost as a peculiar kind of magic. It was quiet and cold and had no incantations or mystical embellishments, but its superhuman might made it seem all the more mysterious.

The literature of this world, even pure fiction, afforded me neither rest nor relaxation. Its images seemed simple and clear, yet somehow they remained alien to me. I wanted to penetrate them more deeply and understand them more intimately, but the result of my efforts was wholly unexpected; instead of opening themselves to me the images faded into fog-shrouded shadows. I was plagued by this same incomprehensibility when I went to the theater. The plots were simple, the acting superb, but reality eluded me. The speech of the protagonists was so reserved and gentle, their behavior so calm and tactful, their feelings so seldom expressed, that it seemed as though they were trying to avoid evoking any emotional response whatever in the spectator. They all seemed to be merely philosophers—very much idealized ones at that, in my opinion. Only the historical plays from the distant past conveyed any familiar impressions to me, for in those productions the acting was as vigorous and the expression of personal feelings as candid as I was accustomed to seeing in our theaters.

All these considerations notwithstanding, the theater in our little town had one feature that held particular fascination for me, namely the fact that no actors performed there at all. The plays were either transmitted from distant large cities by means of audiovisual devices, or—more

[handwritten marginal notes:] It is almost as if the utopia's so far away that it cannot be understood or even enjoyed

[handwritten note at bottom:] → utopia seems dispassionate: Leonid's respect for human passion — is this the cost of scientific socialism?

usually—they were cinematic reproductions of plays performed long ago, sometimes so long ago that the actors themselves were already dead. The Martians have mastered the technique of instantaneous color photography and use it to capture life in motion, much as in our cinema theaters. But not only do they combine the camera with the phonograph, as we are thus far rather unsuccessfully beginning to do on Earth, they also employ the principle of the stereoscope to give the moving pictures natural depth. Two images, the two halves of the stereogram, are projected simultaneously onto the screen, and in front of each seat in the auditorium is fastened a set of binoculars which combines the two flat pictures into three-dimensional ones. It was eerie to watch people moving, acting, and expressing their thoughts and feelings as vividly and distinctly as in real life and yet know that there was actually nothing there but a plate of frosted glass in front of a phonograph and an electric light operated by a clockwork mechanism. It was a weird, almost mystical phenomenon that filled me with a vague sense of unreality.

None of this, however, aided me in my task of understanding the alien world of the Martians. Obviously I needed help from someone else, but I was less and less inclined to turn to Menni for instructions and explanations, for I was embarrassed to reveal the full extent of my difficulties. Besides, Menni was terribly busy at the time with some very important research on the extraction of minus-matter. He worked untiringly, sometimes not sleeping for nights in a row, and I was hesitant to distract him from his work. At the same time, his zeal was a living example which inspired me to keep going on my own.

Meanwhile, I had temporarily lost contact with my other friends. Netti was several thousand kilometers away in the other hemisphere of the planet supervising the construction and organization of a giant new hospital. Enno and Sterni were busy in their observatories with measurements and calculations for new voyages to Earth and Venus and expeditions to the moon and Mercury to obtain better photographs and mineral samples. My relations with other Martians were not very close, my conversations with them being limited to inquiries and factual matters. It was strange and difficult to become friends with alien beings, whom I moreover felt to be superior to myself.

As time went on I began to feel that my work was in fact progressing rather well. I needed less and less rest and even less sleep. The subjects I studied poured into my brain with a kind of mechanical ease and facility; it felt as though my head was completely empty and had room for much, much more. True, I usually failed when I reverted to my old habit and tried to formulate clearly what I had learned. I did not attach much importance to this, however, convincing myself that all I lacked was the means of expression and certain trivial details. I had grasped general notions, and that was the main thing.

Although they were going well, however, my studies no longer afforded me any keen pleasure. Nothing aroused in me the spontaneous interest I had felt earlier. Well, what of it, I thought; that is all quite natural. After all I have seen and learned, there is little that can astonish me any longer. I was not here to have a good time, but to learn what must be learned. The one unpleasant experience was that I found it increasingly difficult to concentrate on any one subject. My thoughts were constantly flying off in different directions. Vivid memories, sometimes very unexpected and distant ones, would flood my consciousness, blocking out what was going on around me and robbing me of precious minutes. I would notice this, come to my senses, and attack my work with renewed energy, but after a little while fantasies or the hovering images of the past would once again invade my brain, and I would be forced to check myself abruptly in order to repress them. I was increasingly troubled by a strange, uneasy feeling that I had failed to accomplish something important and urgent, something that I kept forgetting and had to strain to remember. This feeling would be followed by a swarm of familiar and unfamiliar faces and past events that would sweep me up in an irresistible torrent and spirit me away, further and further back through my adolescence and youth to my earliest childhood, where the images finally disappeared in a haze of vague sensations. After one of these experiences my lack of concentration would become particularly difficult to overcome.

This inner block that prevented me from concentrating for very long on any one thing finally got the better of me, and I began leaping rapidly from one subject to another. Trying to make the best of the situation, I deliberately brought to my room whole piles of books opened beforehand to the right place, tables, maps, stereograms, phonograms, and so on. I hoped in this manner to save time, but my absentmindedness crept up on me anyway, and I would catch myself staring for a long time at the same thing, understanding and accomplishing nothing. When I went to bed and gazed through the glass ceiling at the dark night sky, on the other hand, my brain would start working with incredible speed and energy. Whole pages of figures and formulas would appear in my mind's eye with such clarity that I could read them line by line. These images would soon disappear and yield to others, however, and then my consciousness would become a panorama of astonishingly distinct and lifelike pictures which no longer had any connection at all with my studies or problems. Landscapes from Earth, theatrical scenes, and fairy-tale images would appear deep within me like calm reflections in a mirror, only to vanish and give way to others. I felt no alarm, though, only a mild and even somewhat pleasant interest and curiosity. At first these reflections arose only in my mind and kept their distance from the surrounding reality, but soon they began crowding out the real world, and I would sink into a light, uneasy sleep full of vivid and confused dreams that robbed me of the rest I needed above all else.

I had been bothered for some time by a noise in my ears, but now it became so constant and loud that it interfered with listening to phonograms and deprived me of the little sleep I was able to get at night. From time to time the noise would become more articulate and I would distinguish familiar and unfamiliar human voices. At times someone seemed to be calling me by name, sometimes I thought I heard conversations but could not make out the words above the noise. I began to understand that I was not altogether well when my absentmindedness finally got complete control over me and I became unable to read more than a few lines at a time.

This, of course, is simply due to exhaustion, I thought. All I need is more rest. I have probably been working too much. But Menni need not know what is happening to me—it might look as though I had failed from the very start.

On the few occasions when Menni would visit me in my room I would pretend to be studying diligently, but he remarked to me that I was working too hard and was in danger of becoming exhausted.

"Today you look particularly unwell," he said. "Look in the mirror, how glazed your eyes are, how pale you are. You need a rest—you will benefit by it in the long run."

I myself very much wanted to rest, but I could not. Although I was actually accomplishing almost nothing, even the slightest exertion tired me. The world around me faded away and became almost unreal beneath a raging and never ceasing torrent of lifelike images, memories, and fantasies. I was finally forced to give up. I realized that my will was succumbing to inertia and apathy, and I found myself increasingly powerless to cope with my condition. One morning as I was getting up everything suddenly went black, but I quickly recovered and went to the window to look at the trees in the park. All of a sudden I felt someone was staring at me. I turned around, and there before me stood Anna Nikolaevna. She was pale and sad, and there was a look of reproach in her eyes that was painful to see. Not even stopping to think how odd it was that she should be there, I took a step in her direction and wanted to say something to her. But she disappeared, vanished into thin air.

From that moment on I was overwhelmed by a veritable orgy of phantoms. I had forgotten a great deal, of course, and now my mind was as confused when I was awake as when I slept. All kinds of people I had met in my life and even some I did not know came and went or simply appeared for a moment and vanished. There were no Martians among them, however; they were all from Earth, mostly people I had not seen for a long time—old schoolmates, my younger brother who had died as a child. Once I glanced out the window, and there on a bench in the park a familiar police spy was staring at me with a look of malicious contempt in his shifty, rapacious little eyes. The phantoms did not speak to me. At night, however, when all was quiet, my auditory hallucinations continued and intensified into coherent but absurdly vapid conversations, usually between people I did not know. A passenger would haggle with a cab driver, or a salesman would urge a customer to buy some cloth; once I found myself in the middle of a noisy university lecture hall, and I could hear the voice of an administration official telling everyone to quiet down, because the professor would be there any minute. The visual hallucinations, at least, were interesting, and they did not bother me as much or as often.

After my vision of Anna Nikolaevna I naturally told Menni everything. He immediately put me to bed, summoned the nearest physician, and telephoned Netti, who was six thousand kilometers away. The doctor said that he did not dare begin any treatment, because he knew little about the organism of an Earthling, but that the best thing for me was peace and quiet, and that if I had that there was no danger in waiting a few days until Netti arrived. Netti came a couple of days later, having entrusted his assignment to someone else. When he saw the state I was in he gave Menni a look of sad reproach.

7. Netti

Even with the expert treatment of a doctor like Netti, the illness continued for several weeks. I lay in bed, quietly contemplating reality and my specters with equal apathy. Even Netti's constant presence afforded me only a faint, scarcely noticeable pleasure. It seems strange now to recall my reactions to the hallucinations. Although their unreality became obvious to me on dozens of occasions, each time they appeared I seemed to forget the fact. Even when my mind was clear and steady I took them for real persons and things. It was not until they were about to disappear or had already vanished that I realized they were only illusions.

Netti's main strategy was to get me to sleep and rest. He did not prescribe any medication for the purpose, however, as he feared it might prove poisonous to my alien organism. For several days his usual method of putting me to sleep was unsuccessful, for hallucinatory images intruded themselves into the process of suggestion and rendered it ineffective. Finally he succeeded, and when I awoke after two or three hours of sleep he said:

"Your recovery is certain now, although the illness will continue to run its course for some time yet."

And so it did. The hallucinations appeared less often, but they were just as vivid and lifelike as before. They even became somewhat more complicated, and now my phantasmagorical guests would sometimes begin conversing with me. Of these conversations, however, there was only one, near the end of my illness, which made any sense or held any significance for me. As I awoke one morning, I saw Netti sitting at my bedside as usual. Behind him stood an old revolutionary comrade of mine, Ibrahim. He was an elderly man, an agitator known for his malicious tongue. He seemed to be waiting for something to happen. When Netti went into the adjoining room to draw me a bath, Ibrahim said to me in a harsh and resolute voice:

"You fool! Are you blind! Can't you see what your doctor is?"

I was for some reason not very surprised by the insinuation in his remark, nor was I disturbed by his cynical tone, which was typical of Ibrahim and thus familiar to me. But I remembered the iron grip of Netti's little hand, and I refused to believe him.

"More's the pity for you!" he said with a contemptuous grin and vanished.

Netti came into the room. I felt clumsy and embarrassed. He looked at me intently.

"Good," he said, "Your recovery is progressing rapidly."

He seemed especially taciturn and pensive the rest of the day. The following morning, being convinced that I was feeling well and would not suffer any new hallucinations, he appointed another doctor in his place and left on business, not returning until that night. For the next several days he only came to see me in the evening in order to put me to sleep. It was only then that I realized how important and pleasant his presence had become to me. As waves of well-being poured into my organism from the environment around me, I fell more and more often to pondering over Ibrahim's insinuation. I vacillated, trying in every way I knew to convince myself that it was absurd and merely a result of my illness. Why would Netti and my other friends deceive me on that score? Still, a vague doubt remained, and that pleased me.

Sometimes I questioned Netti about his work. He explained that a series of conferences was in progress to discuss the organization of new expeditions to other planets, and that he was needed as an expert. Menni was in charge of these meetings, but I was glad to learn that neither he nor Netti was planning on leaving in the near future.

"What about you? Wouldn't you like to go home?" Netti asked me, and I seemed to detect a note of uneasiness in his voice.

"But I have not yet accomplished anything," I replied.

Netti's face lit up.

"You are wrong. You have done a great deal . . . merely by answering like that," he said.

I sensed that he was hinting at something which I did not know but which had to do with me.

"Couldn't I accompany you to one of these conferences?" I asked.

"Most certainly not!" Netti declared firmly. "Besides the fact that you absolutely must rest, for several months yet you will have to avoid everything that is closely connected with the early stages of your illness."

I did not argue with him. It was so pleasant to rest, and my sense of duty to mankind had receded into the background. The only thing that continued to bother me was my strange thoughts about Netti. One evening I was standing at the window looking down at the mysterious red "greenery" darkening below me in the park. It was a beautiful scene that no longer struck me as strange or alien. There was a quiet knock at the door, and I sensed immediately that it was Netti. He strode in with his usual brisk, light gait and smiled as he offered me his hand in the Earthly greeting that appealed to him. I squeezed it so happily and vigorously that I must have bruised even his strong fingers.

"Well, I see that my role as a doctor is over," he said with a laugh. "Still, I shall have to ask you some questions just to be absolutely sure."

He questioned me, but for some reason I became so confused that my answers were incoherent. I detected a laugh in his huge eyes. Finally I could hold back no longer:

"Tell me, why do I feel so strongly attracted to you? Why am I so extraordinarily glad to see you?"

"Above all, I should imagine, because I have cured you, and you are unconsciously projecting your joy at recovery onto me. And perhaps . . . there is another reason . . . perhaps because . . . I am a woman."

Lightning flashed before my eyes, everything went black, and my heart felt as though it had stopped beating. A second later I was crushing Netti in my arms like a madman, kissing her hands, her face, her huge deep eyes, green as the Martian sky.

Simply and generously, she yielded to my unbridled impulses. When I recovered from my joyous insanity I again kissed her hands with involuntary tears of gratitude in my eyes. My crying, of course, was due to weakness caused by my illness. Netti said with her sweet smile:

"You know, it seemed to me just now that I was holding your whole youthful world in my arms. Its despotism, its egotism, its desperate hunger for happiness—I felt all of that in your caresses. Your love is like murder. But . . . I love you, Lenni."

This was happiness.

PART III

1. Happiness

Those months . . . As I recall them my body thrills, my eyes become shrouded in mist, and everything around me seems insignificant. There are no words to express the happiness I once knew. Now I began to become very fond of my new world, and it seemed to me that I understood it completely. My past failures did not bother me, my youth and faith returned, and I felt sure that they would never abandon me again. I had a strong and reliable ally, the old weakness was banished, the future was mine. I seldom gave a thought to the past any more, but concentrated on Netti and our love.

"Why did you conceal your sex from me?" I asked her not long after that first evening.

"In the beginning it simply happened that way, by accident. But later I quite deliberately confirmed you in your error and even changed everything in my dress that might have put you on the right track. I was frightened by the difficulty and complexity of your mission and was afraid that I would only complicate things further, especially when I noticed your unconscious attraction for me. I did not fully understand my own feelings, at least not until you fell ill."

"So that was what decided the matter! How grateful I am to my dear hallucinations!"

"Yes, the news of your illness came like a thunderbolt. If I had failed to heal you completely, I might have died."

She was silent a few seconds and added:

"You know, among your friends there is another woman of whom you have suspected nothing, and she also loves you very much. . . not, of course, the way I do."

"Enno!" I guessed immediately.

"Of course. And she also purposely deceived you, on my advice."

"Oh, how much deceit and perfidy there is in your world!" I exclaimed with feigned pathos. "But please, let Menni remain a man, because it would be terrible if I were to fall in love with him."

"Yes, that would be terrible," Netti agreed thoughtfully, and I was puzzled by the sudden note of gravity in her voice.

The days passed, and I joyously set about mastering my wonderful new world.

2. Separation

Nevertheless, the day came—the day I cannot remember without cursing it, the day when the black shadow of a hateful but inevitable separation rose up between us. With her usual calm and composed expression, Netti told me that she would be leaving in a few days for Venus on a gigantic expedition commanded by Menni. Seeing how stunned I was by the news, she added:

"It will not be for long. If we are successful, and I am certain that we will be, part of the expedition will return very soon, and I will be with them."

Then she explained to me what it was all about. The Martian reserves of minus-matter, needed for interplanetary travel and for decomposing and synthesizing elements, were nearly exhausted, and there was no way to replenish them. It had been established beyond doubt that very near the surface of Venus, a young planet only one-fourth the age of Mars, there were colossal deposits of still active substances. The richest field was located on an island the Martians called the Island of Hot Storms in the middle of the largest ocean on Venus. It had been decided to begin mining operations there immediately. First, however, it was necessary to build very high and strong walls to shield the workers from the hot, moist wind, which was far more destructive than our desert sandstorms on Earth. The expedition consisted of ten etheronephs and 1,500 to 2,000 persons. Only about five percent of these were chemists, almost all the rest being construction workers. The best scientists had been enlisted, including some of the most experienced doctors. Both the climate and lethal radiation posed a threat to the health of the workers. Netti claimed that she could not decline to take part in the expedition, but assumed that if the work went well, after about three months one etheroneph would be sent back to Mars with reports and a supply of ore. She would be on it, having been away a total of ten or eleven months.

I could not understand why Netti had to go. She told me that the undertaking was too important to refuse. It was of great significance to my mission as well, since frequent and developed communications with Earth depended on its success, and inadequate medical care could doom the enterprise from the start. These were persuasive arguments, for I already knew that in situations that placed heavier than usual demands on the capacity of established medical science Netti was considered the best doctor on Mars. Still, it seemed to me that this was not the whole truth. I had the feeling that she was withholding something from me. But of one thing I was certain—Netti and her love for me. If she said that she had to go, then she had to go. If she would not tell me why, then I had no business asking her. When she was unaware I was looking at her, however, I detected fear and pain in her beautiful eyes.

"Enno will be a good and dear friend to you," she said with a sad smile. "And do not forget Nella. She loves you for my sake. She is intelligent and experienced, and she can give you valuable support in moments of difficulty. As for me, all you should think of is that I shall return as soon as I can."

"I believe in you, Netti," I said, "and therefore I also believe in myself, in the man you love."

"You are right, Lenni. And I know that whatever trials and disappointments fate may have in store for you, you will emerge from them true to yourself, stronger and purer than ever."

The future cast its shadow over our parting caresses, which were mingled with Netti's tears.

3. The Clothing Factory

With Netti's help, in the course of those short months I was nearly ready to implement my main plan, which was to become a productive worker in Martian society. I could have given lectures about Earth and its inhabitants instead, but I deliberately declined all invitations to do so. It would have been foolish to specialize in such a subject, for it would have meant artificially restricting my attention to images from the past. The past, I reasoned, was within reach without any special exertion on my part—it was the future I had to conquer, and so I decided simply to begin working in industry. After careful consideration and comparison, I chose a clothing factory.

The work, of course, was among the easiest there was, but I was nevertheless forced to make considerable preparations. I had to study the established scientific principles of industrial organization and then acquaint myself in particular with the structure of the factory in which I would be employed, including its architecture and management. Moreover, I had to acquire a general notion of all the machines in use there and know in detail the one with which I would be working. This obliged me to learn beforehand certain branches of theoretical and applied mechanics and technology and even mathematical analysis. The main difficulties I encountered concerned the form rather than the content of the subjects I was studying. The textbooks and instructions were not intended for a person from an inferior culture. I remembered how I was tormented as a child by a French textbook of mathematics I happened to come across. I was seriously interested in the subject and I evidently had an unusual aptitude for it. The notions of limits and derivatives that plague most beginners came to me effortlessly, as if I had always known them. But I lacked the logical discipline and experience of scientific reasoning which the French professor took for granted in his reader and pupil. He expressed himself clearly and precisely, but provided few explanations and constantly omitted those logical bridges that were perhaps self-evident to a man of high scientific culture but wholly obscure to a young "Asiatic." On more than one occasion I spent hours pondering the magical transformation following the words: "whence, given the preceding equations, we obtain. . . ." The same problem, only even more difficult, confronted me now as I read Martian scientific literature. I was no longer deceived, as in the early stages of my illness, by the illusion that everything was easy and clear. Now, however, I had Netti's constant, patient help to smooth out the bumps in my difficult road.

Soon after Netti's departure I took the final step and began working in the factory. It was a gigantic and extremely complex enterprise that did not correspond at all to our usual notion of a clothing factory. Spinning, weaving, cutting, sewing, and dyeing were all performed under the same roof. The raw materials used were not flax, not cotton, or any other plant fiber, not wool or silk, but something quite different. In earlier periods the Martians had manufactured textiles in more or less the same way we do today: fibrous plants were cultivated, hair and skin were obtained from animals, a special kind of spider was bred whose webs yielded a substance similar to silk, and so on. The impulse for a change of techniques came from the growing necessity to increase grain production. Fibrous plants gave way to fibrous minerals not unlike asbestos. Later, chemists turned their attention to the study of spider-web fabrics and the synthesis of new materials possessing similar characteristics. Successful research resulted in a veritable revolution in this branch of industry, and now the old types of fabrics can only be found in museums.

Our factory was a living example of the changes wrought by this revolution. Several times a month "material" for spinning was brought in by rail from the nearest chemical plants in the form of a transparent, semiliquid substance in huge cisterns. Special machines pumped the liquid from the cisterns into an enormous metal reservoir near the ceiling of the factory. The flat bottom of this tank had hundreds of thousands of microscopically tiny apertures through which the viscous liquid was forced at high pressure, so that it emerged in ultrafine strands which contact with the air hardened just a few centimeters from the openings into tough gossamer fibers. These were then wound onto tens of thousands of spindles, which twisted them by the dozens into threads of varying thicknesses and strengths and drew them further into ready "yarn" that was fed into the next section of the factory. There weaving machines knitted the threads into various fabrics, from the finest, such as muslin and cambric, to the coarsest, like broadcloth and felt. These textiles streamed out in broad unbroken ribbons to the cutting shop, where they were seized by other machines that piled them in many layers and cut out individual pieces of clothing according to thousands of different predetermined patterns.

In the sewing section the cut pieces were "stitched" together into ready-made clothing, without, however, the use of needles, thread, or sewing machines. The pieces were laid evenly edge to edge and moistened with a special chemical solvent which transformed the material into its previous semiliquid state. A moment later this very volatile solvent had evaporated, and the pieces of fabric were fused together more solidly than could have been done by any stitched seam. All necessary fastenings were soldered on at the same time, producing ready-to-wear suit pieces in several thousand models of different forms and sizes.

There were several hundred models for each age group, so that almost everyone could find his exact size, especially since the Martians' clothing usually tends to fit rather loosely. If the right size could not be found for, say, a wearer with an unusual build, special measurements

The clothing factory on Mars at which Leonid worked

were immediately taken, the machine was set according to the specifications of the new pattern, and in an hour or so a suit was "tailored" for the customer.

As to the color of the clothing, most Martians are satisfied with the usual dark, soft shades of the material itself. Should someone want a different color, the suit is sent to the dyeing section, where it is treated by electrochemical techniques and emerges a few minutes later colored with perfect evenness in the desired hue. Footwear and warm winter clothing are produced in much the same way, although the fabrics are coarser and stronger. Our factory was not involved in this production, which was done instead at other, even larger plants which made absolutely everything a person would need to dress from head to toe.

I worked by turns in all the sections of the factory, and at first I found the job fascinating. I was especially interested in the cutting section, where I had an opportunity to apply my newly acquired knowledge of mathematical analysis. The work consisted in cutting out all the pieces of a suit with the least possible waste of material. It was a very prosaic task, of course, but it was also very important, because even a slight error multiplied many millions of times resulted in enormous losses. I managed "no worse" than the others.

I tried as hard as I could to work "no worse" than my comrades, and for the most part I was successful. I could not help noticing, however, that it cost me much greater effort than it did them. After 4 to 6 Earth hours of work I was thoroughly exhausted and in immediate need of rest, whereas my fellow workers went to museums, libraries, laboratories, or to other factories to watch and sometimes even to work some more. I hoped that in time I would become accustomed to my new job and catch up with the others, but that did not happen. It became increasingly obvious to me that what I lacked was the *culture of concentration.* The necessary physical movements were not very demanding, and here I was as fast and nimble as most and even better than some. But the constant, intense concentration that was needed to look after the machines and the fabric tired my brain. Evidently it took several generations to develop this capability to a degree the Martians would consider ordinary and average.

Often, usually toward the end of my day's work, weariness would begin to affect my performance. My attention would begin to stray and I would make a mistake or cause some step to be delayed for a second. Whenever this happened, the hand of one of my neighbors was inevitably and infallibly there to correct my error. I was not only surprised but sometimes downright exasperated by this strange ability of theirs to observe everything going on around them without for a moment neglecting their own work. I was not so much touched as annoyed and irritated by their solicitude. I got the feeling that they were all constantly keeping an eye on me. This uneasy sensation aggravated my absentmindedness even

ˈered with my work. Now when I am able to look back
ˈmstances objectively and in detail, I realize that I was
ˈnrades at the factory helped each other in exactly the
the same solicitude, although perhaps less often. I was
ˈ..ined to me then, the object of any special surveillance or
ˈ..ivision. True to my individualistic background, it was I who was
unconsciously singling myself out from the others. And again as a child of
a materialistic culture, I morbidly misinterpreted their kindness and comradely gestures because I felt unable to repay them.

4. Enno

The long autumn drew to a close. Winter, cold but with little snow,
descended upon our region, which was located in the middle latitudes of
the northern hemisphere. The little sun shone even less than before and
gave no warmth at all. Nature cast off her brilliant colors and became
pallid and harsh. A chill crept into my heart, my mind was filled with
doubts, and the moral solitude I felt as a stranger from another world
weighed heavily upon me.

I went to visit Enno, whom I had not seen for some time. She
greeted me like a dear friend, and it was as if a bright ray from the recent
past cut through the cold of winter and my troubled gloom. Later I
noticed that she was also pale and seemed to be worried about something,
for there was a hidden sorrow in her voice and her general manner. We
had a great deal to talk about, and the several hours I spent with her flew
by imperceptibly. It was better than anything I had known since Netti's
departure, and we were both sorry when I rose to go home.

"If you are not pinned down here by your work, why don't you come
with me?" I said.

Enno agreed immediately. She took some work with her (at the time
she was not busy at the observatory, but was checking a long series of
calculations), and we returned to the factory settlement, where I was
living alone in Menni's apartment. Every morning I went to work at my
factory, which was about one hundred kilometers or a half hour's flying
time away. Enno and I began spending the long winter evenings together
in scientific pursuits, discussions, and sometimes walks in and around the
town.

Enno told me the story of her life. She loved Menni and had earlier
been his wife. She passionately wanted to have a baby with him, but the
years passed and no child came. She asked Netti's advice. Netti made a
thorough investigation of the situation and determined with absolute certainty that they would never have children. Menni had matured too late
from boyhood into manhood and had thrown himself too early into the
intense life of a scientist and thinker. His vigorous, overdeveloped intel-

lect had from the very beginning undermined and irreparably stifled the
vitality of his reproductive faculty. Netti's verdict was a terrible blow to
Enno; her love for the brilliant man and her deep-seated maternal instincts had fused into a single passionate desire that had now proven
hopeless.

This was not all, however, for Netti's examination had yielded other
findings. It turned out that Menni's immense intellectual activity and the
full development of his brilliant talents required a maximum of physical
restraint and thus a minimum of lovemaking. Enno could not refuse to
follow this advice and was quickly persuaded of its rationality and fairness.
Menni livened up and began working more energetically than ever. He
brimmed over with new and extraordinarily successful plans and ideas,
and he was evidently not conscious of any loss in his private life. Love was
dearer than life itself to Enno, but the genius of the man she loved was an
even more precious treasure, and she drew the necessary conclusions.
She and Menni separated. It pained him at first, but he soon became
reconciled to the fact. He may even have been unaware of the real reason
for the break. Enno and Netti kept it a secret, although they could never
know for certain that Menni's sharp intellect had not penetrated to the
heart of the matter. As for Enno, her life became so empty and her
repressed emotions caused her such pain that a short while later the
young woman decided she did not want to live any longer.

Netti, whose cooperation Enno had requested, found various pretexts for postponing the suicide for a day and informed Menni. He was
preparing the expedition to Earth at the time and immediately invited
Enno to participate in the important and dangerous undertaking. It was
difficult to refuse, so Enno accepted his offer. Her many new impressions
during the journey helped her to cope with her emotional distress, and by
the time she returned to Mars she had gained enough control of herself to
play the part of the cheerful boy poet I had known on the etheroneph.

Enno had not gone on the new expedition to Venus, because she was
afraid she might again become used to Menni's presence. While she was
alone, however, she did not stop worrying about him, for she knew very
well how dangerous the project was. During the long winter evenings our
thoughts and conversations constantly returned to the same place in the
Universe. There under the rays of the enormous sun and in the breath of
the scorching wind, the two beings who meant the most to both of us
were feverishly struggling to accomplish their daring, titanic mission.
This identity of thoughts and feelings brought us very close to each other.
Enno became more than just a sister to me. Simply and naturally—
neither of us experienced any transports of passion or conflicting emotions—our mutual affection developed into an amorous relationship.
Invariably meek and kind, Enno neither shunned nor actively sought this
intimacy. Her one definite decision was that she did not want children

with me. There was an element of gentle sadness in her caresses—caresses of a tender friendship which permitted everything.

Winter, a long deathly still Martian winter unbroken by thaws, storms, or blizzards, continued to extend its cold, pallid wings over us. Neither of us wanted to fly south, where nature brimmed with life and spread its brilliant plumage under the warm sun. Enno was not at all in the mood for such a tropical clime, whereas I avoided new people and new situations. Meeting and getting used to them involved additional effort and fatigue, and, as it was, I was making but slow progress toward my goal. Ours was a strange, unreal friendship—a wintertime romance overshadowed by cares and expectations.

5. Nella

Enno had been Netti's best friend since they were both young girls, and she told me a great deal about her. On one occasion I was surprised to hear her mention Netti and Sterni together. When I asked her about it she paused for a moment and seemingly even embarrassed answered:

"Netti was at one time Sterni's wife. If she has not told you about it, then I should not be mentioning it either. Obviously I have made a mistake, so please do not question me any further."

For some reason I was strangely shaken by what I had heard. After all, the news should not have come as any surprise. I had never imagined that I was Netti's first man. It would have been absurd to think that a woman bursting with life and health, beautiful both physically and spiritually, a child of a free, highly cultivated race, could live without love until our meeting. Why in the world was I so shocked? I could not reason about it logically, I only knew that I had to have a clear and detailed explanation. It was obviously impossible to ask Enno, but then I remembered Nella. As Netti was leaving she had said to me: "Do not forget Nella, go to her if you run into trouble!" I had in fact thought of visiting her a number of times, but was prevented from doing so partly by my work and partly by a vague fear of the hundreds of curious children's eyes that surrounded her. Now, however, my indecision had vanished, and I set off that very day for the Children's Colony in the Great City of Machines.

Nella immediately dropped what she was doing. Asking one of her colleagues to replace her, she took me to her room, where we would not be bothered by the children. I decided not to tell her straightaway about the purpose of my visit, especially since I was not convinced myself that my intentions were particularly reasonable or noble. It was perfectly natural that I should begin by talking about a person who was very dear to us both. Then I would simply wait for an opportune moment to ask my question. Nella told me a long, enthusiastic story about Netti's childhood and youth.

Like most Martian children, Netti spent the first years of her life at home with her mother. When the time came to send her to the Children's Colony in order to expose her to the educational influence of her fellow children, Nella could not bear to part with her. First she moved temporarily to the colony, and then she decided to stay on and work there as an educator. She had studied psychology, so she already had a suitable background for the job.

Netti was a lively, energetic, impetuous child with a great thirst for knowledge and activity. She was especially interested in the mysterious universe beyond Mars. Her most cherished dream and favorite topic of conversation with her teachers and comrades was Earth, which no one had yet visited, and its strange people. When the account of Menni's first successful expedition was published the little girl was beside herself with joy and excitement. She learned Menni's report by heart and pestered Nella and the other educators to explain to her every word of it she did not understand. She fell in love with Menni before ever laying eyes on him and wrote him a wildly enthusiastic letter in which, among other things, she asked him to bring her an orphan from Earth, promising to give it the very best upbringing. She filled her room with pictures from the planet and portraits of Earthlings, and began studying the dictionaries of our languages as soon as they appeared in print. Menni and his comrades had captured the first person they met and forced him to help them learn the languages they needed. Netti was indignant at this use of force, yet at the same time she was very sorry they had set him free instead of bringing him back with them to Mars. She was firmly determined to travel to Earth some day, and when her mother jokingly remarked that she would probably end up marrying an Earthling there, she thought for a moment and then declared: "I may do just that!"

Netti had never mentioned any of this to me herself and was generally reticent about her past. No one, of course, not even she, could have told the story better than Nella. Nella's descriptions glowed with such warm maternal affection! For minutes on end I was oblivious to all else, and as vividly as if she were standing right there before me I could see this marvelous little girl with her huge sparkling eyes and her enigmatic enthusiasm for our remote, faraway world. This soon passed, however; as my awareness of reality returned I recalled the purpose of my visit, and once again I felt a chill in my heart. Finally, when we came to Netti's most recent past, I decided to ask as casually and naturally as possible how Netti and Sterni's relationship had begun. Nella thought for a moment.

"So that's what it is!" she said, with a note of uncustomary severity in her voice. "That is why you have come to see me. Why didn't you simply say so?"

"Well of course I can tell you," she went on. "It is actually a very simple story. Sterni was one of Netti's teachers. He used to lecture to young people on mathematics and astronomy. When he returned from his

first trip to Earth—I believe it was Menni's second expedition—he delivered a whole series of lectures about the planet and its inhabitants. Netti
attended all of them. She was especially attracted to him because of the
attention and patience with which he answered her endless inquiries, and
their friendship gradually grew into marriage. Their relationship was
nourished at first by the kind of polar attraction that sometimes exists
between two very different and in some respects even opposite characters. This same disparity later manifested itself more fully and consist-
ently, their relations cooled, and finally they separated. That is the whole
story."

"Tell me, when did this break occur?"

"It became final after Letta's death. Actually, it was Netti's intimacy
with Letta that provoked the rupture. Netti disliked Sterni's coldly analytical intellect; he persistently and systematically demolished all the
dreams and emotional and intellectual fantasies that formed a very important part of her life. She unconsiously started looking for someone with a
different attitude; old Letta was unusually sympathetic and full of child-
like enthusiasm. In him Netti found the comrade she was searching for.
He was not only patient with her flights of imagination but was often
carried away himself by her enthusiasm. He offered her an emotional
respite from Sterni's numbing criticism. Like her, he loved Earth in his
dreams and imagination and believed in the future union of the two
worlds and the great prosperity and poetry of life that would result from
that alliance. And then she found out that despite the richness of his
feelings and spirit Letta had never known a woman's love and caresses.
That was something she simply could not accept, and thus began her
second liaison."

"Just a moment," I interrupted. "Do I understand you to mean that
she was Letta's wife?"

"Yes," replied Nella.

"But I thought you said that the final break with Sterni did not occur
until after Letta's death."

"That is correct. Is that so difficult to understand?"

"No, I understand. I simply did not know it."

At this point we were interrupted. One of the children had had a
nervous fit, and Nella was urgently summoned to him. I was alone for
several minutes. My head was spinning—there are no words to describe
how I felt. Why? No reason in particular. Netti was a free person and
behaved like a free person. What of it if Letta was her husband? I had
always respected him and would have liked him very much even if he had
not sacrificed his life for me. Netti was married to two of her comrades at
the same time? So what? I have always believed that monogamy among us
is due exclusively to our economic conditions, which limit and enslave
man at every step. The conditions on Mars were quite different and in no

way inhibited personal feelings and relationships. Why then this agitated
bewilderment, this incomprehensible pain that made me want to scream
and laugh at the same time? Or was it that I did not know how to *feel* as I
thought? Evidently. And what about my relationship to Enno? Where was
my logic? What was I myself? What an absurd situation!

Ah yes, one more thing . . . Why hadn't Netti told me all this? How
many more secrets and lies were there around me? How many of them
could I expect to encounter in the future? Wrong again! A secret, yes, but
there was no deceit here. In this particular case, however, wasn't the
secret equivalent to deception? These thoughts were whirling around in
my head when the door opened and Nella again stepped into the room.
Evidently she could see from my face how bad I felt, for the earlier note of
dryness and severity had disappeared from her voice.

"Of course," she said, "it is difficult to get used to an entirely different code of personal relations and the customs of a world with which you
have no blood ties. You have already overcome many obstacles, and you
will cope with this one as well. Netti believes in you, and I think she is
right. Surely your faith in her has not been shaken?"

"Why did she conceal all of this from me? Is that a sign of faith in me?
I cannot understand it."

"I do not know why she has behaved the way she has. But I do know
that she must have had an important reason and was not acting out of
selfish motives. Perhaps this letter contains the answer. She left it with
me to give you in the event we should have just such a conversation."

The letter was written in my native language, which my Netti knew
so well. This is what I read:

> Dearest Lenni! I have never told you about my earlier
> relationships, but it was not because I wanted to conceal from
> you any of the details of my life. I have full confidence in your
> lucid intellect and noble heart. I am sure that however strange
> and unfamiliar certain of our mores must seem to you, sooner or
> later you will be able to understand them and judge them fairly.
> But I was afraid of one thing . . . After your illness you quickly
> regained the strength to work, but the emotional equilibrium
> that is constantly and in all situations necessary for self-control
> in words and deeds had not yet fully returned. If the impression
> of the moment and the unbridled forces of the past that con-
> stantly lurk in the depths of the human soul had caused you for a
> single second to expose me as a woman to that unhealthy at-
> titude of force and domination that still prevails in the old world,
> you would never have been able to forgive yourself. Yes, my
> darling, I know that you are hard, even cruel, toward yourself.
> This is a trait you have brought with you from the stern school of

struggle on Earth, and a single ugly, morbid outburst would have remained forever as a black stain upon our love.

Dear Lenni, I want to and I know I can set your mind at ease. May that evil feeling which mingles concern for a living chattel with love for another human being slumber deep inside you and never awake. *There will never be anyone else.* I can easily and confidently promise you this: alongside my love for you, alongside my passionate desire to help you in your great and vital task, everything else appears so petty and insignificant. I love you not only as a wife, I love you as a mother who guides her child into a new and strange life full of trials and dangers. This love is the strongest bond that can exist between two people. For that reason my promise requires no sacrifice of me.

Goodbye my darling, my beloved child.

Love,
Netti

When I had read this letter, Nella gave me an inquiring glance. "You were right," I said, and kissed her hand.

6. The Search

This episode left me with a lingering feeling of profound humiliation. I became more morbidly sensitive than ever to the superiority of everyone around me, both at the factory and in all my other dealings with the Martians. I doubtless even exaggerated their superiority and my own weakness. In the gestures of goodwill and solicitude they showed me I began to detect a note of almost contemptuous condescension, and I interpreted their cautious reserve as a concealed aversion for an inferior being. The accuracy of my impressions and the fairness of my judgments were increasingly distorted by such attitudes.

In all other respects my mind was clear, and I began concentrating particularly on filling in the blanks connected with Netti's departure. I was more convinced than ever that her participation was dictated by considerations still unknown to me that were stronger and more important than those she had mentioned. The new proof I had of her love for me and the enormous importance which she attached to my mission of uniting our two worlds served further to confirm my suspicion that she would never have decided to leave me for long among the depths and shoals and hidden reefs of this alien life, especially since her lucid intelligence was better aware than mine of the dangers that lurked here. There was something I did not know, but I was convinced that it had a great deal to do with me, and I simply had to find it out at any price.

I decided that systematic research was the best way to get at the truth. I recalled certain casual, unwitting remarks Netti had made and the uneasy expression that would linger on her face whenever anyone talked about the colonial expedition in my presence. I came to the conclusion that Netti's decision to separate was made not when she told me about it, but long before, not later than the first days of our union. In other words, the reasons for it also had to be sought from around that time. But where?

These motives could be connected either with Netti's private life or with the origin, character, and significance of the expedition. After her letter, the first alternative seemed the less likely. Consequently, my probe would have to be in the other direction, and the first task was to get some information on the background of the expedition.

It went without saying that the expedition was decided upon by the "Colonial Group," which consisted of a team of scientists actively engaged in organizing interplanetary voyages and representatives from the Central Institute of Statistics and the industries involved in manufacturing etheronephs and other necessary equipment. I knew that the most recent congress of this Colonial Group had taken place when I was ill, and that Menni and Netti had attended it. Since I was already on the road to recovery and was bored when I could not be with Netti, I had also wanted to go to the meetings, but Netti had refused to allow it on the grounds that it might prove injurious to my health. But was this "danger" connected with something that I was not supposed to know? Obviously, what I had to do was to get hold of the minutes of the congress and read everything of possible relevance to my problem.

Here, however, I encountered difficulties. All they would give me in the colonial library was the collected resolutions of the congress. These documents indicated very clearly, down to almost the smallest details, the entire organization of the grandiose Venus enterprise, but they contained nothing of immediate interest to me and were thus by no means exhaustive from my point of view. Despite their great detail, the resolutions were presented without any motivation and lacked any reference to the discussion which had preceded their adoption. When I told the librarian that I needed the minutes themselves he explained that the records had not been published; in fact, unlike the case with conferences treating technical and administrative questions, no detailed minutes of this congress had ever been taken.

At first glance this seemed plausible, for as a rule the Martians publish only the resolutions of their technical conferences, and consider that all reasonable and useful opinions expressed there will either be reflected in the final document or will be presented in a more polished and detailed form as an article, brochure, or book should a delegate think his views have some special significance. The Martians are generally reluctant to add unnecessarily to the bulk of the already existing literature, and they have nothing corresponding to our "proceedings of the

Leonid finds in the Martian library the stenogram of the debate
about colonizing Earth

commission." They prefer to condense everything and make it as brief as possible. But in this case I did not believe the librarian. The matters considered by the congress were too great and vital to be able to treat their discussion like an ordinary debate on some ordinary technical problem. I tried to conceal my skepticism, however, and to divert possible suspicion I humbly plunged into the materials they gave me. Either there really were no minutes, or my question had alerted the librarian and he was deliberately withholding them from me. There was one other possibility—the phonogram section of the library. The minutes might be kept there even if they had never been published. The Martians often use recordings instead of stenography, and their archives contain a large collection of phonograms from various public conferences.

I waited until the librarian in the book section was deeply engrossed in his work and slipped by him unnoticed into the phonogram department. I asked the comrade on duty there for the huge catalogue of their holdings. He gave it to me, and I quickly found the numbers of the phonograms from the congress. Under the pretense that I did not wish to inconvenience the librarian, I went to look for them myself, and he made no effort to prevent me. There were fifteen phonograms in all, one for each session of the congress. As is usual on Mars, each of them had a written title, and I quickly glanced through them. The first days of the conference were devoted entirely to papers on the expeditions that had taken place since the previous congress and on new improvements in etheroneph construction. The title of the sixth recording read: "Proposal of Central Institute of Statistics on Mass Colonization. Target Planet— Earth or Venus. Speeches and Proposals of Sterni, Netti, Menni, and Others. Tentative Resolution in Favor of Venus." I sensed that this was exactly what I was looking for. I put the phonogram into the apparatus. What I heard has been etched forever into my soul and is presented below.

The sixth session was opened by Menni, who chaired the congress. The first report was delivered by a representative of the Central Institute of Statistics. He presented a host of figures showing that, given the present growth rate of the population, if the Martians restricted themselves to the exploitation of their own planet, a food shortage would begin to make itself felt within thirty years. The crisis could be averted if a technically feasible process could be discovered for synthesizing protein from inorganic matter, but there were no guarantees that this could be done in thirty years. For that reason it had become absolutely imperative for the Colonial Group to shift its attention from purely scientific interplanetary expeditions to the organization of mass resettlement. Two planets with enormous natural resources were at present accessible to the Martians, and it was necessary to decide immediately which of them was to become the initial center of colonization and then draw up a plan for the project.

Menni asked whether there were any objections to either the facts or the arguments presented by the Central Institute of Statistics. There were none, whereupon he proposed to open the discussion on the planet to be chosen for mass colonization. Sterni took the floor.

7. Sterni

"The first question submitted to us by the representative from the Institute of Statistics," Sterni began in his usual, mathematically precise tone of voice, "concerns the planet to be chosen for colonization. In my opinion, no decision is necessary, because the matter was decided long ago by reality itself. There is no choice. Of the two planets presently accessible to us, only one is at all suitable for mass colonization—Earth. There is a large body of literature on Venus, and of course you are all familiar with it. Only one conclusion can be drawn from the data presented there, and that is that we are *at present* unable to conquer the planet. Her blazing sun would sap the strength of our colonists, her terrible thunderstorms and winds would demolish our buildings, sweep aside our aircraft, and dash them against her giant mountains. We could cope with her monsters, though we would have to pay a high price in human lives. The bacteria of the planet, however, are enormously rich and varied, and our knowledge of them extremely poor. How many new diseases are lurking there? Volcanic activity is still in a state of uneasy ferment; how many earthquakes, eruptions, tidal waves would be in store for us? Rational beings should not undertake the impossible. The casualties that would result from an attempt to colonize Venus would be not only countless but meaningless. They would not be necessary sacrifices for the sake of science and the common good, but victims of a mad dream. This, I think, is quite clear, and anyone who has read the report from the latest expedition to Venus will be forced to agree.

"Thus if we are to organize mass resettlement, it must of course be done on Earth. There are no significant natural obstacles there, and the incalculable riches with which the planet is endowed exceed our own eightfold. The process of colonization itself has already been prepared by the civilization already existing on Earth, even if it is not a very developed human culture. The Central Institute of Statistics, of course, is also aware of all these considerations. If it has proposed that we choose a planet and if we think it necessary even to discuss the question, then that is only because there is one very serious obstacle on Earth, namely its humanity.

"The peoples of the earth are masters of the planet, and they will under no circumstances relinquish any significant portion of its surface. Such reluctance derives from the very nature of their culture, which is based on ownership protected by organized violence. Although even the most civilized nations on Earth actually exploit only a small fraction of the natural resources available to them, they are possessed by an unrelenting aspiration to seize new territories. The systematic plundering of the lands and belongings of less developed peoples goes by the name of colonial policy and is considered a major area of their political life. You can imagine how they would react to a natural and reasonable suggestion on our part that they cede to us a part of their territory in return for our help to make incomparably better use of their part. As they see it, colonization is only a question of brute strength and violence, and whether we want it or not, they will *force* us to adopt the same attitude toward them.

"If it were only a matter of demonstrating our superiority on a single occasion, the whole thing would be relatively simple and would not demand more victims than one of their ordinary, senseless, useless wars. They already have enormous herds of people trained to murder—they call them armies—which would provide most suitable material for such necessary violence. Any one of our etheronephs could simply use the lethal rays emanating from the accelerated decomposition of radium in its engine to annihilate two or three of these herds in a matter of minutes, and the loss would probably even benefit their culture more than it would damage it. Unfortunately, however, things are not that simple—such a battle would only be the beginning of the real problems.

"In their never-ending internal bickering, the peoples of Earth have developed a psychological peculiarity which they call patriotism. This indefinite but strong and deep-seated emotion includes a spiteful distrust of all other peoples and races, a visceral attachment to a particular way of life—especially to the territory with which each people has fused, like a turtle with its shell—a certain collective self-conceit and often, evidently, a simple thirst for destruction, violence, and plunder. Patriotic fervor intensifies and becomes extremely acute after military defeats, especially when the victors seize a part of the losers' territory. The patriotism of the vanquished then takes the form of an intense and prolonged hatred of the victors, and revenge becomes the ideal of not just the worst groups—the upper or ruling classes—but of the entire people, including the best elements among the toiling masses.

"Now then, if we were to take a part of Earth's surface by force, the entire population of the planet would doubtless find itself united by a common patriotism and merciless racist hatred and resentment toward our colonists. Extermination of the newcomers by any and all means, no matter how treacherous, would in the eyes of the Earthlings become a sacred and noble exploit, a sure path to immortal glory. The situation of our colonists would become unbearable. You know that the destruction of life is usually a very simple matter, even for an inferior civilization. We are immeasurably superior to the Earthlings in open combat, but by means of surprise attacks they could destroy us just as effectively as they usually annihilate one another. Moreover, it should be noted that the art

of destruction on Earth is much more advanced than any other aspect of
their peculiar culture.

"Living among them and together with them, of course, would be
quite impossible. They would be forever menacing us with intrigues and
acts of terrorism, and our comrades would have to endure a constant
sense of insecurity and would suffer innumerable casualties. We would
be forced to evict the Earthlings from all the territories occupied by us,
and I am talking about removing tens and perhaps hundreds of millions at
a time. Given their political system, which does not recognize any principle of fraternal mutual assistance, given their social order, in which services and aid are paid for in money, and finally, given their clumsy and
rigid system of production, which does not allow for any rapid increase of
productivity or redistribution of fruits of labor, the overwhelming majority of these millions would be doomed to slow starvation. The survivors
would organize themselves in cadres of embittered, fanatical agitators
working to incite the rest of the population of Earth against us.

"We would then be forced to continue the struggle anyway. Our
entire territory would have to be transformed into a constantly guarded
military camp. Deep racial hatred and fear that we would seize more
territory would unite all the people of Earth in wars against us. If their
weapons are already now more developed than their tools of labor, under
such conditions their technology of destruction would advance even more
swiftly. At the same time, they would be constantly on the lookout for a
chance to start a sudden war, and if they succeeded they would doubtless
cause us considerable uncompensated losses even if we were to win. In
addition, we cannot rule out the possibility that they may discover the
secret of our main weapon. They already know about radioactive matter,
and they could find out how to accelerate its decay either through intelligence obtained from us or through the independent efforts of their scientists. You know that when one has such a weapon, one need be only a few
minutes ahead of the enemy in order to attack and annihilate him. And in
this case it is as easy to destroy the highest form of life as the most
elementary one.

"What would life be like for our comrades amid these dangers and
eternal anxieties? Not only would all the joys of life be poisoned; the very
form of life would soon be perverted and degraded. Little by little, life
would be infiltrated by suspicion, mistrust, an egoistic thirst for self-
preservation, and the cruelty which that instinct inevitably breeds. The
colony would cease to be *our* colony and would become a militaristic
republic in the midst of vanquished and invariably hostile peoples. Repeated attacks and the resultant casualties would not only generate feelings of revenge and hatred that would pervert the image of man so dear to
us, but would also objectively force us to move from self-defense to a
ruthless offensive. And ultimately, after much hesitation and a fruitless

and agonizing loss of strength, we would inevitably be forced to reach the same conclusion which, as conscious beings able to anticipate the course of events, we know enough to be able to draw today: *colonization of Earth requires the utter annihilation of its population.*"

(A murmur of horror rose from among the hundreds of listeners. Netti's voice could be heard above it in a distinct exclamation of indignation. When quiet was restored, Sterni continued.)

"We must understand this necessity and look it squarely in the eye, however grim it might seem. We have only two alternatives: either we halt the development of our civilization, or we destroy the alien civilization on Earth. There is no third possibility." (Netti's voice: "Not true!") "I know what Netti is thinking about, and I shall now consider the third alternative she is proposing.

"She is thinking of the immediate socialist reeducation of the peoples of Earth. All of us have lately favored such a plan, but in my opinion we are now forced to reject it. We know enough about Earthlings to realize that the idea is quite infeasible. The culture of the most highly developed peoples of Earth is on approximately the same level as that of our forefathers during the epoch of the Great Canals. They are also under the sway of capital, and they have a proletariat struggling for socialism. One might be led to think that the upheaval will come very soon, eliminating the system of organized violence and creating the preconditions for the free and rapid development of human life. Capitalism on Earth, however, possesses certain important features which greatly alter the essence of the matter.

"In the first place, Earth is terribly riven by political and national divisions. This means that instead of following a single and uniform path of development in a single broad society, the struggle for socialism is split into a variety of unique and autonomous processes in individual societies with distinct political systems, languages, and sometimes even races. Secondly, the methods of social struggle there are much cruder and more mechanical than was the case with us, and outright physical violence in the form of standing armies and armed uprisings plays an incomparably greater role there than it ever did on Mars. Due to all these factors, the question of social revolution becomes a very uncertain one. We must expect not one, but a multitude of revolutions taking place in different countries at different times. In many respects they will probably not even have the same basic character, but the main point is that their outcome is unpredictable and unstable. The ruling classes will rely on the army and sophisticated military technology, and in certain cases they may deal the rebelling proletariat such a stunning blow that the cause of socialism will be frustrated for decades in a number of important states. Such examples have already been recorded in the chronicles of Earth.

"If this happens, the individual advanced countries in which socialism triumphs will be like islands in a hostile capitalist and even to some extent precapitalist sea. Anxious about their own power, the upper classes of the nonsocialist countries will continue to concentrate all their efforts on destroying these islands. They will constantly be organizing military expeditions against them, and from among the ranks of the former large and small property-holders in the socialist nations themselves they will be able to find plenty of allies willing to commit treason. It is difficult to foresee the outcome of these conflicts, but even in those instances where socialism prevails and triumphs, its character will be perverted deeply and for a long time to come by years of encirclement, unavoidable terror and militarism, and the barbarian patriotism that is their inevitable consequence. This socialism will be a far cry from our own.

"In our previous plans, we had hoped to interfere in this process by accelerating and aiding the triumph of socialism. What means do we have at our disposal for such a project? First of all, we could give the peoples of Earth our technology, our science, our ability to harness the forces of nature. Their culture would thereby immediately be raised to the point where the backward forms of their economic and political life would come into such sharp conflict with it that they would disappear due to their own unfitness. Secondly, we could lend direct support to the socialist proletariat in its revolutionary struggle and help it to break the resistance of the other classes. There are no other alternatives. But can these two strategies achieve their goal? We know enough now to be able to answer definitely: no!

"What would happen if we were to give the Earthlings our technological knowledge and methods? The first to seize upon them and use them to increase their own power would be the *ruling* class in all countries. This would be inevitable, because they already control the means of production and command the loyalty of ninety-nine percent of all the scientists and engineers. In other words, they are the only ones who can *apply* the new technology, and they will use it to the exact extent that it can help them increase their power over the masses. Moreover, the new and mighty means of destruction which this technology would place in their hands would immediately be employed to crush the socialist proletariat. The rulers would intensify their persecution tenfold and attempt as soon as possible to provoke the proletariat into open combat, where they can crush its best and most conscious elements and emasculate it ideologically before the working class has a chance to develop its own new and improved methods of military force. Thus our interference would only serve to stimulate a reaction from above and provide it with weapons and unheard-of power. In the final analysis this would delay the victory of socialism by decades.

"What could we expect to achieve if we were openly to assist the socialist proletariat against its enemies? Let us assume—for the point is by no means self-evident—that it agrees to an alliance with us. In that case we would gain some easy first victories. But then? We and the socialists of Earth would inevitably be confronted by the most bitter and rabid patriotism on the part of all other classes of society. The proletariat is still a minority in even the most advanced countries. The dying remnants of the petty bourgeoisie and the most backward and ignorant elements of the masses are in the majority. It would be an easy matter for the large property-holders and their closest allies, the bureaucrats and scientists, to stir up rabid hostility toward the proletariat among these classes, because the masses are at bottom conservative and even to an extent reactionary, and they react violently to rapid progess. The vanguard of the proletariat would be surrounded by embittered and merciless enemies whose rank would also be swelled by the backward strata of the working class. It would find itself in the same unbearable situation as our colonists besieged by the vanquished peoples of Earth. We could expect countless treacherous attacks, pogroms, slaughter, but the main point is that the whole position of the proletariat in society would be extremely unfavorable, in terms of being able to effect any meaningful social transformation. Once again our interference would delay rather than hasten the social revolution.

"Thus the time for this upheaval remains indefinite, and we cannot shorten it. It is in any case going to take more time than we have at our disposal. In only thirty years we are going to be faced with a population surplus of 15 to 20 million persons, a figure that will then continue to grow at the rate of 20 to 25 million a year. Considerable colonization must take place before this situation arises, for otherwise we will not have the strength or the resources to undertake it on an adequate scale.

"In addition, it is more than doubtful that we would be able to reach a peaceful agreement even with the socialist societies on Earth, assuming that these were to arise sooner than expected. As I have already said, in many respects this will not be *our* socialism. Centuries of national division, a mutual lack of understanding, and brutal, bloody struggle will leave deep scars on the psychology of liberated Earthly humanity. We do not know how much barbarity and narrow-mindedness the socialists of Earth will bring with them into their new society.

"We have enough experience to perceive the great distance which separates us from the psychology of even the best representatives of Earth. On our latest expedition we brought back with us a socialist, a man of superior spiritual and physical health. And what happened? Our life proved so alien to him, so contrary to his entire psychology, that in a short while he became seriously deranged. If he is one of the best—and Menni selected him personally from among many—what can we expect of the others?

"Thus we are faced with the same dilemma: either we halt the growth

BOGDANOV'S PRESYENCE

of our own population and thereby impair the entire development of our life, or we colonize Earth, having first exterminated its inhabitants. I speak of the destruction of its entire population, because we cannot even make an exception for its socialist vanguard. In the first place, in the process of universal destruction it is technically impossible to single out this numerically insignificant vanguard from the masses as a whole. Secondly, even if we somehow managed to spare the socialists, they would start a bitter and ruthless war against us, because they would never be able to reconcile themselves to the killing of millions of their own kind, to whom they are bound by a multitude of often very intimate ties. There can be no compromise in the conflict between our two worlds.

"We must choose, and I say that we have but one choice. A higher form of life cannot be sacrificed for the sake of a lower one. Among all the people on Earth there are not even a few million who are consciously striving for a truly human type of life. For the sake of these embryonic human beings we cannot deny the birth and development of tens, maybe hundreds of millions of our own people, who are humans in an incomparably fuller sense of the word. We will not be guilty of cruelty, because we can destroy them with far less suffering than they are constantly causing each other. There is but one Life in the Universe, and it will be enriched rather than impoverished if it is _our_ socialism rather than the distant, semibarbaric Earthly variant that is allowed to develop, for thanks to its unbroken evolution and boundless potential, our life is infinitely more harmonious."

(Sterni's speech was followed by a deep silence, broken by Menni's call for objections. Netti took the floor.)

8. Netti

"'There is but one Life in the Universe,' says Sterni. And yet what does he propose to us? That we exterminate an entire individual type of life, a type which we can never resurrect or replace.

"For hundreds of millions of years the marvelous planet Earth has lived its own particular life, a life different from others. And now consciousness has begun to develop from its spontaneous forces. Proceeding through a bitter and difficult struggle from the lowest stages to the higher, this consciousness has finally assumed _human_ forms closely related to our own. But these forms are not identical with ours: the history of a different natural environment and a different struggle is reflected in them; they conceal a different play of spontaneous forces, other contradictions, other possibilities of development. The epoch has dawned when it has for the first time become possible to unite the two great lines of life. Just imagine the new variety, the higher harmony that could result from this union!

And we are told that since there is but one Life in the Universe we should not unify, but destroy it.

"When Sterni showed how greatly the peoples, the history, the mores and psychology of Earth differ from our own, he refuted his own argument almost better than I could hope to do. If they were identical with us in all respects save their level of development, then one might be able to agree with Sterni: a lower stage is worth sacrificing for the sake of a higher one, the weak must yield to the strong. But the Earthlings are not the same as we. They and their civilization are not simply lower and weaker than ours—they are *different*. If we eliminate them we will not replace them in the process of universal evolution but will merely fill in mechanically the vacuum we have created in the world of life forms.

"The real difference between our cultures does not lie in the barbarity or cruelty of Earthly civilization. Barbarity and cruelty are only transient phenomena of the general *dissipation* in the process of development which characterizes the evolution of life on Earth. The struggle for survival is more vigorous and intense there, nature is continually creating many more forms of life, but many more of them also fall victim to the march of evolution. This cannot be otherwise, because the source of life—the sun—provides Earth with eight times more energy-giving rays than Mars. That is why there is so much life spread generously throughout the planet, that is why the variety of its forms gives rise to so many contradictions and why the solution of these is so terribly complicated and punctuated by catastrophes. In the plant and animal kingdoms millions of species struggled violently and quickly crowded each other out, contributing through their life and death to the development of new, more perfect and harmonious, more synthetic species. The same is true of humans.

"If we compare our history with that of Earthly humanity, it seems astonishingly simple, so regular and free of errors that it seems almost schematic. The elements of socialism accumulated peacefully and uninterruptedly as the petty bourgeoisie gradually disappeared and rose to the same level of consciousness as the proletariat. This was a smooth process, with no vacillation or sudden leaps, and it also took place uniformly in all countries of our planet, which was already organized into a single coherent political whole. There was a struggle, but people managed somehow to understand each other; the proletariat did not try to peer far into the future, and the bourgeoisie did not have any reactionary utopian dreams. The various epochs and social formations were not mingled to the same extent as on Earth, where one can sometimes find a reactionary feudal system in a highly developed capitalistic country, and where the numerous peasantry, whose development lags behind by an entire historical epoch, often serve the upper classes as an instrument for crushing the proletariat. Several generations ago we arrived by a smooth and even road at a type of social order which liberates and unites all the forces of social development.

"That is not the road our Earthly brothers have traveled. Their path is a thorny one, full of twists and turns. Even the few of us who know the facts find it impossible to picture the insane sophistication which the art of oppression has attained in the hands of the ideological and political organizations dominated by the upper classes of the most civilized nations of Earth. What is the result? Has progress been delayed? No, there are no grounds for saying that; because although the initial stages of capitalism preceding the birth of proletarian socialist consciousness developed in the midst of confusion and a cruel struggle among various formations, that development was not slower, but more rapid than it was here, where it proceeded through a series of gradual and more peaceful transitions. The very severity and ruthlessness of the struggle inspired in the combatants an energy and passion, a spirit of heroism and self-sacrifice that were completely absent from the more moderate and less tragic struggle of our ancestors. In this respect the life of the people on Earth is higher rather than lower than ours, even though our culture is older and has attained a much higher level.

"Earthly humanity is splintered, its various races and peoples have fused with their territories and historical traditions, they speak different languages, and a profound mutual lack of understanding pervades all their relations. This is all true, and it is also true that because of these enormous obstacles our Earthly brothers will achieve their goal of uniting mankind much later than we. But if one is aware of the causes, one is in a better position to evaluate the consequences. This fragmentation is due to the immensity of life on Earth and the richness and variety of its natural environment, which together have produced a multitude of different world-views. Surely this makes Earth and her people superior rather than inferior to our world during the corresponding historical epoch.

"Even the difference in the languages they speak has in many respects contributed to the development of their thought, as it has liberated notions from the tyranny of the words by which they are expressed. Compare the philosophy of the Earthlings with that of our capitalist ancestors. Philosophy on Earth is not only more varied but also more subtle than ours. Not only is the material with which it works more complicated, its best schools analyze that material more profoundly and establish the relationships between facts and notions with greater precision. All systems of philosophy, of course, are manifestations of an imperfect and fragmented cognition and reflect a deficient level of scientific development. They represent attempts to provide a uniform description of Being by filling in the gaps in scientific experience with speculations.

Eventually, therefore, philosophy will be eliminated on Earth as it has been eliminated among us by the monism of science.

"Consider, however, that many of the philosophical suppositions advanced by their greatest thinkers and by the leaders of the social and political struggle roughly anticipate our scientific discoveries. Such, for example, is almost the entire social philosophy of the socialists. It is obvious that peoples who have surpassed our ancestors in philosophical creativity can eventually surpass even us in scientific creation. Yet Sterni would have us measure this humanity on the basis of the number of righteous men—that is, conscious socialists—that can be found in its midst. He is asking us to judge that humanity on the basis of its present contradictions, not according to the forces which have generated and will in due course resolve those contradictions. He would drain forever this stormy but beautiful ocean of life!

"We must answer him firmly and decisively: *never!* We must lay the foundations for our future alliance with the people of Earth. We cannot significantly accelerate their transition to a free order, but we must do the little we can to facilitate that development. And if we have not been able to protect the first emissary from Earth from unnecessary suffering and illness, it is we rather than the peoples of Earth who should bear the dishonor. Fortunately, he will soon be well again, but even if his too sudden immersion in an alien world proves fatal, he will still have accomplished a great deal for the future union of our planets.

"As to our own difficulties and dangers, we shall have to overcome them by other means. We must increase our efforts to find synthetic proteins and, to the best of our present abilities, we must undertake the colonization of Venus. If we fail to solve these problems in the little time we have left, we must temporarily check the birth rate. What intelligent midwife would not sacrifice the life of an unborn child in order to save the mother? If necessary, we must likewise sacrifice a part of our life that has not yet come into being for the sake of the lives of others who already exist and are developing. The union of our worlds will repay us endlessly for this sacrifice. The unity of Life is our highest goal, and love is the highest expression of intelligence!"

(A deep hush. Menni took the floor.)

9. Menni

"I have been attentively observing the mood of the audience, and I can see that a majority of comrades are on Netti's side. I am pleased to note this, because my own point of view is very near hers. I would only like to add one practical consideration which I feel to be very important. It is quite possible that even if we were to attempt the mass colonization of other planets, we would find that we presently lack the technical resources to accomplish our purpose. We might build tens of thousands of etheronephs, only to discover that we have nothing to run them on. Such a huge new fleet would demand a hundred times more radioactive fuel than we use today, yet our known reserves are constantly being depleted, and discoveries of new deposits are becoming rarer. Let us not forget that radioactive matter is not only used to give the etheronephs their enormous velocity. You know that our entire chemical industry is now based on these substances. We use them to manufacture minus-matter, without which the etheronephs and our countless aircraft are only heavy, useless boxes. It is impossible to discontinue such uses of active matter.

"The worst thing of all, however, is that the only possible substitute for colonization, namely the development of synthetic proteins, may prove unfeasible because of that same lack of radioactive substances. Considering the enormous chemical complexity of proteins, it is inconceivable that our old methods of synthesizing by means of a gradual complication will ever result in a technically simple synthesis suitable for mass industrial production. You know that a few years ago we succeeded in developing artificial proteins by such a process, but a tremendous expenditure of time and energy yielded only a very small quantity of them, so that the significance of the whole project is purely theoretical. The only way proteins can be mass-produced from inorganic matter is by rapidly and radically altering the chemical composition of the substance in question, and that process involves exposing this ordinary, stable matter to the action of unstable elements. If we are to succeed in this area, tens of thousands of scientists will have to begin working on developing synthetic proteins, and they will be performing millions of new experiments. But in order to conduct this research, and, if it is successful, in order to mass-produce proteins, we will again need enormous quantities of radioactive material, much more than we presently have at our disposal. Thus no matter how we look at it, the solution to our problem depends on the discovery of new deposits of radioactive elements.

"But where are they to be found? Obviously, on other planets; that is, either on Earth or on Venus. It seems evident to me personally that the first attempt should be made on Venus. It is reasonable to assume that there are rich deposits of active elements on Earth, but we already know for certain that such reserves exist on Venus. We do not know where the fields on Earth are located, because those that have already been discovered by Earthly scientists are worthless to us, whereas all our expeditions immediately discovered deposits on Venus. Most of the reserves on Earth presumably lie at the same great depths as here on Mars, whereas some of them on Venus are so close to the surface that they were easily found by means of a photographic detector. In order to prospect for radium on Earth we would have to undertake the same massive excavations as we have done on Mars. That could take decades, and even then we cannot be sure of success. On Venus we need only mine what has already been discovered, and we can begin doing that immediately.

"Whatever we may decide later on the question of mass colonization, therefore, I am thoroughly convinced that the very possibility of making the decision depends on an immediate, small-scale, and temporary colonization of Venus whose sole object will be to obtain radioactive ore.

"To be sure, there are enormous natural obstacles, but we need not fully overcome them. We will not have to establish control over more than a small area of the planet. What is essentially involved here is a large expedition that will have to remain on Venus not for months, as in the case of earlier voyages, but years, and its chief activity will be the mining of radium. At the same time, of course, we will have to wage a vigorous struggle against the elements in order to protect ourselves from the murderous climate, unknown diseases, and other dangers. It will demand great sacrifices; perhaps only a fraction of the expedition will ever return. But we must make an attempt.

"Our data indicate that the most suitable place to begin is on the Island of Hot Storms. I have made an exhaustive study of the natural environment there and have drawn up a detailed plan for the project. Comrades, if you feel you can consider it now, I shall immediately present it to you."

(There were no objections, and Menni began describing his plan in great technical detail. Other speakers took the floor after him, but their comments referred exclusively to individual points of the plan. Certain of them expressed doubts as to the expedition's chances of success, but all were agreed that an attempt was necessary. The meeting concluded by adopting the resolution proposed by Menni.)

10. Murder

I was so stunned by what I had heard that I could not even attempt to assemble my thoughts. I only felt a cold pain closing like an iron ring on my heart, and before me, as clearly as my earlier hallucinations, I could still see Sterni's towering figure and implacably calm face. Everything else was jumbled together and lost in a dark, oppressive chaos. Like a robot, I left the library and got into the gondola. As I flew swiftly along, I was forced to bundle up tightly in my overcoat to shield myself from the cold wind. As I did so, I was struck by a thought which immediately froze into an absolute certainty in my mind: I had to be alone. When I arrived home, I set about implementing my decision, but my actions were so mechanical that it seemed as though someone else were doing it all for me.

I wrote the administrative board of the factory that I was leaving my job for a while. I told Enno that we would have to separate for the time being. She gave me a worried, questioning glance and turned a little pale, but said not a word. It was not until later, just as I was about to go, that she asked me whether I would not like to see Nella. I replied that I did not, and kissed her for the last time.

I fell into a state of utter paralysis that was empty save for a cold pain in my heart and a jumble of fragmentary thoughts. I could only faintly recall Netti's and Menni's speeches, as if what they had said was of little interest or consequence. Only once did I come to the sudden realization that this was why Netti had gone: "*everything* depends on the expedition." Individual expressions and whole sentences from Sterni's speech resounded sharply and clearly: "we must *understand* necessity . . . a few million human embryos . . . the utter annihilation of Earthly humanity . . . he is seriously deranged. . . ." But there were no connections or conclusions. Sometimes it would seem as though the destruction of mankind was already an accomplished fact, but I could only envisage it in a hazy and abstract form. The pain became more intense, and I was seized by the thought that I was to blame for the catastrophe. For a short while I realized that nothing had happened yet, and perhaps never would happen. The pain, however, did not cease, and my thoughts went grinding slowly on: "They will all die . . . Anna Nikolaevna . . . and Vanya the worker . . . and Netti . . . no, not Netti . . . she is a Martian . . . they will all die . . . but it is not cruel, because there will be no pain . . . yes, that is what Sterni said . . . but everyone will die because I was sick . . . in other words, it is my fault. . . ." These fragmentary, oppressive thoughts grew numb and rigid, planting themselves cold and immobile in my brain. Time seemed to freeze with them.

This was delirium—agonizing, unceasing, endless raving. I did not see any apparitions around me—there was only one black apparition now, but it was inside me and it was *everything*. And it would never go away, for time had stopped. The thought of committing suicide occurred to me and dragged sluggishly on in my consciousness for some time, but I never became obsessed with it. Suicide seemed meaningless, banal—could it really end this black pain that was *everything?* I could not believe in suicide, because I did not believe in my own existence. Sorrow, cold, this hateful *everything*— they existed, but my "I" was lost among them, where it seemed infinitely small, imperceptible, insignificant. There was no "me." At times my condition became so intolerable that I was seized by a violent urge to throw myself at everything animate and inanimate around me, beat it, destroy it, annihilate it. But I realized that to do so would be meaningless and childish, so I gritted my teeth and resisted the temptation.

The thought of Sterni kept returning and finally lodged itself firmly in my mind. It seemed to be the center of all my pain and sorrow.

Gradually, slowly but surely, an intention began to form around this nucleus and develop into a clear and resolute decision: I must see Sterni. Why I had to see him I could not say. All I knew was that I was going to do it. Yet at the same time it was painfully difficult to rouse myself from my inertia. Finally the day came when I found sufficient energy to overcome this inner resistance. I got into the gondola and flew to Sterni's observatory. On the way I tried to think of what I was going to say to him, but the chill in my heart and the winter cold around me paralyzed my thoughts. Three hours later I had arrived.

As I entered the large hall of the observatory I told one of the comrades working there that I had to see Sterni. He left and returned a moment later, saying that Sterni was busy checking instruments but would be free in fifteen minutes and had asked me to wait in his office.

I was shown to the office, where I sat down at the desk and began to wait. The room was full of various apparatuses and machines, some of them familiar to me, some of them not. To the right of my chair there was a little instrument on a heavy metal tripod. A book about Earth and her inhabitants lay open on the table. I began reading it mechanically, but halted after the first few sentences and fell into a state much like my former paralysis, except that the usual sorrow was now accompanied by an indistinct emotional convulsion. I do not know how long I sat there like that.

I heard heavy footsteps in the corridor, and Sterni entered the room in his usual unhurried, matter-of-fact way. He seated himself in the chair on the other side of the table and looked at me questioningly. I was silent. He waited a minute or so and then addressed me directly:

"What can I do for you?"

I remained silent, staring at him fixedly as if he were an inanimate object. He gave a hardly noticeable shrug of his shoulders and settled down in the armchair to wait.

"Netti's husband . . ." I finally uttered with some effort. The remark was only half conscious, and I was not actually talking to him.

"I *used to be* Netti's husband," he corrected me calmly. "We separated long ago."

"Annihilation . . . will not . . . be cruel," I continued in the same slow and half-conscious manner, repeating the thought that had become petrified in my brain.

"Oh, so that is why you are here," he said calmly. "But now it is quite out of the question. As you know, an altogether different preliminary resolution was adopted."

"Preliminary resolution," I repeated mechanically.

"As for the plan I was thinking of on that occasion," added Sterni, "although I am not prepared to disown it entirely, I must admit that now I would not be inclined to defend it with such confidence."

"Not entirely . . ." I repeated.

"Your recovery and the active part you have taken in the work of our society have partly demolished my arguments."

"Annihilation . . . partly," I interrupted. My unconscious irony must have revealed my sorrow and pain, for Sterni paled and looked at me anxiously. We both fell silent.

Suddenly the cold ring of pain wrung my heart with unprecedented, inexpressible force. I threw myself backward in the chair to stifle a mad scream. My fingers clutched convulsively at something hard and cold. I felt a heavy weapon in my hand as the pain within me swelled like an uncontrollable elemental force to a pitch of frenzied despair. I leapt up from the chair and dealt Sterni a terrible blow. One of the legs of the tripod struck him in the temple, and without a cry or even a groan he slumped to one side. I threw aside my weapon, which fell with a clatter against the machine. It was all over.

I went out into the corridor and told the first person I met that I had killed Sterni. He turned pale and rushed to the office. Evidently he could see immediately that help was no longer needed, however, for he returned to me at once. He took me to his room, told another comrade to telephone a doctor and then go to Sterni's office, and we were alone. He could not make up his mind to speak to me. Finally I asked him:

"Is Enno here?"

"No," he answered, "she went to visit Nella for a few days."

We remained silent until the doctor arrived. He tried to question me about what had happened, but I told him I did not feel like talking. He took me to the nearest mental hospital, where I was given spacious and comfortable quarters and was left in peace for a long time. That was all I could possibly wish for.

The situation seemed clear. I had murdered Sterni, and because of that everything was lost. The Martians could now see what they could expect from closer relations with the people of Earth. They could see that even the man they thought best prepared to enter into their life had brought them nothing but violence and death. Sterni was dead, but his idea would be resurrected. The last hope had vanished—Earth was doomed. And it was all my fault.

These thoughts arose soon after the murder and lodged themselves in my mind alongside recollections of the deed. At first I found a certain comfort in their cold certainty, but soon the sorrow and pain returned, and it felt as though they could continue to grow forever. These sensations were accompanied by a profound self-contempt. I felt I had betrayed all of humanity. There was a flicker of hope that the Martians would execute me, but it was followed by the thought that their disgust and contempt for me would prevent them from doing that. They took considerable pains to hide their aversion, but I could sense it clearly.

LEONID'S REL'SHIP WITH SOCIALISM ENDS IN VIOLENCE

I do not know how long I remained immersed in such thoughts. Finally the doctor came and told me that I needed a change of surroundings and would be sent back to Earth. I thought that this was merely a way of concealing from me the fact that I had been condemned to death, but I had no objections. My only request would be that, lest I defile the planets with my odious body, it be cast as far away from them as possible into space.

My recollections of the return trip are very hazy. There were no familiar faces and I spoke to no one. My mind was not confused, but I noticed practically nothing going on around me. Nothing mattered.

PART IV

1. Werner's Clinic

I do not remember how I came to the clinic headed by my old comrade Dr. Werner. It was a Zemstvo* hospital in one of the northern provinces and was already familiar to me from Werner's letters. Located a few kilometers from the provincial capital, it was in wretched condition and always terribly overcrowded. The steward was an unusually crafty sort, and the medical staff was undermanned and perpetually overworked. Doctor Werner waged a stubborn war with the very liberal Zemstvo Board over the steward, over the construction of additional barracks, which the Board was reluctant to finance, over the church, which it insisted on building at any price, over the wages of the staff, and so on. Instead of curing the patients, the hospital managed to reduce many of them to imbecility, while many others, weakened by a lack of fresh air and proper nutrition, perished from tuberculosis. As for Werner, he would of course have left long ago if he had not been forced to stay there by certain very special circumstances connected with his revolutionary past.

The charms of the Zemstvo clinic, however, were of no consequence to me. Werner was a good comrade who unhesitatingly provided me with the greatest possible comfort. He gave me two rooms in the large apartment allotted him as the senior physician. A third room was occupied by an assistant, while in the fourth he housed a comrade hiding from the police, disguising him as one of the medical staff. I did not, of course have all my former conveniences, and despite the tact of my young comrades, the surveillance to which I was subject was far more conspicuous than on Mars. However, none of this meant a thing to me.

Like the Martian physicians, Dr. Werner hardly treated me at all,

*Organ of local government.

Leonid tries to recover from psychological disorientation outside the hospital on Earth after his return

merely giving me occasional sedatives. His main concern was for my comfort and tranquility. Each morning and evening he would drop in to see me after I had taken the bath prepared for me by my thoughtful comrades, but he limited himself to asking whether I was in need of anything. During the long months of my illness I had become quite unaccustomed to speaking, and would either answer him "no" or say nothing at all. I was touched by his solicitude, however, though at the same time I felt I was altogether undeserving of it and should tell him so. Finally I managed to summon enough strength to confess to him that I was a murderer and a traitor, and that all humanity was doomed to perish because of me. He smiled but said nothing, and after this occasion his visits became more frequent.

Little by little my new environment began to exercise a beneficial influence on me. The pain became less intense, my sorrow began to fade, my thoughts became both livelier and brighter. I began leaving the apartment to stroll in the garden and wood. One of my comrades was always nearby, and although that was unpleasant, I understood that a murderer could not be allowed simply to walk around by himself. Sometimes I even conversed with them, though of course only on trivial topics.

It was early spring, and the reawakening of life around me no longer aggravated my painful memories. As I listened to the chirping of the birds I even found a certain melancholy comfort in the thought that they would remain and go on living while other people were doomed to die. Once near the wood I happened to meet a patient carrying a spade on his way to work in the fields. He hastened to introduce himself, pompously claiming (he was suffering from megalomania) that he was the village constable, evidently the highest authority he had known while still a free man. For the first time since the beginning of my illness, I involuntarily laughed. I realized I was in my mother country, and like Antaeus I gathered—albeit very slowly—new strength from contact with my native soil.

2. Reality or Fantasy?

As I began to pay more attention to my surroundings, I wanted to know whether Werner and my other comrades knew anything about what had happened to me or what I had done. I asked Werner who had brought me to the hospital. He replied that I had come with two young strangers who were unable to tell him anything about my illness. They said that I was already ill when they happened to run into me in the capital, that they had known me earlier, before the revolution, and that when they heard me mention Dr. Werner they had decided to turn to him for help. They left the same day they had arrived. They impressed Werner as trustworthy people whom he had no reason to disbelieve. He had himself lost touch with me several years previously, and there was no one who could give him any information about me.

I wanted to tell Werner about the murder I had committed. It was difficult to do so, however, because the story was extremely complicated and contained a multitude of details which would appear very strange to any impartial listener. I explained the problem to Werner, who answered unexpectedly:

"It would be best not to tell me anything just now. It would not further your recovery. I do not intend to argue with you, of course, but I am not going to believe your story either. You are suffering from melancholia, a disorder in which people quite sincerely confess nonexistent crimes; their memory adapts to their delirium and fashions false recollections. But you will not believe me either until you have recovered, which is why it would be better to postpone your story until then."

If this conversation had taken place a few months earlier, I would doubtless have interpreted Werner's remarks as an expression of thorough distrust and contempt. Now, however, when my soul yearned for peace and comfort, I reacted quite differently. I was pleased by the thought that my comrades knew nothing of my crime and that even its very existence might be open to question. I thought about it less and less often.

My recovery began to proceed more rapidly. Occasionally I would suffer attacks of my former distress, but they never lasted long. Werner was obviously satisfied with my progress and even almost released me from medical observation. On one occasion, recalling his diagnosis of my "delirium," I asked him to let me read a typical case history of an illness like mine, one that he had observed and recorded at the hospital. He hesitated considerably and was obviously reluctant, but he finally complied with my request. In my presence he selected and gave to me one of a large pile of case histories.

The report dealt with a peasant from a remote, isolated little village who had been forced by poverty to seek his living in the capital, where he had begun working at one of the largest factories. The life of the huge city evidently proved a great shock to him, and, as his wife put it, for a long time he was "not himself." This eventually passed and he began living and working like everyone else. When a strike broke out at the factory he joined the ranks of his comrades. The strike was long and persistent, and he and his wife and child were on the verge of starvation. Suddenly he "got cold feet," started rebuking himself for getting married and having a child, and condemned his whole way of life as "ungodly." Soon he began to "babble utter nonsense." He was taken to a hospital and later transferred to a clinic in his native province. He claimed that he was a strikebreaker who had betrayed both his comrades and a certain "kind engineer" who secretly sympathized with the strike and was hanged by the government. By a coincidence I happened to be intimately acquainted with the entire history of this strike, as I was working at the time in the capital. In reality there had been no treachery, and the "kind engineer" had not only not been hanged, but had never even been arrested. The worker finally recovered from his illness.

This story put my thoughts into a new context. I began to doubt whether I had ever actually committed the murder; perhaps, as Werner had said, my memory was merely "adapting itself to my delirium melancholia." At the same time, my recollections of life among the Martians were strangely vague and even fragmentary and full of gaps. Although I remembered the murder more distinctly than anything else, even it became jumbled and faded beside the simple and clear impressions of the present. At times I would overcome my cowardice and reassuring doubts and clearly realize that everything had indeed happened and that nothing could alter the fact, but soon my uncertainty and sophisms would return. They helped me escape my thoughts about the past. People are so ready to believe what they want to believe . . . And although deep down I knew I was deceiving myself, I surrendered to the lie much as one might abandon oneself to pleasant dreaming. I think now that without this deceptive autosuggestion my recovery would never have been as rapid or complete.

3. The Revolution

Werner painstakingly shielded me from any impressions which he felt might not be conducive to my recovery. He did not permit me to visit him at the hospital itself, and the only patients I was allowed to observe were the incurably degenerate and the feebleminded who had permission to leave the grounds to work in the fields, the wood, and the garden. To tell the truth, I was not at all interested in them, for I very much dislike anything that I already know to be hopeless, superfluous, and doomed to failure. I wanted to see the critically ill patients who still had a chance for recovery, especially those suffering from manic depression and elation. Werner said he would show them to me as soon as my own health had been sufficiently restored, but he kept putting it off and putting it off, and nothing ever came of his promise.

Werner took even greater pains to isolate me from the political life of the country. He evidently assumed that my illness had been brought on by the distressing events of the revolution, unaware that I had been cut off from my native land during that whole period and could not even know what was happening there. He considered my total ignorance to be merely amnesia caused by my illness and even thought that it was good for me. Not only did he refuse to tell me anything on the subject himself, but he also forbade my bodyguards to speak of it, and there was not a single recent issue of a newspaper or journal in the whole apartment. He kept all such publications in his office at the hospital. Thus I was forced to live on a politically uninhabited island.

At first, when all I wanted was peace and quiet, I liked the situation. As I became stronger, however, I began to feel cramped by this little shell. I badgered my companions with questions, but they loyally obeyed the doctor's orders and refused to answer. I became irritated and bored and began looking for a way out of my political quarantine. I tried to convince Werner that I was well enough to read the newspapers, but to no avail. He told me it was still too early for that, and that he would decide when the time had come to alter my intellectual diet. Trickery was my last resort. I had to recruit one of my companions as an accomplice. It would have been very difficult to win over Werner's assistant, for he had

too solemn a view of his professional duty. I concentrated my efforts
instead on my other bodyguard, comrade Vladimir, and here I encountered little resistance.

Vladimir was a former worker. Poorly educated and still only a boy,
he was already a battle-hardened soldier from the rank and file of the
revolution. During one famous pogrom, in which many of his comrades
had been shot or perished in the flames, he stormed his way through a
crowd of thugs, killing several of them but escaping without a scratch
himself. For a long time afterward he lived underground, traveling from
town to town in the modest but dangerous function of smuggler of
weapons and forbidden literature. Finally things got too hot for him and
he was forced to seek temporary asylum with Werner. He did not tell me
about any of this until later, of course, but from the very first I noticed
that the young man was very disheartened by his deficient education and
lack of rudimentary scholarly discipline, which made even independent
study difficult. I began to tutor him. It went well, and soon I had won his
heart forever. The rest was easy; Vladimir had little understanding of
medical considerations, and we hatched a little conspiracy which neutralized Werner's stern precautions. Conversations with Vladimir, and the
newspapers, journals, and political brochures which he smuggled to me,
soon revealed to me the life my country had been living during the years I
was away.

The revolution had developed fitfully and had dragged on over a
frustratingly long period. The working class was the first to attack, and the
swift offensive resulted in significant early victories. Lacking the support
of the peasant masses at the critical moment, however, it subsequently
suffered a resounding defeat at the hands of the united reactionary forces.
While the proletariat was gathering strength for new battles and waiting
for the peasant rear guard, the landowners and bourgoisie entered into
negotiations with the government, haggling to settle their internal differences so as to be able to crush the revolution once and for all. Disguised
in the form of a parliamentary comedy, these attempts repeatedly ran
aground against the uncompromising attitude of the reactionary feudal
landlords. Puppet parliaments were convened and brutally dissolved one
after the other.

The bourgeoisie, exhausted by the storms of revolution and in-
timidated by the independence and energy of the first offensives of the
proletariat, drifted further and further to the right. The peasant masses
were in a thoroughly revolutionary frame of mind, and as they slowly
gained political experience the flames of countless burning manor houses
illuminated their path to higher forms of struggle. Besides bloodily re-
pressing the peasantry, the old regime also attempted to bribe part of it by
selling plots of land, but the whole scheme was managed so idiotically and
on such a petty scale that nothing came of it. Insurrections, led by bands

of partisans or other groups, multiplied day by day. From above and below, the country was gripped by a dual terror the likes of which had never been witnessed before anywhere in the world.

We were clearly on our way toward new and decisive battles. The road was so long and so full of twists and turns, however, that many became weary and even began to despair. The so-called radical intelligentsia, whose participation in the struggle had been limited for the most part to demonstrations of sympathy, betrayed the cause almost to a man. There was nothing to regret in that, of course, but despondency and despair had even infiltrated the ranks of my former comrades. That fact alone told me what a trying ordeal revolutionary life must have been at the time. I was fresh; I remembered the period before the revolution and the beginning of the struggle but had not experienced the full impact of the later defeats, and I could clearly see how senseless it was to bury the revolution. I could see that much had changed during these years; many new elements had joined the struggle, and it was obviously impossible to maintain a balance between reaction and terror. A new upsurge was inevitable and near at hand.

Yet we would have to wait for the time being. I understood how agonizingly difficult it was for my comrades to work in such a situation. Quite apart from what Werner thought about my health, however, I was in no hurry to join them. I thought it wiser to conserve my strength for the day when I would need all I could muster. Vladimir and I discussed the chances and prerequisites for the coming struggle. I was deeply touched by his naïvely heroic plans and dreams. He seemed to be a noble, sweet little child, destined for a warrior's death that would be as beautiful and humble as his life had been. The revolution selects her glorious martyrs and paints her proletarian banner in their rich blood. . . .

Vladimir was not the only one who impressed me as being a child. I discovered that the veteran revolutionary Werner, other comrades I remembered, and even our leaders were in many respects just as naïve and childish. In fact, all the people I had known on Earth struck me as little more than children, striplings who were only dimly aware of their own life and surroundings and who half-consciously yielded to elemental forces pressing upon them from within and without. There was not a trace of condescension or contempt in this feeling, only a deep sympathy and fraternal solicitude for these embryonic human beings, children of a youthful humanity.

4. The Envelope

It was as if the hot summer sun melted the ice that had lain like a shroud over the life of the country. The people awoke, sheets of lightning were already flashing on the horizon, and thunder could once again be heard rolling dully up from the depths. This sun and this reawakening warmed my heart and filled me with fresh strength, and I felt that soon I would be healthier than ever before. In this hazy, buoyant frame of mind I had no desire to think of the past, and it was pleasant to realize that I had been forgotten by everyone, by the whole world. I intended to reappear among my comrades at a time when no one would even think of asking me where I had been the past few years, when everyone would be much too busy for such questions, when my past would have sunk forever beneath the stormy waves of the new surging tide. If I happened to take note of facts which seemed to cast doubt upon my plans, I would become anxious and uneasy and feel a vague hostility toward everyone who might still remember me.

One summer morning Werner returned from his rounds at the hospital, but instead of going as usual to the garden to rest (his rounds tired him greatly), he came to me and began asking me in considerable detail how I felt. It seemed to me as though he were deliberately making a mental note of my answers. All of this was out of the ordinary, and at first I thought that somehow he must have stumbled onto my little conspiracy. It soon became obvious, however, that he suspected nothing. Then he went away again, not to the garden but to his office, and it was not until a half hour later that I saw him through the window walking along his favorite shaded path. I could not help thinking about these trifles, for nothing else of any great importance was going on around me. After considering several possibilities, I settled for what seemed to be the most likely hypothesis, namely that Werner had received a special inquiry on the state of my health and was therefore preparing a detailed report. The mail was delivered every morning to his office at the hospital, so the letter asking about me must have come there.

Who had written the letter and why? If I was to have any peace of mind I simply had to find out immediately. It was no use asking Werner. For some reaon he evidently felt he could not tell me, for otherwise he would have done so straightaway. Did Vladimir know anything? No, it turned out that he did not. I began thinking of a way to get to the bottom of the matter. Vladimir was prepared to help me in any way he could. He considered my curiosity legitimate and Werner's secretiveness uncalled for. He did not hesitate a moment to subject Werner's office and apartment to a thorough search, but he found nothing of interest.

"We must assume," said Vladimir, "that he either has the letter on him or has ripped it up and thrown it away."

"Well then, where does he usually throw his wastepaper?" I asked.

"In the basket under his desk in the office," replied Vladimir.

"Fine. In that case bring me all the scraps you can find in the basket."

Vladimir left and returned in a short while.

"There weren't any scraps there," he said, "but I did find this: an envelope that he must have received today, judging by the stamp."

I took the envelope and glanced at the address. The ground trembled beneath my feet and the walls came crashing down around me . . . Netti's handwriting!

handwritten marginal note: communism / from man / FANTASY / BECOMES / REALITY / AGAIN

5. Summing Up

Amid the chaos of thoughts and recollections that surged up within me when I found out that Netti was on Earth and did not want to meet me, the only point that was clear to me at first was my plan and its final outcome. It was not the product of any conscious logical reasoning on my part, but arose by itself and was beyond question. Simply implementing the plan as soon as possible, however, was not enough. I felt I had to justify it both to myself and to others. I was especially unable to accept the thought that even Netti might misunderstand me and think that my action was merely an emotional outburst rather than a logical necessity, an inevitable consequence of all that had happened to me.

The first thing I had to do, therefore, was to tell my story in logical sequence—tell it to my comrades, to myself, to Netti. That is the reason for the present manuscript. Werner, who will be the first to read it the day after Vladimir and I have disappeared, will see to its publication. Naturally, he will make such alterations as may be dictated by considerations of political secrecy. This is my only testament to him. I regret very much that I will not have the opportunity to bid him farewell.

In the process of setting these memories to paper, the past gradually became clear to me. Chaos yielded to order, and I began to understand my role and position in events. Being of sound mind and lucid memory, I can now undertake a final summary.

It is patently evident that the task entrusted to me was more than I could handle. Why did I fail, and how could a penetrating judge of human nature like Menni make such an unfortunate choice?

I remember a conversation with Menni during that happy time when Netti's love inspired me with a boundless faith in myself.

"How is it, Menni," I asked him, "that out of all the many different people of our country you met on your search, you chose me as the best qualified to represent Earth?"

"The choice was not really so very great," he replied. "From the very beginning we were obliged to limit ourselves to the supporters of scientific and revolutionary socialism. All other outlooks are much too distant from our own."

"All right, but among the representatives of this current you have also met people who are doubtless stronger and more gifted than I. You knew the leader we jokingly call the Old Man of the Mountain, you knew our comrade the Poet . . ."

"Yes, and I have observed them closely. But the Old Man of the Mountain is exclusively a man of struggle and revolution. Our order would not suit him at all. He is a man of iron, and men of iron are not flexible. They also have a strong measure of inborn conservatism. As for the Poet, he could not take it physically. He has gone through too much on his ramblings through all the social strata of your world and would have difficulty surviving yet another transition to ours. In addition, both of them—the political leader and the artist who speaks for millions—are too indispensable to the struggle going on among you."

"Your last argument seems very persuasive. But in that case let me remind you of Mirsky, the philosopher.* In his profession he is accustomed to advancing, comparing, and reconciling the most disparate points of view. I should think that this experience would be of great assistance to him in coping with the difficulties of the assignment."

"True, but we must not forget that he is above all a man of abstract thought. He hardly has the spiritual vigor necessary to bring his emotions and will to bear on his experience of the new life. He even impressed me as being somewhat weary, and you can understand that that is a very serious handicap."

"Perhaps you are right. But what of the proletarians who constitute the base and main strength of our movement? Surely you could find what you are looking for among them."

"Yes, that would be the best place to look. However, workers usually lack what I feel to be a very important prerequisite, namely a broad, well-rounded education based on the best your culture has achieved. This deflected my search in another direction."

This was how Menni reasoned, but he had miscalculated. Did that mean that there was no one suited to the purpose, that the difference between our civilizations was an unbridgeable gap for any individual and could only be overcome by society as a whole? It would be comforting for me personally to think so, but I seriously doubt it. I think that Menni should have reconsidered his last argument, the one concerning the workers.

Where, exactly, did I fail?

The way it happened the first time was that I was inundated by a wave of new impressions in the alien world on Mars—its grandiose rich-

---

*It seems reasonably clear from the context that the Old Man of the Mountain is meant to designate Lenin; the Poet—Gorky; and Mirsky—Plekhanov. Because of the slightly unflattering, if not wholly inaccurate, characterization of Lenin, the Soviet editors of the latest edition of *Red Star* chose to delete these passages (but without saying so). "Krasnaya zvezda," in *Vechnoe solntse: russkaya sotsialnaya utopiya i nauchnaya fantastika (vtoraya polovina XIX-nachalo XX veka)*, Moscow, 1979, pp. 248–379 (see p. 373).

ness flooded and washed away the shores of my consciousness. With Netti's help I survived and learned to cope with the crisis. But I wonder whether the crisis itself was not aggravated and intensified by the hypersensitivity and delicacy of perception that are characteristic of persons exclusively devoted to intellectual labor. Perhaps someone whose personality was somewhat more primitive, somewhat less complex, but organically more stable and firm would have had an easier time of it and would have made the transition less painfully. Perhaps it would be easier for an uneducated worker to become integrated into a new and higher order, for although he would have to learn much more at first, he would not be forced to relearn as much, and that, after all, is the most difficult problem. This is what I am inclined to believe, and I think that Menni was mistaken in concentrating on the level of culture rather than on the force behind its development.

What sapped my spiritual energy on the second occasion was the very nature of the civilization into which I attempted to integrate my entire being. I was overwhelmed by its loftiness, by the profundity of its social ties and the purity of its interpersonal relationships. Sterni's speech, which crudely expressed the thorough incompatibility of our two types of life, was merely the immediate cause, the last nudge that sent me plummeting into the dark abyss toward which I was in any case being involuntarily and irresistibly drawn by the contradiction between my inner life and my social environment at the factory, in my family, among my friends. Once again, I cannot help wondering whether this contradiction was not stronger and more acute in the case of a man like me, a revolutionary intellectual who nine-tenths of the time had worked either alone or in a one-sided, unequal relationship to his comrades and fellow workers, to whom he had been a teacher and leader. In other words, perhaps it was my *isolation* from the collective that was to blame. Perhaps this contradiction would have proved less acute for a man who had instead spent nine-tenths of his working life in an environment that may have been primitive and uncultivated but was nonetheless pervaded by a spirit of comradeship. An environment in which equality was real if somewhat coarse. I believe that this is the case, and I think that Menni should renew this search in a different quarter.

Then there is what occurred between the two catastrophes, what gave me strength and courage to continue my long struggle, what even now allows me to make this summing up with no sense of humiliation: Netti's love. It was undoubtedly a misunderstanding, a mistake of her noble and fervent imagination. But such a mistake was *possible*. No one can take that away from me and nothing can change it. This to me proves that our two worlds really are close and that one day they will be able to unite into a single, unprecedentedly beautiful and harmonious order.

As for myself . . . but here there is nothing to sum up. The new life is

Epilogue

From Dr. Werner's Letter to Mirsky

(Undated, evidently due to Werner's absentmindedness.)

. . . .

The cannonade had stopped some time ago, but a steady stream of wounded kept on coming. The overwhelming majority were not revolutionary militia or soldiers, but peaceful civilians. Many were women and even children: shrapnel treats all as equals. However, most of the casualties brought to my hospital, which was the one nearest the fighting, were militia and soldiers. I am an old doctor and at one time spent several years working as a surgeon, but even I was appalled by many of the shrapnel and shell-splinter wounds. Towering above all this horror, however, was one radiant feeling, one joyous word: Victory!

This is our first victory in the great battle now in progress, but it is clear to all that it is a decisive one. The scales have tipped to the other side. Entire regiments with their artillery have come over to us—a sure sign of what is to come. The Last Judgment is here. The verdict will not be a mild one, but it will be just. It is high time we had done with it.

The street is littered with debris and spattered with blood. The sun shines a bright red through the smoke from the fires and the artillery. To us, however, it is not an ominous portent, but a source of joyous awe. Our hearts reverberate with a song of battle, a song of triumph. . . .

. . . .

Leonid was brought to my hospital around noon. He had a serious chest wound and several minor ones that were little more than scratches. In the middle of the night he and five grenadiers had set off for the section of the city controlled by the enemy. Their mission was to unnerve and demoralize the enemy with a series of violent attacks. Leonid had proposed the plan himself and volunteered to carry it out. Since he had worked a great deal here some time back, he knew every inch of the city and was better qualified than others for the desperate operation. After some hesitation the chief of the revolutionary militia agreed to the plan.

137

Armed with grenades, the commando succeeded in reaching one of the enemy batteries and blew up several boxes of ammunition from a position on a nearby rooftop. In the ensuing panic they climbed down, destroyed the howitzers, and exploded the remaining shells.

Leonid received several slight splinter-wounds. Then, as they were hurriedly retreating, they ran into a detachment of enemy dragoons. Leonid entrusted the command to his adjutant, Vladimir, took his last two grenades, and crept into the nearest doorway to wait in ambush while the others retreated, using all available cover as they vigorously returned the fire of the enemy. He waited until most of the detachment had passed by him and threw his first grenade at an officer and a second into the nearest group of dragoons. The entire detachment fled in wild disorder, and our troops returned to get Leonid, who had been seriously wounded by a splinter from his second grenade. They managed to bring him back to our lines before dawn and then brought him to my hospital and entrusted him to my care.

I quickly removed the fragment, but one of his lungs had been hit and his condition was critical. I made him as comfortable as I could, but I was unable to give him the peace and quiet he needed most of all. The battle had resumed at dawn. We could hear it clearly, and Leonid's feverish condition was aggravated by his uneasy concern for its progress. He became even more upset when the wounded began to arrive, and I was forced to isolate him as best I could, moving him behind a screen so that he would at least not see them.

. . . .

By about 4 p.m. the battle was already over, and its outcome was obvious. I was busy examining and assigning beds to the wounded when I was handed the card of a woman who had written to me several weeks previously asking about Leonid's health. She had visited me after his disappearance, and I had recommended that she go to see you in order to acquaint herself with his manuscript. Since she was obviously a comrade and evidently a physician as well, I invited her to come straight to the ward. As on the previous occasion I had seen her, she wore a dark veil that effectively concealed her face.

"Is Leonid here?" she asked without even greeting me.

"Yes," I replied, "but there is no particular cause for alarm. He is seriously wounded, but I think he will pull through."

She questioned me rapidly and intelligently about his condition and announced that she wanted to see him.

"Don't you think that your visit might upset him?" I objected.

"Undoubtedly," came her answer, "but it will do him more good than harm, I can assure you."

She seemed very confident and determined. I felt that she knew what she was talking about and I could not deny her request. We went to

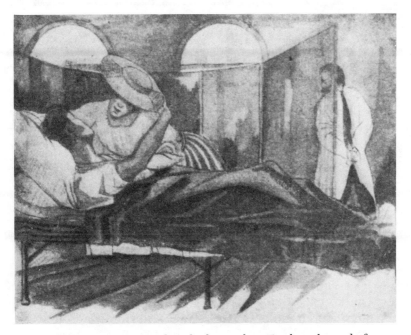

Netti returns to Leonid in the hospital on Earth at the end of
Red Star

Leonid's ward, and I gestured to her to go behind the screen. I remained
nearby at the bed of another seriously wounded patient I had to attend to
in any case. I wanted to hear their conversation so that I could interfere if
necessary.

As she went behind the screen she lifted her veil a little. Her
silhouette showed through the semitransparent partition, and I could see
her bending over him.

"A mask . . ." said Leonid faintly.

"Your Netti!" she answered, and her soft, melodious voice uttered
these two words with such tenderness and affection that this old heart of
mine quivered in an almost painful convulsion of joyous sympathy.

"It looks as though I'm dying," he said softly, almost as a question.

"No, Lenni, you have your life ahead of you. Your wound is not fatal,
not even dangerous."

"And the murder?" he objected with deep anxiety.

"You were ill, my dearest. Don't worry, that attack of pain will never come between us or keep us from our great common goal. We will reach it, dear Lenni!"

He gave a quiet moan, but it was not a moan of pain. I went away, because I had found out what I wanted to know about my patient, and there was no reason or excuse for eavesdropping any longer. A few minutes later the stranger, again in her hat and veil, summoned me once more.

"I shall take Leonid with me," she announced. "He wants to go, and his chances for recovery are better with me than here, so you need not worry on that score. Two comrades are waiting downstairs to take him away. Please call for a stretcher."

There was no use arguing; the conditions at our hospital were indeed less than splendid. I asked for her address—it was quite nearby—and decided I would visit Leonid there the following day. Two workers came and carefully carried him away on the stretcher. . . .

. . . .

(Note added the next day.)

I have just come from Netti's apartment. She and Leonid have both disappeared without a trace. The doors were unlocked and the rooms empty. On the table in a large room with a huge wide-open window I found a note addressed to me. There were just a few words written in a shaky hand:

Remember me to my comrades. Goodbye.
Yours, Leonid.

Strangely enough, I was not at all upset. I had become terribly exhausted the last few days, I had seen a lot of suffering that I could do nothing to alleviate, I had had my fill of death and destruction, but my heart was still light and happy.

The worst is behind us now. The struggle has been a long ordeal, but victory is within our grasp. The next struggle will be easier . . .

ENGINEER MENNI

Contents

Translator's Foreword

After the events which I described in the book *Red Star,* I am once again living among my Martian friends and working for the cherished cause of bringing our two worlds closer together. The Martians have decided for the immediate future to refrain from all direct or active interference in the affairs of Earth. For the time being they will restrict themselves to studying our humanity and gradually acquainting us with the more ancient civilization of Mars. I wholly agree with them that caution is of the essence, for if their discoveries on the structure of matter were at the present time to become known on Earth, the militaristic rulers of our mutually hostile nations would gain control over weapons of unprecedented might, and the entire planet would be devastated in a matter of months.

The Martians have established a special unit for the dissemination of the New Culture on Earth, affiliated with the Colonial Group. I have taken a position there as translator, that being the work for which I am best qualified; we hope in the near future to enlist other Earthlings of various nationalities for the same purpose. This is not at all as simple as it may appear at first glance. Translation from the single Martian language into those of Earth is much more difficult than translation from one Earthly language to another, and it is often even impossible to give a full and exact rendering of the content of the original.

Imagine trying to translate a modern scientific work, a psychological novel, or a political article into the language of Homer or into Old Church Slavonic. I am aware that such a comparison does not flatter us Earthlings, but it is unfortunately no exaggeration—the difference between our respective civilizations is just about that great. The life, the social bonds, and the entire experience of the Martians differ radically from our own. Many notions which are well developed and quite ordinary there are entirely lacking among us. Ideas which on Mars are so universally accepted that they are merely implied rather than stated explicitly are received on Earth as something incomprehensible, improbable, or even monstrous. We respond to them as devout Catholics of the Middle Ages reacted to atheism or as an old-fashioned petty bourgeois might have reacted to free love. The language of thoughts can differ much more than the language of words from its translation—even when the words seem to be exactly the same the thought they convey is sometimes totally different. In fact, the greatest difficulty an idea encounters on its way to acceptance is most often that of translation into ordinary language. When Copernicus, Giordano Bruno, and Galileo said that the Earth turns on its axis, their very words were incomprehensible to most of their contemporaries: "turn" signified above all certain palpable sensations associated with the circular movement of a human being or objects in his surroundings. In this case, however, it was precisely such sensations which were absent. The same story has recurred many times and continues to be repeated even today.

Now I am sure you will understand the problems involved in translating from the language of a civilization which is not only different from but also higher and more complex than our own. It goes without saying that one should begin with what is easiest, and this explains our unit's first choice of subject matter. We selected a historical novel by my friend Enno which depicts the epoch that roughly corresponds to the present stage of Earthly civilization, namely the final phase of capitalism. The relations and types described there are similar to our own and are thus fairly comprehensible to the Earthly reader. Enno has herself visited Earth and knows several of our languages, so she has to some exent been able to assist me in my task. Only to an extent, however—if we are at all to speak of responsibility for the form in which the work as a whole is presented, then it is I who must accept all such responsibility.

Martian weights, measures, and time, of course, have been translated throughout into the Earthly system. Where possible, I have replaced the names of countries, seas, and canals with those in general use on the maps of our astronomers, that is, with Schiaparelli's Greek and Latin designations. However, the novel often refers to details—cities, mountain ranges, small gulfs, and the like—which cannot be observed at all in our telescopes. In such cases I have either simply translated the Martian name or tried to render its content through a suitable Greek form on the model of Schiaparelli's terminology.

The astronomical age of Mars is twice that of Earth, and for that reason there is relatively little water on the planet. In the course of millions of years the water of its oceans has been absorbed into the depths of its crust. The seas on Mars constitute at present only half of its surface area, and they are also much smaller than those on Earth. Dry land in the form of a single unbroken continent occupies three quarters of the northern hemisphere and about a fourth of the southern, and contains several small inland seas. The remaining area is covered by the Mare Australe

(Southern Ocean), which is thickly sprinkled with islands, some of them fairly large. The continent is transversed in all directions by the famous canals.

This is what the planet looks like today, but it appeared somewhat different three hundred years ago. Even if Galileo and Kepler had had modern telescopes, they would not have seen most of the present-day canals or even certain of the inland seas and lakes. In fact, there were no "great canals" at all then, but only a few broad ocean inlets which Earthly astronomers have erroneously taken for canals. The Great Project was started by an engineer named Menni as recently as two hundred and fifty years ago. This wonder of labor and human will was dictated by historical necessity.

The history of Mars is basically very similar to that of Earthly humanity, having followed the same course from the tribal system through feudalism to the reign of capital and through it to the unification of labor. This development, however, proceeded more gently and at a slower pace. The natural environment on Mars is not as rich as ours; on the other hand, the evolution of life there has not demanded the same extravagant sacrifices as on Earth. Every page of our history is so soaked in blood and fire that for a long time the chroniclers and historians were unable to find anything else in it. Naturally, violence, destruction, and killing also played a role on Mars, but these phenomena never became as monstrously grandiose as among us. Martian humanity developed slower than ours, but it never knew the worst forms of our slavery, the destruction of entire civilizations, or the epochs of deep and cruel reaction that we have experienced. Even the countless wars waged during the feudal era, which lasted several thousand years, were relatively free from the senseless and bestial thirst for blood that distinguished our feudal wars. Savage battles there were seldom followed by mass murder or the devastating plunder of the civilian population. The barbarity of the age did not totally eclipse a certain respect for life and labor.

Why was this so? The natural environment of the planet was poor and harsh, and the experience of thousands of generations built up the dim awareness that it is extremely difficult to restore what has once been destroyed. There was also less discord among people: different tribes and nationalities were more closely related and intercourse among them was easier. The land mass was not broken into separate continents by broad seas and oceans, the mountain ranges were not as high or impassable as on Earth. Also, the weaker force of gravity on Mars facilitated physical movement—all bodies on Earth are two and a half times heavier. The various languages arose from a common source and never became completely distinct; and, when commercial relations quickened and distant expeditions became more common during the feudal epoch, these lan-

guages once again began to converge. By the end of this period they were
more like regional dialects than separate languages. Thus people understood each other better and their unity was more profound.

In about A.D. 1000 according to our calendar, feudalism had already
died out in most countries on Mars. During the preceding five to ten
centuries a money economy had become established, and commercial
capital increasingly asserted itself as the rival of the old landowning class
for control of society. A cultural revolution was under way everywhere,
although it was still religious in form and manifested itself as a reformation
of the ancient feudal faiths. The strong kings and princes, the "gatherers
of the land," took advantage of the situation to undermine the power of
their most dangerous rival, the priesthood, and establish the monarchical
order. Already by about 1100 the thousands of earlier petty principalities
had been replaced by approximately twenty bureaucratic monarchies,
and most of the proud feudal princes entered the civil service or became
attached to the royal courts.

During the same period, however, manufacturing spread and capitalism continued to expand. It soon began to feel cramped under the tutel-
age of the police state and embarked upon its struggle for liberation.
From about 1200 to 1600 its invisible hand directed a number of political
evolutions in various countries.

The end of the fourteenth century witnessed the beginning of the
industrial revolution, which was brought about by the introduction of
machines, and the course of development was accelerated. By 1560 a
democratic order had been established in all but a few backward countries, but something even greater had been accomplished at the same
time, namely, the almost complete cultural and political unification of
Mars. A common literary language evolved which absorbed most of the
earlier regional dialects; and partly through war, partly by means of
negotiations, a giant Federal Republic was established which encom-
passed approximately three quarters of the planet. All that remained to
complete the process was to conquer a handful of semifeudal states, and
this the federal government succeeded in systematically doing during the
subsequent fifty years.

In about 1620 the last independent state was subdued. This was the
country designated on our maps as Thaumasia Felix (Happy Land of
Wonders), which was ruled by the ancient ducal house of Aldo.
Thaumasia is the large southern peninsula of the continent, from which,
however, it is separated today by a system of canals and lakes. At that time
a coastal strip on the Mare Australe was the only inhabited part of the
country. The whole interior, where the huge Solis Lacus (Lake of the Sun)
is now located, was an arid desert. The population—a few hundred
thousand peasants and fishermen—were known for their stern and simple

character, conservatism, and piety. The economy was still for the most part a natural one, and the relations between peasants and feudal lords were thoroughly patriarchal. Thaumasia was a real Vendée,* and in fact that was the role it played in Martian history.

Old Duke Aldo did not survive the defeat, but he left a son and heir named Ormen. When war was declared on Thaumasia, Ormen was conducting negotiations in Centropolis, the main city of the Republic. He was detained there during the entire course of the war. The Republic did not confiscate the estates of the ducal house, and although Ormen had no political power, he retained a considerable portion of the territory of Thaumasia as a landowner. Outwardly he seemed thoroughly resigned to his new position. He spent a few months each year in Centropolis, where he lived the life of a young millionaire and pretended to be completely uninterested in politics. In reality he kept a watchful eye on the balance of social forces and cultivated contacts with dissatisfied elements such as the remnants of the clergy and the aristocracy and various separatists who dreamed of restoring the autonomy of their native regions. The rest of the time he was in Thaumasia, traveling up and down the country on the pretext of hunting or attending to financial business with his tenants.

The soil of discontent was fertile and ready to receive the seeds of his agitation. Working for him were not only the power of the sacred past and the influence of the priests on the ignorant masses; an even more important factor was the painful economic development of the country, which had been invaded by commercial and usurious capital. The taxes set by the central government were not in themselves heavy, but they had to be paid in cash, and money had become a rarity in Thaumasia. Since olden days the peasants had been accustomed to living directly off the products of their labor, supplementing what they could not get themselves through local bartering, for which money was unnecessary. Their obligations to the landowners were also discharged in kind; even ninety percent of the taxes that went to the old ducal government were paid in goods and services.

But now on a set date each year it became necessary to pay the tax collectors sums of money which seemed enormous to the peasants. The only way to get money was to sell something, anything, and thus the vast majority of the population came under the sway of buyers and foreign tradesmen who took ruthless advantage of the situation. They bought for practically nothing, lent money at exorbitant rates of interest, and foisted upon the peasants goods which they often did not need. By means of extortionary contracts they appropriated standing crops and future catches of fish and further increased their profits through systematic

---

*A royalist and Catholic holdout during the French Revolution.

fraud, against which the ignorant population was utterly defenseless. Commerce introduced new needs and temptations into the life of the peasants, but money was again necessary to satisfy them, and this only served to intensify the plunder. Economic ruin spread rapidly, and discontent grew accordingly among the Thaumasians.

After twenty years of discreet work, Ormen Aldo and his friends decided that the time was ripe for action. Tens of thousands of energetic people were prepared to rise the moment the signal was given, and huge caches of weapons had gradually been stockpiled in the cellars of castles scattered throughout the country. All that remained was to await a suitable opportunity. In the meanwhile Ormen arranged for the continuation of his dynasty, marrying a daughter of a rich landowner who was a devoted member of the conspiracy. The union had nothing whatever to do with love; twenty years of politics and diplomacy had transformed Ormen into a gloomy and unpleasant figure. A few months later the woman became pregnant, and Ormen sent her to one of his most distant castles to protect her in the event of an uprising. A short while later Ormen received glad tidings: an heir had been born, and the entire Republic had been plunged into a serious industrial crisis. He could not have wished for a more propitious moment, and he immediately raised the ancient banner of the dukes of Aldo.

The ensuing struggle was stubborn but unequal. Ormen displayed great talent as a military leader and gained several brilliant victories. Soon, however, the Republic mobilized a huge army, and the other uprisings Ormen had counted on failed to materialize. The ironic logic of life was such that it was the war that enabled the Republic to recover from its economic crisis, for the enormous purchases and orders the government was forced to make immediately improved the position of several branches of industry. This helped still other branches, and so on. It was all over in the course of a year: Duke Ormen was killed in combat and Thaumasia was subdued once and for all. The idea of feudalism would never be revived again.

The government ordered Aldo's widow and child to be moved to Centropolis, probably to facilitate surveillance. The capital is located several thousand kilometers from Thaumasia on the shore of an inland sea called Nillacus Lacus (Lake Nile) in the interior of the continent, and is situated at the mouth of the very broad and very long Straits of Inda, which connect the lake with the Margaritifer Sinus (Bay of Pearls) in the Mare Australe. The young woman soon died of homesickness for her distant land. The boy grew up among strangers and received a republican education. He bore his father's name, Ormen, but he subsequently signed himself "Menni." This is the democratic form of the name, much as we in Russia call monarchs "Ioann" but give the name "Ivan" to ordinary people.

Menni proved to be a first-rate scholar, physicist, and engineer. He was well enough off financially, for although the entire fortune of his father had been confiscated, he received a considerable inheritance from his mother. At the age of twenty he was therefore able to undertake a series of long and daring journeys that in the next five years took him through the vast wastelands of the continent. At that time less than half the area of the planet was inhabited. There was as yet no system of canals, and the whole interior of the continent, about three-fifths of its surface, was devoid of water. It was probably during these trips that he first conceived the idea of the Great Project.

Menni's first period of activity as an engineer was in Libya. This country, which is located near the equator on the vast Syrtis Major (Gulf of Sands), has an undeservedly bad reputation among our astronomers. Schiaparelli concluded that the large western peninsula of Libya was covered by water for several years. In actual fact this was a mistaken observation. Off the shore of Libya there is a huge, long sandbank, on which the Martians for many years cultivated giant plantations of a certain seaweed whose fibers were used in the manufacture of textiles. Like all other vegetation on the planet, it is red, and this created the illusion that the area was dry land. New technology rendered the plant superfluous in the clothing industry, and thus the illusion disappeared along with it. The Nepenthes Canal now empties into a small gulf to the north of this sandbank; running eastward, a few dozen kilometers from the sea it has given rise to Moeris Lacus (Lake Moeris), which is twice the size of Lake Ladoga in Russia. It continues in a bend somewhat toward the north, and through Lake Triton it merges with an entire network of other canals. Menni dug the first segment of the Nepenthes Canal from the sea to Lake Moeris. Part of the desert was a depression whose bottom was considerably below sea level, and thus the lake was created when the canal was opened.

Due to similar conditions, the Nectar and Ambrosia canals, which Menni constructed through Thaumasia, formed the Solis Lacus, which is about half as large as the Caspian Sea. Only a small part of the present network of canals was completed in Menni's lifetime, but almost all of it was envisaged in the projects drawn up by him and his successor, an engineer by the name of Netti.

These two men are the chief protagonists of the novel.

Leonid N.

Prologue

1. Menni

An official conference to discuss the canal through western Libya was convened by the Ministry of Public Works in the winter of 1667 according to our calendar. The hundreds of delegates in attendance included representatives of the largest banking cartels, the relevant industrial trusts and most powerful private enterprises, a great many renowned scientists and prominent engineers, members of Parliament, and government officials. The minister opened the session with a short speech explaining its purpose.

"I assume," he said, "that all of you are already familiar in a general way with the project proposed by the engineer Menni Aldo in his remarkable book *The Future of the Libyan Desert*. This project has aroused the interest of society and Parliament, as is evident from your presence here today. On the suggestion of the Central Government, the author himself will present a report describing the technical and financial aspects of the matter in more detail. The government appeals to your great expertise and attaches considerable importance to your opinions and advice. We would hope that the conference as a whole could arrive at a definite conclusion in principle for or against the project. It envisages the peaceful conquest of a new country for the good of mankind, but it will also involve expenses totaling one to two billion."

He gave the floor to the speaker. With the help of figures and drawings projected by a lantern onto a screen, Menni gave a concise and accurate description of the geographical relief of the region.

"My assistants and I," he said, "have taken new measurements of the Libyan depression from south to north and from east to west, for the data provided by earlier explorers were too approximate and incomplete. This area of a little more than 600,000 square kilometers is surrounded on all sides by mountains which are high enough to shut out rain clouds. To the south and west this range lies fairly close to the sea, while there are other deserts to the north and east of it. At one time the entire depression was the floor of a sea, but since then the level of the ocean has dropped considerably, so that the sea was cut off from it and dried up. However, as you can see from these cross-section drawings, the central part of the depression today is still from 50 to 200 meters below sea level, in some places as much as 300 meters. This central area of some 50,000 square kilometers would be flooded immediately if it were to be connected with the Mare Australe, and this would in turn radically alter the climate of the country.

"At present this is nothing but an arid desert whose surface stratum of sand has been ground into a fine dust that is injurious to the lungs and eyes. There are no oases there which could serve as resting places for travelers. Of the eight expeditions that have penetrated the desert during the past hundred years, two did not return at all and the others suffered casualties. Our expedition was better equipped than the previous ones, but then we stayed much longer. Only half of us returned, and except for myself we were all seriously ill. Especially troublesome are the nervous disorders which result from the monotony of the environment and the total absence of sound. The desert there is a veritable Kingdom of Silence.

"All this will change if we succeed in creating an inland sea in Libya. The moisture evaporating from the surface of the water under the tropical sun will be retained by the mountains surrounding the depression and will return down their slopes as streams and rivers that will provide sufficient if not abundant irrigation. According to our analyses, the soil of the desert is rich in the salts necessary to vegetation, and the water will immediately render it fertile. If agriculture is organized on a scientifically correct basis, the country will be able to feed 20 million persons of our entire present population of 300 million.

"Such colonization, of course, will require decades. But immediately after the inland sea is created we will gain easy access to the northern and eastern mountains of Libya, where the enormous mineral riches of the country are concentrated. Earlier expeditions discovered entire mountains of the best magnetic iron ore and broad veins of coal at the surface in fissures and geological faults. We have brought back with us samples of silver and lead ore, which the experts have assessed as among the richest on Mars, and we have also found mercury and even uranium. In one region we discovered deposits of native platinum, a precious monetary metal. Without the shadow of a doubt, however, we saw only an insignificant fraction of the whole, for we lacked the time and resources to make a more thorough investigation."

Menni then turned to the question of the canal itself. Choosing its route presented no difficulties, as the only suitable point was where the depression lay closest to the sea and the mountain range narrowed to a width of a few kilometers.

"Here," said Menni, "the entire length of the canal will not exceed 70 kilometers. We already have navigable canals for shipping which are two or three times as long. In this case, however, the object is to fill and maintain an inland sea. An ordinary canal would simply disappear in the sands of the desert. Our calculations indicate that it must be five times wider and three times deeper than any of these. Part of it—about a third—will have to lie on the bedrock, and, even more importantly, we will have to cut a pass through the mountains. An enormous body of limestone will have to be blasted away, and we will also be forced to remove the substratum of granite which constitutes the root of the mountain range. This will require about 500,000 tons of dynamite. According to our preliminary estimates, we will need a labor force of some 200,000 men for a period of four years, assuming that we use the best and most expensive machinery."

Menni went on to describe the financial side of the project. A liberal estimate of total outlays set them at around 1,500 million. Obviously, only the state had the kind of resources necessary for such an undertaking. The government would issue a special loan over a period of four years which would cover the expenses of the project and the annual interest on the loan itself. Later, as the new country was opened up to exploitation, the interest and the principal would gradually be repaid through the sale or leasing of land for the purposes of mining or agriculture. Thus the state would acquire a piece of real estate worth tens of billions. All major financial institutions would support the loan, as it would provide them with a whole new field of operations, and numerous branches of industry would profit by the enormous orders entailed by the project.

"In addition," said Menni, "I can mention one more important reason why all financiers and entrepreneurs should be interested in supporting the project. You are aware that at regular intervals during the past 150 years we have been beset by serious financial and industrial crises. At such times credit falls, the market shrinks, thousands of enterprises are ruined, and millions become unemployed. The renowned Xarma, who despite his socialist views is the most learned and profound economist of our time, has declared that a new and unprecedentedly deep crisis will occur in a year or two unless the market expands. He adds that there are no grounds for expecting the latter. You will recall that Xarma accurately predicted the last recession, and there is every reason to believe him this time as well. The construction of the Libyan canal, however, would stimulate the expansion of the market that we need, first by way of the project itself and later by bringing an entire new country into production. This, I think, would considerably delay the crisis and its attendant calamities."

Menni concluded his report by pointing out that the grandiose dimensions and enormous complexity of the proposed project demanded the greatest possible measure of unity in its execution.

After a short intermission the chairman opened the discussion. The first to address a question to the speaker was Feli Rao, president of Railroad Credit, the largest Martian banking cartel. His hair was gray, but he looked much younger than his years, and his gaze was cold and piercing.

"In your report you made no mention of the administrative and organizational end of the matter. I assume, however, that your concluding remark on the need for unity referred to this. If I have understood you correctly, you are of the opinion that the supervision of the project should be entrusted to a single person who will select his own assistants and assume full control and responsibility for all details."

"That is correct," replied Menni.

"Don't you think, however, that the interests involved here are too numerous and complicated to be handled by a single individual? Would it not be better to establish some form of collective leadership, if not in the technical sphere, then at least in the administrative one? And should we not grant a certain right of inspection to, say, the organizations offering financial cooperation?"

"I do not think that that would be the best solution. The project must be conducted according to a plan that has been predetermined and approved by the government. A collective principle may be useful for the development and discussion of the plan, but not for its execution. Inspection should be exercised by the government, Parliament, and public opinion, and continuous and candid reports should be provided for the purpose. In this form it will be sufficient. Allow me to remark that I do not envisage inspection by the government as the power to interfere at will in the details of the project. Interference is appropriate only when the approved plan must be revised or when previous estimates are disrupted."

"I think that we can speak frankly," said Feli Rao. "It is obvious to all that both justice and expediency demand that you be placed at the head of the project. Is what you have just said a statement of the conditions on which you would agree to accept such a position?"

"Yes. I could take no part in the project on any other conditions. I want all responsibility or none whatever."

Uncertainty, vacillation, almost discontent could be sensed in the mood of the delegates. Rao continued:

"But it seems to me that the organization of the project involves a number of very complicated problems demanding a great deal of attention. At the same time these are questions that can hardly hold any immediate interest for you as a man of science. For example, you will have to calculate the number of workers required on the basis of your technical plan, but as to the conditions of their employment . . ."

"On the contrary, I consider that question to be very important precisely from the point of view of the success of the project. I am aware of the fact that many enterprises attempt to economize at the expense of the workers. A worker who is poorly fed or overworked is not in possession of his full labor capacity. A dissatisfied worker can behave unexpectedly and disrupt production. I need a full labor force and I do not need surprises."

Feli Rao declared that he had no further questions for the time being. For a moment there was an oppressive hush. The next speaker was an engineer and representative of the Dynamite and Powder Trust by the name of Maro, a man who was very well known in his branch despite his relative youth.

"I should like to turn to a consideration of technical and financial questions," he said. "Although the administrative issue is important, I feel that these aspects are even more so. Speaking for myself, I should like to say that I am confident in Menni Aldo's personal integrity and support his views on the matter of public control. In my opinion the attitude of the government is of crucial significance here. In the final analysis, it is the state that bears responsibility for organizing inspection; by issuing a loan to raise the capital for the project it will thereby also provide a guarantee for all private financial interests and will stand between the creditors and the administration of the project. If it can agree to the conditions set by Engineer Aldo, then I do not think we need especially insist upon further discussion of them. I should therefore like to address that question to the representatives of the Central Government and the Libyan authorities present here today."

The Minister of Public Works replied:

"We had intended to present the viewpoint of the government toward the end of the discussion, as is usually done at such conferences. However, in order to avoid misunderstandings we are obliged to answer a direct question. Let me first of all remind you that the final decision belongs to the Central Parliament. After a preliminary review of the matter the Council of Ministers did not for its part find anything unacceptable in the demands of Engineer Aldo, the initiator and author of the project."

The governor of Libya declared that the government of his state fully agreed with the central authorities.

The atmosphere of the conference changed immediately. Maro's maneuver had trumped the high card of the opposition. The discussion turned to technical questions and the conditions of the loans. Menni had won an indisputable victory.

It was time for dinner, and the conference adjourned. The delegates were invited to dine with the minister. On the way to the banquet hall Feli Rao approached Maro.

"I understand your position," he said with an air of good-natured candor. "You are an executive of the Dynamite and Powder Trust, and

orders for a half million tons of explosives are not very common. But tell
me honestly, where have you found any assurances of Menni's administrative talents? His technical plan is evidently irreproachable, and I can say
that the financial one is very good. But the supervision of this colossal
project and hundreds of thousands of workers . . . Where and when has
he ever demonstrated such organizational ability? And he is only twenty-
six. Don't you think that you and the government are taking a leap into
the unknown?"

An enigmatic smile flitted across Maro's face.

"Administrative talents? How can you doubt them? Isn't he the son of
Duke Ormen Aldo?"

Rao gazed intently at Maro, whose eyes had once again become
impenetrable.

"I think that you and I will come to an understanding in due course,"
said the financier.

At dinner he sat next to the minister. When the hum of conversation
had become animated and loud, Rao turned to his neighbor and said in a
low voice:

"Just now, of course, it is easier for the government to hand everything over to Menni. But is it wise to contribute to the rise of such a
talented and ambitious man? Might he not pose a threat in the future?"

"No," replied the minister, "I know Menni. He is not our rival for the
very reason that he is so ambitious. Rest assured that at this moment he
has even more grandiose plans which he is not divulging for the time
being. He is not interested in becoming a minister or President of the
Republic. What is more," the minister added with a smile, "he does not
even want to be the financial emperor of Mars. His book on Libya ends in
the words: 'All the deserts of the world have a future.' His is the ambition
of the gods."

2. Nella

The city of Ichthyopolis is situated on terraces cut into the slopes of
the coastal mountains descending to the southern shore of the narrow gulf
at the beginning of the present Nepenthes Canal. At that time it had not
yet become a city, but was only a large settlement with a few thousand
inhabitants. Most of the few large buildings were public edifices. The rest
of the town consisted of small wooden houses and mud huts. An old
fisherman and his son lived for many years in one of these huts not far
from the embankment, along which small boats used to dock. The son's
name was Arri; his father's has been forgotten.

About six years before the beginning of the Libyan Project and the
radical changes it brought to the life of Ichthyopolis, the old man was out

on one of his usual fishing trips in his little schooner when he happened to run across a sloop from a wrecked ship. A girl of about twelve by the name of Nella was among the survivors he picked up. She told the fisherman the following story of her life.

Her father had worked as a mechanic in a factory in the capital. He had a fairly good salary and spared nothing to give his daughter a good upbringing. A machine exploded during a test and killed him on the spot, and soon her mother also fell ill and died. The authorities learned that the girl had an uncle, a minor official in the capital of the state of Meroe north of Syrtis Major; it was decided that she be sent to live with him, although she had never met the man. After the shipwreck the sloop had drifted on the sea for several days. The sailors had given her their water rations.

The fisherman took a liking to Nella, who he thought resembled his late wife. He wanted to suggest that she come and live with him but hesitated to ask her, for to him she seemed almost an upper-class young lady. When the mayor came to ask her where she wanted to go, she herself turned to the elderly fisherman and said:

"I would like to live with you. You and your son are very kind, and my uncle is a complete stranger. I will not be a burden on you. I am good at sewing and I can help around the house."

The old man was very happy, for Nella brightened and enlivened his little hut. When the shadow of her misfortunes had lifted, her warm smile, silvery laughter, and gentle jokes—though they were sometimes too subtle for those around her—soon earned her the name of Merry Nella. She had an excellent voice, and as she went about her work she constantly sang the songs she had learned from her mother. Later she began making up her own melodies and beautiful lyrics. She also read a great deal, devouring everything she found in the local library. For the sake of his adopted daughter, the old man began subscribing to the newspaper.

Five years passed, and the little girl became a young woman. Arri was already twenty-two. While out fishing one day the old man accidentally injured himself on a harpoon; the wound became infected, and a week later he was dead. Arri and Nella continued living as brother and sister for several months. But one day, upon returning from an unusually long sea journey, Arri suddenly said:

"Nella, I have thought a great deal about it, and I do not think we can go on like this any longer. I love you too much, Nella, and if your heart is indifferent to me then I must go away."

A look of sadness crept into the girl's face.

"I love you very much, Arri. No one in the whole world is dearer to me. That is why I cannot lie to you. Just now my heart leapt with pain, not with joy. I will go, not you. This is your home, your country. You need not worry about me."

"I am not worried about you, Nella, but it is I who must go, because everything here would only remind me of that which cannot be. My only salvation is to see new people and new lands and start a new life. I will even look for a different job. If you agree to stay here, then at least I will be sure where you are and it will be easier for me to know how you are doing, so that I can come to you if you should need me."

Arri left, and Nella stayed on alone in the little house. Her smile faded, and she began singing mournful songs as she sat at dusk and sewed by the window.

The weeks and months dragged monotonously on. The nocturnal rains, which occur in winter in the tropical countries of Mars, came and went. Neighbors came to Nella and asked her about the strange rumors they had heard. People were saying that a former aristocrat was planning to drain the Libyan sea and its sandbank, one of their best fishing grounds, and flood the desert. And it seemed that the government was going to let him. Nella, who besides reading newspapers had also read Menni's book, explained to them in detail what it was all about. The men calmed down, the women shook their heads skeptically. Soon the mystery became reality.

The Ichthyopolis roadsteads and the entire bay became livelier than ever. Several big ships arrived every day; some of them stopped outside the city, some did not, but they all eventually moved on to the far end of the bay, where the new canal was to begin. It was only about ten kilometers away, and some sort of activity between the ships and the shore could be observed from the crest of the hills along the coast. It was evident that something was being unloaded, though it was impossible to make out just what it was. Gradually, however, this something grew into a giant anthill that spread farther and farther off toward the mountains bounding the desert. Against the background of the reddish-gray soil the white spots of tents rapidly sprouted up in two parallel bands separated by a wide empty space. Thousands of black specks—obviously human beings—swarmed and flickered among them. Soon there were also larger, stationary black spots, probably temporary storehouses and huge machines.

Many new faces appeared in Ichthyopolis itself, and foreign accents could be heard on the streets. Several hundred young people left the city to work on the canal, where there were plenty of jobs and the pay was very good. The price of everything rose and kept on rising, but that was of little concern to anyone. Platinum money clinked dully on the sales counters more often than simple silver coins had done before. The merchants and even most of the fishermen seemed more cheerful, although it was also evident that a certain feverish nervousness had crept into their movements. The shops were filled with new goods. The women began wearing more colorful and stylish dresses, and the laughter became louder and shriller.

Nella had more than enough work. Most of the day she could be seen sitting at the open window with her sewing. Her countenance was no brighter than before, but when she raised her head from her work and gazed at the surface of the bay stretching off into the distance, a faraway dream, a look of expectation seemed to come into her gray green eyes. Her songs, quiet in the daytime, became louder in the evening, when the noisy life of the embankment had receded into the depths of the city and Nella felt more at ease.

Sometimes a swift, elegant cutter would dock not far from Nella's house and several men would disembark and set off toward the city hall or the post office. They were led by a tall, athletic man with steel gray eyes. Usually he seemed not to notice anything going on around him, and his fixed gaze was directed forward toward some invisible goal. Once as the man walked by, however, he suddenly caught the sweet strains of a song. He turned around and spied Nella. Their eyes met; she turned pale and bowed her head. After that, every time he happened to pass the house he looked intently at the beautiful seamstress, and Nella did not always lower her gaze.

It was a strange day. Since morning, gray clouds had billowed up beyond the mountains guarding the secret of the desert, only to scatter slowly and then form again. There was a prolonged rumbling followed by a muffled boom that sounded like thunder. The windows in the houses quivered, and there were moments when it seemed as though the ground was shaking. A breeze from the east brought with it clouds of fine, pungent dust. And then, something that had never been seen on Mars before—in the middle of the day a cloud formed over the city and it began to rain. Nella explained to one of her alarmed neighbors that there was nothing to worry about. It was all because of the dynamite charges being detonated in the mountains to cut a path for the canal. Yet she herself experienced a certain twinge of anxiety.

Toward evening the explosions ceased. Before sunset the cutter again docked at the embankment. This time the chief engineer got off alone. There was an unusual expression of nervous animation on his face; his eyes glittered feverishly, and his gait was not as even and confident as usual, as if he were slightly fuddled by the powder fumes.

Night came, and Nella was still sitting by the open window. She gazed at the dark sky and the brightly twinkling stars. The little face of Phobos capriciously altered its contours as it glided eastward across the sky, and objects below cast pale, delicate shadows in its light. On no other planet in the solar system can people see such a remarkable moon. The tiny crescent of Deimos seemed frozen in the firmament. Not far from it, the greenish evening star—Earth and her inseparable companion— descended into the sunset. The surface of the bay mirrored this picture in paler hues. Nella's song poured forth, uniting the heavens and the sea and the heart of man. When it had died away, she heard the approach of heavy footsteps. A tall figure stopped in front of the window, and a soft, quiet voice said:

"You sing beautifully, Nella."

The girl was not even surprised that the chief engineer knew her name. She answered:

"Songs make living easier."

"With your permission, I should like to come in and visit you," said Menni.

"Yes!" she blurted out without hesitation.

Nella's fate was sealed.

When the passion of their caresses had ebbed, she told him all about her love for him. She had known him for a long time. She had first seen him several years ago when he had passed through on his way into the desert where others had remained forever in the embraces of a sandy death. She was only a little girl then, but he inspired her with pride rather than fear, and she began a long wait. A few months later he returned, pale, emaciated, but a victor—what joy! He was taken to his ship in her father's boat, while she stood with a trembling heart and watched them from the bank. Then she read his book, and of course she realized that everything he was doing now was only the beginning, only the first step. It would be followed by things which he had not yet revealed to anyone but which he had long since pondered and firmly decided upon.

In the darkness of the night Nella could not see the first expression of happy surprise on Menni's face darken into a heavy shadow. But she could sense the strange immobility of his body and fell silent. Menni thought intensely for a long while. Finally he said:

"Forgive me, Nella. I was mistaken. I did not know you. You are worth infinitely more than I can ever give you. If it were possible for me to join my life to the life of another, I would not want anyone but you, Nella. But you have guessed the truth. I have taken upon myself tasks which exceed anything man has ever attempted before. I can expect enormous obstacles and a bitter struggle on the road to their fulfillment. I have hardly taken the first step, and already the forces of hatred have begun honing their weapons. To overcome everything and be stopped by nothing I must be absolutely free, totally invulnerable . . . Nella! Only he who is alone is invulnerable in battle."

His voice underwent an odd change, as if he were attempting to stifle pain. Nella answered him:

"Don't be afraid, don't be sorry about anything. I need nothing. I knew, of course, that it would be like this, and even a moment ago I felt it was all just a dream."

Again they fell silent. Menni's kisses became tender, almost respectful.

"Sing me a song, Nella."

The night and all of nature seemed to be listening to her song. It told of a girl who heeded no one, but gave everything to her beloved. The old melody breathed a feeling that was as deep and clear as the sky and as powerful as Fate.

Menni left before dawn, never to return again.

For a long time afterward no one saw Nella or heard her singing. Then she again appeared with her work at the window, somewhat pale and with a new expression of serene and confident expectation on her face. She sang her songs very softly at dusk and at night, as if she did not want anyone to hear them. One of these songs was new; Nella sang it more often yet more softly than the others. Its lyrics ran something like this:

> Wondrous the secret I bear deep within . . .
>   Alone, yet at once I am two!
> Deep in my body there quickens again
>   The happiness fate struck and slew.
>
> A tiny little flower in first budding bloom,
>   A star in the dark cloud on high,
> A marvelous moth in its humble cocoon,
>   A promise of sunlight and life . . .
>
> Come unto me, little one, my yearning burns bright.
>   Ah, the wait of these cruelly long days!
> The first shining rays of life's faint dawning light
>   Will I greet with my fond loving gaze.
>
> My darling, I feel you are restless today
>   By the twitch of your tiny wee feet.
> What sight of the future has darkened your gaze
>   And broken your slumber so sweet?
>
> I know by the strain of your thrust to be free
>   That the fruit of my womb is a boy.
> A warrior is what you are destined to be,
>   My genius unseen, my one joy!
>
> Like your father a warrior, mighty and bold
>   To the warrior's call you'll stand true.
> But the chill in his heart and the pride in his soul
>   Will never be known unto you.

His will is of iron, his thoughts are of steel,
    His better he has yet to know.
But his heart is of ice, no pain does it feel
    For the creatures that Fate has brought low.

The soul of the woman he loved for a day
    Pines empty, forgotten, alone.
The tears of the wretches cast into the fray
    Warm not his heart made of stone.

Like him you will harness the wind and its might,
    But heed that you too are a man.
Sleep, little one, my secret delight,
    As your first cradle rocks gently on.

Days, nights, weeks passed. Arri arrived unexpectedly just before the beginning of the nocturnal rains. He was dressed like a worker from the capital and seemed much older than before. Nella said to him:

"You came at the right time, Arri. Take me away from here."

He replied: "I sensed that you needed me. We will go together to Centropolis."

A few weeks later the little old house was sold. Arri and Nella boarded a ship and left their native Libya forever.

PART I

1. The Great Project

Menni's star had risen high. Faith is born of miracles, and the miracle had been worked. The mighty torrent of waters from the Mare Australe rushed along the channel carved by the hand of man, along the channel blasted through the mountains by the will of man. And proud steamships began sailing across the sands of the ancient desert. The clouds shaded and the rains watered the parched soil, which had not known such bliss for a hundred thousand years. The Kingdom of Silence was invaded by the childish babble of brooks, and brightly colored grasses entered into battle with the tawny gray dust of the past. The elements had been dealt a tremendous blow, and it began to seem as though man could accomplish anything he set his will to. The time had come when Menni could present his idea in full with the confidence that people would listen to him.

And so now he launched his "Plan of the Project," which foresaw the transformation of the entire planet. It envisaged the gigantic system of canals whose construction during the following century conquered all the deserts through artificial irrigation and more than doubled the inhabitable surface of Mars. On the basis of an extremely painstaking study of the geographical and geological conditions, Menni indicated both the best location and course of the canals and the sum of human labor, time, and capital they would require. Subsequent generations needed only to supplement his calculations with minor adjustments and additions.

The main problem concerned the source of these enormous resources and labor. Menni demonstrated that to continue construction as on the Libyan Canal through loans repaid by income from the reclaimed deserts would mean prolonging the Great Project over several centuries. The new financial plan which he proposed instead showed that he could also be a revolutionary outside his own special field. It was a plan for nationalizing the land which provided that all previous ground rent would serve as the source of capital for the Project.

It goes without saying that the realization of such an undertaking depended upon especially favorable historical circumstances. Such conditions existed. Menni was not the first to understand this; he was simply more able than others to seize the right moment and formulate the best slogan for a powerful social movement attracting the support of various classes.

By that time the independent peasantry had almost disappeared from the face of Mars. More than nine-tenths of all properties in land were in the hands of a few thousand grotesquely wealthy owners. Most of these were the scions of the old hereditary aristocracy, while others were descended from various government officials who had taken advantage of their power during the bourgeois revolutions and the last feudal uprisings to appropriate for themselves the confiscated estates of certain reactionaries. The generally dry climate of the planet made it even easier for these landlords to ruin the peasantry and seize their property, since artificial irrigation offered enormous advantages to those who could afford it, but the capital it required was more than the smallholders could hope to raise. The peasants banded together in cooperatives, but sooner or later these associations became saddled with debts and were ruined. In the course of a few centuries the process had progressed so far that small-scale land ownership survived in only a few isolated corners of the planet.

At the same time, the general economic development and the growth of the population had increased the demand for land and bread; the cost of living, and with it the ground rent, rose rapidly. This was bad for everyone save the landlords; even the vast majority of capitalists found the situation very constrictive, not to mention the proletarian and semi-proletarian masses of the population. The profits of enterprises were reduced by both high land rents and high wages, although the latter were

not much above subsistence level. And the more rents and the already
high cost of living rose, the more desperately people started looking for a
way out of the predicament. Nothing came of this search for a long time,
however, because it pulled in different and incompatible directions.

Certain experts suggested unfeasible plans for legislating reductions
in the price of cereals and lease payments. Others realized that nothing
could be accomplished until the land was taken away from the lords, but
they were unable to agree on how to do this. Should the land be distributed in small parcels to landless peasants who would cultivate it, or
should it be turned over to entire cooperatives in the form of large estates, or should it simply be distributed by the government to those who
were willing and able to pay the highest rent—obviously, that is, to the
capitalists? The first of these approaches, although it threatened to destroy agriculture by depriving it of artificial irrigation, had a great many
supporters among the remnants of the petty bourgeoisie and related
strata of intellectuals and was also favored by those workers who had
retained the ideals of their peasant forebears. The second plan was advocated by a majority of socialists from among the workers and intellectuals. The great economist Xarma was decidedly against it, convincingly
arguing that in view of the huge capital needed to run large-scale agricultural enterprises, the peasant cooperatives would soon be dominated
entirely by business and banking interests and would become owners in
name only, a simple front for the latter. But in those days few socialists
listened to Xarma. The third approach—a simple bourgeois "nationalization" of the land—was advanced by certain radical democrats, and it also
had the sympathy of most capitalists. In reality this was the only feasible
alternative, but at the time Menni presented his project it had not gained
sufficiently broad support from society at large.

On Earth, which is presently going through an analogous period,
such "nationalization" schemes are supported by only an insignificant
handful of democrats, while almost the entire bourgeoisie rejects them as
a harmful utopia. Why such a difference? The explanation lies in the fact
that on Earth the working-class movement developed rapidly and aggres-
sively, whereas on Mars this evolution was slower and calmer. The Martian workers of the time were permeated by a spirit of moderation and
sober pragmatism. Socialism preserved almost everywhere the strongly
idealistic and philanthropic elements injected into it by theoreticians
from the intelligentsia. The specter of social revolution did not confront
the bourgeoisie as an imminent and menacing possibility.

By contrast, the bourgeoisie on Earth became aware of the threat
posed by the proletariat even before accounts had been settled with the
old aristocracy, and this has affected its attitude toward the workers. It is
frightened by the thought of the blow which nationalization of the land
would deal to the sacred principle of private ownership, the basis of the

present social order. What would happen if the masses were to be shown that the property of an entire class could be expropriated in the name of the common good! Also, the bourgeoisie on Earth is placid, due to the very nature of its activities, and even somewhat cowardly since attaining the position of the ruling, that is, the most contented, class; and it is not especially confident of its own abilities to suppress unrest. It therefore highly values the vestiges of militarism and ferociousness that have been preserved among the aristocracy, and it is always prepared to make considerable concessions to ensure itself of allies in the event it should become necessary to crush the masses by force. And of course the first thing it had to agree to was to oppose the idea of nationalization.

On Mars, however, these conditions did not exist. The situation there was far more favorable, and Menni knew how to take advantage of it. First he linked the idea of nationalization to the Great Cause, whose significance was apparent to all. Secondly, in his book he advanced a very simple and seemingly persuasive argument that allied the bourgeois nationalizers, the supporters of distribution to the individual peasants, and those who favored the cooperatives. He pointed out that the first and most important step was to get rid of the big landowners. Then, since the redistribution of the land or the organization of associations for its collective cultivation could not be effected rapidly, the state would have to start by leasing the land in the usual way, by auctioning it off. Nothing, however, would prevent anyone who wished from engaging parliamentary means in order to bring about a transition to other forms of exploiting the nationalized land. The road would be clear for all sorts of new projects, because the main obstacle—the landowners—would already have been eliminated.

Menni himself, of course, was not aware how deceptive these arguments really were. For once the state had delivered the exploitation of the land into the hands of the capitalists, taking it away again would prove much more difficult than in the case of the earlier landowners, who had no firm support among the other social classes. Xarma realized this immediately, but he supported Menni's plan. Others did not bother to look so very deeply into the matter: all the supporters of the peasants and the cooperatives enthusiastically advocated immediate nationalization, and the capitalists also struck while the iron was hot.

Feli Rao convened a congress of the industrial and banking syndicates. The delegates drew up an action program and elected a Council of Syndicates, which immediately emerged as the decisive force in the struggle. Thus the agrarian revolution was achieved through Parliament.

Scattered remnants of the peasantry rose in defense of their property, but these revolts were easily suppressed; their only effect was to provide the state with an excuse for expropriating the rebels' land with almost no compensation. As for the big landlords, instead of compensation they received pensions, which, however, could not lawfully exceed the salaries of the highest officials of the Republic and were a mere pittance compared to the landowners' previous incomes. The syndicates also owned land in certain places; they managed to negotiate the best terms and were compensated without losses, not to mention the fact that they could expect enormous profits in the future.

Menni did not participate directly in this struggle, which went on for two or three years, but continued to work on his technical plan. When he approached the Central Parliament with his detailed project for the first ten canals, which he proposed to start simultaneously, it was adopted immediately and he was appointed supervisor and given almost dictatorial powers.

The Great Project got under way.

2. Dark Clouds

Of the first group of canals which Menni began digging, it was proposed that eight be completed in twenty to thirty years. The two in Thaumasia—Nectar and Ambrosia, which created the inland sea called Solis Lacus—were to be finished in ten to twelve years, while a third, Phosphorus, was constructed much later.

The construction projects were conducted in widely separated corners of the planet, and it was impossible for Menni to supervise them on the spot. However, he selected able assistants who kept him continuously informed by telegraph, and he spent a large share of his time on inspection trips. The most prominent among these subordinates was the engineer Maro, who left his position with the Dynamite and Powder Trust to offer his services to the new project. Within only a year he had become Menni's chief assistant and the director of the most important part of the undertaking in Thaumasia. The canals had to be completed as quickly as possible there, because they promised immediate and obvious results similar to those that had been achieved in Libya, only on an even grander scale. Maro proved to be an excellent organizer, and Menni's other lieutenants were also equal to their tasks. The great deeds being wrought inspired everyone with enthusiasm, and during the first years the Project progressed as well as anyone could have wished.

The workers' labor conditions were quite respectable, but of course there were conflicts with the engineers over penalties, abuses of power, wage miscalculations, dismissals, and so on. However, such disagreements never developed into a strike; when the local directors were unable to resolve all difficulties the workers agreed to await Menni's arrival, knowing by experience that they could rely on his disinterested, objective attitude toward disputes, and that despite his icy reserve he would never sacrifice an iota of justice as he understood it in order to save the prestige of their bosses. The engineers were not always happy about this, but even those who called him a dictator behind his back admitted that he listened attentively to their point of view and took all serious and practical arguments into consideration. In addition, the engineers valued the honor of working under his leadership and especially appreciated the opportunities for rapid advancement that lay open to those with sufficient skill and energy.

In the third year of the Project a new factor entered into the relations between Menni and the workers. By that time trade unions had been formed under the influence of urban proletarians who had brought their organizational habits and demands to their new places of work. At first, of course, only a minority of workers joined the unions, but gradually the unorganized ones followed their example and willingly granted the former the leading role in all negotiations with the engineers. Most of the engineers were for their part not opposed to dealing with the delegates of the unions. On one of his trips to Thaumasia Menni was officially approached by representatives of the Excavators' union, whose navvies were employed on the Nectar Canal. The problem was that several thousand workers were digging through a particularly compact and rocky subsoil. They were on a piecework system based on cubic measures of excavated earth, which meant that many started receiving considerably less than average earnings. The union proposed establishing a minimum daily wage. Menni listened quietly and attentively as usual and then asked the delegates who had elected them.

"The Excavators' Union," they replied.

"Does everyone involved in excavation belong to your union?"

"No, not everyone."

"In that case, I cannot discuss the matter with you. Employment contracts have been concluded not with the union, but with each navvy individually. The union therefore lacks the authority to alter the terms of the contracts."

"But it's impossible for each navvy to conduct his own individual negotiations."

"Of course. I am not refusing to talk to the real representatives of all the workers affected by the matter, but I am refusing to recognize you as having such a mandate. You were elected not by the workers, but by an organization which may be pursuing goals alien to them and acting according to norms which they had no voice in formulating. If the workers wish, they can tell me what they need through delegates whom they have freely and directly elected."

"But now even many capitalists think it is possible to conduct negotiations with the unions. And it was in fact Maro who referred us to you."

"The capitalists can do what they think is best for them—that is no concern of mine. Not wishing to decide the matter himself, Maro was quite correct in advising you to come to me. Now you know my point of view."

The workers left, exasperated by Menni's formalism. They informed their comrades of his answer. All the navvies then elected delegates, and the wage system was adjusted. After this incident, however, the most conscious workers began agitating against Menni, accusing him of wanting to deprive the workers of their freedom of organization. This was doubtless an exaggeration, but it was understandable. The agitation also influenced the mass of the workers who were not organized but did not wish to relinquish their right to join the unions, and distrust of Menni grew.

Part of the bourgeois press—the largest newspapers, controlled by the Council of Syndicates—entered the fray and did their best to exacerbate the conflict. They showered Menni with backhanded compliments on his "firmness" and "resolution," sometimes taking advantage of the opportunity to add that perhaps his attitude toward the unions was just a little too severe and categorical, but that on the other hand, at times there was no harm in going to this other extreme, as most employers were entirely too meek and soft on this vital question. Here appropriate mention was usually made of Menni's feudal extraction, and he was praised as "a knight of iron who had preserved the best traits of his ancestors, the mighty dukes of Thaumasia."

The reactionary press, owned by the former landlords, suddenly adopted a radically different tone when they spoke of Menni. "The Republic stole him from the old aristocracy; the Republic raised him to betray his great heritage," wrote one of their publicists, "but these sacred principles are now taking their revenge. The entire personality and behavior of Ormen Aldo have unmasked the lie of democracy, which has proved unable completely to corrupt his ancient blood." The journalist argued quite persuasively that the accomplishment of any truly grandiose mission demands a leader, a strong authority that is in essence monarchical, whatever men might choose to call him. "Could Menni's heroic father, who sacrificed his life for the honor and glory of the house of Aldo, even dream of acquiring the power actually possessed by his republican engineer son?" For their part the socialists unmasked the "dictator," while the democrats were at a loss for what to say. Public opinion wavered and gradually swung against Menni.

Soon Menni was confronted by a new and very serious problem. The construction of the Ambrosia Canal had reached the point from which it would continue for two hundred kilometers across an extremely unhealthy region known among the Thaumasians as the Rotten Bogs. The clay subsoil of a vast area there rose in many places to the very surface, forming innumerable shallow depressions that were impossible to drain. These collected stagnant rainwater and were also fed by the streams descending from the nearby mountains, which the canals would subsequently have to cut through. The region was almost uninhabited; the vegetation was luxuriant, consisting only of swamp plants, and the bogs were teeming with disease. Three hundred thousand workers, often laboring up to their waists in water, were to be employed in this area for a period of about two years. Illness was rampant; thousands died each month, and muffled discontent began fermenting among the workers. The unions conferred but were at first unable to arrive at any generally acceptable solution.

Whenever possible, Maro began sending workers who had fallen ill to work instead on the Nectar Canal, from which he transferred fresh men to replace them. As a result the discontent and agitation spread to that project as well, and the atmosphere became even more tense. A movement was beginning to take form, but it still lacked an articulate battle cry. Such a banner was being sought, however, and it was obvious that unless something happened to reverse the situation, it would soon be found.

Menni had to an extent foreseen such complications. He had been especially careful to furnish a detailed justification for the course of the Ambrosia Canal in his plan. He had himself shown that, considering the relief of the area, it would be easier to move the line of the canal a few dozen kilometers to the east and take advantage of the deep valley lying at the foot of a low chain of hills running inland from the sea. In this way the Rotten Bogs would be bypassed entirely. If this route were followed, however, it would mean that a long segment of the canal would run along one of the tectonic lines in the crust of the planet, that is, near a fault, where major earthquakes could be expected. True, no serious disturbances had been recorded there for nearly two and a half centuries, but the risk was still inadmissible. The entire canal with the cities constructed along it and the irrigation system fed by it could be destroyed in a matter of minutes, and hundreds of thousands of human lives would be lost as a result of someone else's mistake. For the sake of humanity as a whole, therefore, it was necessary consciously to opt instead for the sacrifice of thousands, much in the same way that nations knowingly allowed for even greater losses to serve their interests in the wars of the past.

In further support of his argument Menni pointed out that constructing the canal through the Rotten Bogs would provide an outlet for the water collected there. Thus the swamp would quickly be drained and at the same time a vast province capable of supporting two to three million colonists would be opened up to cultivation.

At this point an anonymous brochure mysteriously appeared in a mass edition that was circulated among the agitated and resentful workers. It argued that the workers on the Ambrosia project were being sent to an altogether unnecessary death. The author took advantage of the fact that they could not read Menni's huge and specialized book, boldly quoting its figures and data to show that the best technical solution would have been to dig the canal in a different direction so as to bypass the bogs. A few words were devoted to Menni's "obviously unfounded remark on the danger of earthquakes that had ceased centuries ago," whence it was concluded that "the chief engineer, since he cannot be unaware of all this, must have personal reasons for wanting to exterminate the workers, whose unions he loathes so fiercely; the fate of the Project is obviously of no concern to him." The brochure had been composed by a talented writer in racy and an easily accessible language, and its impact proved enormous.

The movement had found its battle cry.

Menni was in the capital at the time, 7,000 kilometers from the theater of operations. Some time before, he had introduced a bill in Parliament providing pensions for the families of workers on the Great Project who had died or destroyed their health as a result of diseases caused by local or occupational conditions. Up until then the laws covered only "accidents." The bill had to be passed as soon as possible in order to alleviate the situation in Thaumasia. A majority of delegates were evidently prepared to vote for it, but formalistic tangles arose in committee due to continuous demands for new information, challenges to estimates on the cost of the measure, and so on, and the matter dragged on indefinitely. Menni decided to mobilize all available means to solve the problem. First of all he had to reach an agreement with the Prime Minister, the first such official ever to have enjoyed his full confidence. He was the former Minister of Public Works to whom Menni had suggested the Libyan canal project.

An hour before his meeting with the Prime Minister, Menni received by special delivery from Maro a report and a copy of the anonymous brochure. The Prime Minister had already been informed about the matter, and was holding the same brochure in his hand when he greeted Menni.

"An extraordinarily skillful move!" he said.

"By whom?" asked Menni.

"Ultimately, of course, Feli Rao. However, although he is a sharp operator on the stock exchange and behind the scenes in Parliament, I still do not think that this particular idea belongs to his usual arsenal. I suspect Maro."

Menni shuddered as if from an unexpected blow and turned somewhat pale.

"Why do you suspect him?"

"Has Maro ever told you about his secret meeting with a certain mechanic by the name of Arri, who is also the leader of the Thaumasian Federation of Labor?"

"No. Are you absolutely sure that it took place?"

"Together with this brochure I also received a message the other day from an agent I had sent there on a special mission. He is intelligent, reliable, and devoted to me personally."

"And how is the pension bill coming along?"

"It's almost hopeless. They will be able to procrastinate for another two or three months, and now things are happening fast. They have already referred it to the discussion of next year's budget, and you know how it is with the budget . . ."

"But how could you allow this to happen? You have a majority."

"Only formally. It is already clear that we are bound to fail."

"But your party alone constitutes over half the chamber, does it not?"

"It used to, but the Council of Syndicates has a lot of money. I cannot actually prove it, but I know for a fact that fifty new millionaires have appeared in the ranks of our 'radicals.'"

"What? Are they that generous?"

"You are worth much more than these millions to them. The budget of the Great Project is already nearly four billion a year. With a well organized system of embezzlement, one or two billion can be raked off annually."

"Well, what are you going to do, then—try to stay in power?"

"On the contrary, I am going to try to force them to topple our ministry immediately. It won't be easy, however, because it is very advantageous for them to let us stay in power as long as things are so desperate."

"Do you think the situation is absolutely hopeless?"

"At the moment, yes. The workers are aroused to the breaking point. They no longer trust us, and this business with the pension bill is direct evidence against us. You will not be able to convince them either, because they are not about to listen to you. Your attitude toward the unions has thoroughly undermined any possibility of mutual understanding. I have never agreed with your viewpoint—you know what I think of the need for compromise in the interest of preserving the social peace—but there is no sense in arguing about principles now. The situation is clear. The workers are demanding that construction in the Rotten Bogs cease at all costs, and that the course of the canal be altered. Can you agree to these conditions?"

"Absolutely not!"

"I agree. To give in would be tantamount to admitting to an uncommitted crime and at the same time committing a real one. The only result would be to delay insignificantly a no less inevitable but more shameful failure. In other words, there are going to be strikes, then an uprising, suppression by the troops . . ."

"If that is necessary . . ."

"But what's the use! When you and I have bathed in their blood then our cause will truly have perished once and for all. That will be the end of our popularity, and it will be child's play for Feli Rao to pull down a ministry that is distasteful to the masses. They will rid themselves of you even more efficiently: it will not be hard to incite some naïve and fanatical worker to commit the deed, and your visits to the construction sites will provide any number of opportunities. Sooner or later they are bound to succeed."

"Do you hope to resign soon?"

"We need an excuse, so we must be voted down on some important issue. There is a ministers' meeting this evening. With the support of my colleagues, tomorrow I intend to move that Parliament immediately detach the pension bill from the budget and hold a special vote on it. This might spoil their game. The fifty bribed delegates will vote with the opposition, and that will be that. Then all we have to do is wait."

"I have never believed that there is any such thing in the life of man as a completely hopeless situation."

"They exist. Listen to me when I say that there are certain things I know better than you do. You do not like history, and there you are making a mistake. I, on the other hand, have studied the subject, and this is one of the things I have learned: Society is a strange animal; from time to time it needs to indulge in a senseless waste of resources. What could be more absurd than war? And yet how often war has served to regenerate nations! Now we have no wars, so society has discovered other means. The epic of Feli Rao's financial imperialism is beginning, and it is going to cost mankind more than a good war. In other words, this is what history needs. I do not know whether it will always be like this, but I am certain that this is what is about to happen now."

3. The Showdown

Within the week Menni was in Thaumasia. He received a telegram on the way informing him of the fall of the ministry. Work on both of the Thaumasian canals had already come to a halt as over 600,000 men went on strike. Maro came to meet him. They conferred in the Project Administration Building in the new city located at the mouth of the Nectar Canal. The chief engineer listened attentively to his assistant's report on the events of the past few days and then asked him point-blank:

"What was the object of your negotiations with this labor leader, Arri?"

Maro's face twitched slightly, but in a second he had recovered his previous impenetrable composure.

"I admit that it was not entirely right of me not to inform you of this attempt at conciliation, which I took on my own private initiative and responsibility. Knowing your attitude toward the unions, I was unable to have any official relations with their representatives. I was convinced, however, that in this particular instance a great deal, if not all, depended on them. The exceptional nature of the situation forced me to use other than the usual channels."

"Would you like to tell me about the content of your conversation?"

"I explained to him that, due to technical and scientific considerations which you can judge more competently than anyone else, the plan of the project cannot under any circumstances be altered, and that intractability on the part of the workers will only lead to forceful suppression. I urged him to use his enormous influence with the workers to bring about a conciliation. I pointed out that the adoption of the pension bill by Parliament can only be impeded and delayed by disturbances, because for reasons of their own prestige the authorities must avoid anything that looks like a concession to illegal pressure."

"You are very perspicacious, Maro," Menni remarked with irony. "You were speaking with Arri about the impossibility of changing the plan several days before the publication of the anonymous brochure, before the workers had even advanced any such demand. It is useless to continue this comedy. We are alone here. What does the Council of Syndicates—or rather Feli Rao—want?"

Maro blanched somewhat, thought for a moment, and then quickly making up his mind said:

"You are right. The course events are taking is beginning to emerge clearly, and I can speak with you frankly. The Council of Syndicates wants to take over the administrative and financial end of the Project. It would be happy to leave the technical sphere, which is doubtless the most important one to you, under your supervision. The council considers itself to be entitled to compensation for the enormous losses it has already suffered due to the Great Project, which has greatly increased the demand for manpower and the claims advanced by the workers."

"And," interjected Menni, "has also provided the syndicates with colossal orders at good prices and has given them fantastic profits. I think we had better leave justice out of this—the question under discussion is one of strength. How does the Council of Syndicates propose to achieve its wish?"

"If you agree, everything will be arranged quite simply, and you will be allowed to play the most distinguished role. The strike will be stubborn, but of course peaceful at first. You will openly argue against sending troops, but the new government will dispatch them anyway. You will demonstratively wash your hands of all responsibility for the consequences. The disorders will then be quelled; there will be a good deal of bloodshed, and it will be necessary to send troops to the other canals to prevent sympathy strikes and uprisings. You will resign in protest from all administrative duties and declare that only your desire to accomplish a mission of vital significance to all mankind has induced you to retain the scientific and technical leadership of the Project. An executive committee will be appointed to see to the budget and to maintain order at the construction sites. It will include Feli Rao as a representative of the Ministry of Finance, myself as a representative of the Ministry of Public Works, and one other member from the Central Police. Then, to satisfy you even more completely, Parliament will bring down the present goverment; it has purposely been composed of nobodies so that it can afford to become involved in these delicate matters."

There was a moment of silence. Menni's face was calm, but his eyes darkened strangely and his voice sounded somewhat muffled when he resumed the conversation.

"Excellent. If I agree, then you will have no problem in accomplishing all this. But suppose I refuse?"

"That would be most unfortunate, and we would hope that a man of your genius would be able to assess the balance of forces accurately and dispassionately and not wish to prolong a completely hopeless and senseless struggle. However, I can tell you what our strategy would be in such an unlikely situation. There would be no effort whatever to curb the workers; on the contrary, we would offer them our paternal protection. The question would be raised in Parliament whether it might not in fact be possible to alter the course of the canal. A commission would be appointed consisting of a group of old academic scholars—you know how they hate you. They are certain to issue a statement that is ambiguous and vague enough to enable Parliament to satisfy the demands of the workers in spite of you. Your position then . . ."

Maro stopped. Menni's darkening gaze made him vaguely uneasy, and he lowered his eyes. Because of this he did not notice that for a few seconds this gaze rested on the dull surface of a bronze paper-knife lying in a pile of papers off to one side of them both. Maro finished what he had started to say:

"You see that this outcome would be the worst one in all respects."

"So you would not hesitate to commit a crime in the eyes of science and mankind for the sake of the . . . budget?"

The touch of icy contempt in Menni's question was stronger than a slap in the face. Maro straightened up, his eyes lit up in a flash of cynicism, and his businesslike reserve gave way to an impudent sneer.

"Crime? Such language! Is that your only objection? Everything will be quite legal. As for the earthquake, it will probably occur long after we are gone!"

"Yes, indeed, *you* will not be here!"

Menni leapt to his feet, and Maro was unable to evade his lightning-swift blow. In the hands of an ordinary man the bronze knife would not have been much of a weapon, but Aldo was the descendant of ancient knights. Maro's carotid artery and throat were ripped open, and he fell to the floor in a spurting fountain of blood. He gave a shudder, there was a faint wheezing sound, and then only silence.

4. The Trial

Menni's case was postponed for a few months until things had quieted down. In the meantime the workers were subdued by the military, their unions were disbanded, and their leaders were arrested. The newspapers worked feverishly to prepare public opinion for Menni's trial, depicting him as a man with a violent and despotic character who was capable of the worst excesses at the slightest provocation. The bloody biographies of certain of his ancestors were also given the proper embellishment and enlisted in the cause. The voices of the few who defended him were drowned in a choir of malicious joy. Because the murder was connected with politics, the government handed Menni over to the Supreme Tribunal, which was made up of the most prominent jurists of the planet. A very select audience was allowed to attend the trial. One of the friends of the Minister of Justice acted as prosecutor. The accused declined legal counsel.

Menni confined his testimony to an accurate account of his conversation with Maro. Most of the depositions of the other witnesses amounted to unfavorable remarks on Menni's character. The audience awaited two witnesses with great interest. One was the Prime Minister and the other was the arrested labor leader, Arri. Neither appeared, however: the Prime Minister suddenly fell ill with some mysterious disease, and Arri was wounded trying to escape from prison. Events were working in Feli Rao's favor. The court, of course, determined that it was possible to continue the trial without these witnesses.

The prosecutor declared in his speech that the court simply could not attach any importance to Menni's explanation.

"At all trials, of course," he said, "the testimony of the accused always puts him in a favorable light. In this case, however, we have a report of a private conversation that cannot be checked, and juridically speaking a fact is not a fact unless it can be verified. To describe a respected man like Feli Rao and the entire Council of Syndicates as criminal conspirators—is this not an obvious fantasy invented by the accused simply to exonerate himself? We are left with the established and indisputable fact of the murder, which the accused does not deny having committed."

Several times during his address the prosecutor expatiated upon the theme of the difficult situation in which the court found itself due to the high position of the accused and the great services he had rendered to mankind. "But it must be remembered," he went on, "that in the eyes of the Republic there are no great or insignificant people: all are equal. If any difference at all is allowable, then it is that he who has been given more can also be expected to render more." From this the prosecutor concluded that there were no mitigating circumstances: "The only thing that is not entirely clear is the degree to which the murder was premeditated. Here the accused should be given the benefit of the doubt."

In his concluding speech Menni observed that the prosecutor was completely right in refusing to recognize any mitigating circumstances: "The just act I committed has no need of any such extenuation. Nor will the judgment of the future find any mitigating circumstances for those who are guilty of the real crime, for if greatness is no excuse, then neither is smallness." The chairman called the accused to order, threatening to deprive him of the right to speak. "I do not have much more to say," Menni concluded, "only that I protest emphatically against the assumption that my act was unpremeditated. On the contrary, it was deliberate and carefully considered."

The judges were indignant over Menni's cold arrogance. Although in earlier private conversations they had told the ministers that they would not be able to give Menni more than a few years in prison, now they felt that the politicians would not be satisfied with so little. They therefore sentenced Menni to the maximum penalty—fifteen years of solitary confinement.

A large crowd had gathered in the courtyard of the Supreme Tribunal Building to await the announcement of the sentence. When it had been passed along from mouth to mouth a dead silence fell over the gathering. The hush seemed to become even deeper when Menni's serene, athletic figure appeared at the top of the stone steps and he was led away by two gendarmes to the prison van. The crowd parted to let him through. An invisible force diverted Menni's unblinking forward gaze to one side. His eyes met those of a tall, beautiful woman holding a boy of twelve or thirteen by the hand. Somehow she seemed familiar . . .

A sonorous female voice called out in the midst of the silence:

"Son, take a good look at a hero! Never forget him!"

A memory flashed deep in Menni's soul:

Nella!

PART II

1. Netti

Twelve years passed.

Some thirty persons gathered in the dimly lit cellar of a small tavern in one of the proletarian suburbs of Centropolis. Lean figures, intelligent faces, working clothes . . . When the doors had been locked and it had become quiet in the room, the elderly chairman rose and spoke:

"Brothers!" (At that time this was the customery form of address among members of the workers' organizations.) "I hereby declare this Council of the Great Project Federation to be open. You union secretaries are well aware of the situation that has led us to gather clandestinely here today in order to draw up and discuss a general plan of action. You know that labor conditions are becoming increasingly intolerable. In the years that have passed since the failure of the general strike and the shooting of thousands of our brothers, the arrogance of the exploiters has steadily grown. Wages have fallen by a third, while almost everything has become more expensive. The working day has been lengthened everywhere from ten to twelve hours. The engineers and contractors and even the foremen treat us like serfs, penalizing and firing us as they see fit. Our organizations are subject to systematic persecution. You will remember how difficult it was to resurrect them after our defeat. At present active workers are dismissed on the flimsiest pretexts, sometimes even without any pretext. Almost all of you have personally experienced something of the sort.

"However, discontent is also growing. The proletariat has long been suppressed, but it is finally raising its head. It looks around and says: 'What is this, anyway? Why? What's the reason?' And from these questions it proceeds to another one which is even more important, namely 'What must be done?' We have been asked this question thousands upon thousands of times by our brothers out on the construction sites; every conversation we have had with them has led to it. It is this question which has brought us here today and forced us to resuscitate, after a long interruption, our forbidden General Federation. Let us pool our entire experience and strength for the common cause; the fate of millions of our brothers depends on it. And let us not leave here today until this matter is settled!

"Now then, brothers, tell us what you know and let's hear what you think we should do."

Ten speakers representing the workers at ten different canals addressed the gathering in turn. Their speeches were brief: a concise description of the on-the-spot situation, a few typical facts relating to labor conditions, some figures relevant to the state of the workers' organizations, and finally conclusions. All were agreed that the common struggle must be initiated immediately, for otherwise anarchical disorders would begin flaring up sporadically on their own. Everyone was of the opinion that the only weapon was a general strike, and that its slogan should be a return to the conditions that prevailed before the first strike. Certain delegates suggested appealing for support to the railroad workers, the mechanics, and the coal miners, who were the best organized groups; the assaults of the growing syndicates had also robbed them of a great deal during these years, and it was hoped that they would agree to advance their demands at the same time. In that case the prospects for victory looked very good. The plan of action seemed to be almost ready when an elderly worker sitting next to the chairman took the floor. It was Arri.

"Brothers," he said, "I would like to ask you to allow my son Netti to present a report. An engineer, he is attending our gathering without the right to vote, not as a representative of a union but as one of the organizers of the congress. Some of you know him already, for his assignment has brought him into personal contact with half of our organizations. We are not accustomed to trusting outsiders, nor should we be, considering how often we have been deceived and betrayed in the past. But he is not a stranger to us: he is from a worker's family, and as a boy he himself worked in a factory. He has studied a great deal; if to complete his education he attended the same schools as our enemies, he did so in order to find new weapons for the defense of our cause. You will not regret taking the time to hear him out."

The meeting expressed its unanimous consent, and a tall young man with clear, blue green eyes rose to speak.

"Brothers! I have nothing to add to what the speakers before me have said about the situation of the workers at the construction sites, about their mood, their hopes, or their desires. You are more competent than I to judge such matters. I want instead to talk about another aspect of the question. I am going to tell you certain things which many of you have probably already guessed but which no one has been able to mention because of the lack of precise information and proof. Let me tell you about how the Great Project is being run technically and financially. This entire sphere is one big muddle of flagrant blunders, unparalleled dishonesty, unprecedented thievery and embezzlement. I can prove what I am saying; for several years now, beginning when I was still a university student, I have been studying the subject. Not only do I have at my disposal all the printed reports and materials available to the specialists, I have also made use of personal contacts with engineers and especially with officials at Central Project Administration to obtain access to documents deep within the archives, sheltered from prying eyes. In addition I have had an opportunity to observe and learn a great deal on the spot during trips I have made in connection with organizational work for our common cause. When I had collected and compared all these materials, uncovered all the contradictory figures, and summarized the data, the picture which emerged was monstrous and overwhelming.

"I found that the plans of our great engineer had been distorted and perverted by the new leaders of the Project, partly due to their own mediocrity, but mostly because of their selfish dishonesty. Do you know why construction in the Rotten Bogs took four years instead of the proposed two? First of all, no use was made of special machines which had been invented, tested, and approved by Menni and Maro. Secondly, the course of the canal was deflected to run along the edge of the bogs, ostensibly to avoid a stretch of rocky subsoil, which, as I have confirmed with my own eyes, does not exist. Who needed all this and why? What happened was that workers were dying by the thousands, but over half the dead continued to be entered in the lists as able-bodied or ill for up to a year and a half. Thus their wages continued to be paid, but to whom? The contractors and engineers would know the details about that. And then there were the pensions to the families of the dead. Although special care had been taken to recruit bachelors and men without families to these sites, it turns out that all those who died had 'dependents.' So for many years now these pensions have been paid to at least twenty thousand nonexistent families.

"You have all noticed, of course, that large numbers of workers are very often transferred from one construction site to another without any apparent reason. There is a reason, however, a very simple one. The books are kept in such a manner that to the end of a given fiscal year the transferred workers are registered at their former place of employment, but are also entered at the new one. Thus a double wage is allocated for them, but as you well know, they never receive it. By this and other means official labor costs are higher than in Menni's time, even though the number of workers has remained more or less constant and wages have decreased by a third.

"You remember the accident on the Ganges Canal, when a sudden explosion occurred as dynamite charges were being laid, killing over two thousand men. The official investigation blamed the incident on negligence and carelessness, three engineers were dismissed, and one explosives expert who happened to survive was thrown into prison. What you do not know is that all three of these engineers immediately became rich, and that their answers during the preliminary inquiry were not included in the printed report of the investigation. They said that it was impossible to foresee the explosion, which occurred spontaneously due to defective dynamite. The explosive used there was the most powerful and most expensive type, and it is supposed to be manufactured from absolutely pure chemical components. If ingredients that are not wholly pure are used instead, however, production costs can be reduced by two thirds without affecting the explosive power of the dynamite, but there is the danger that it will explode on its own. It goes without saying that the Dynamite and Powder Trust has all this time been charging the state for the superior product. In other words, its price is three times what it should be, and the lives of the workers, of course, are immaterial. Several minor accidents occurred unnoticed, but the disaster on the Ganges posed a threat to the Trust's profits. Since the Great Project requires enormous amounts of dynamite, this profit amounts to hundreds of millions per year. Thus it is not surprising that they should be willing to spend ten million or so to silence the investigators and the accused."

At this point one of the delegates interrupted the speaker: "Can you prove all this?"

"Yes, I can," replied Netti. "My brother workers procured samples of the dynamite, and I have analyzed it. Through engineer friends employed at the largest explosives factory I learned exactly how it is manufactured. I was able to trick bank employees into revealing to me when the three engineers deposited their millions. What is more, I can prove that twelve years ago ninety percent of the stocks in the Dynamite and Powder Trust were bought by Feli Rao, the chairman of Central Project Administration. I could go on proving this and much more to you for some time.

"Let me give you the results of my calculations. During the past twelve years the budget of the Great Project has run to a little more than fifty billion. Of this sum, between sixteen and eighteen billion have been stolen or embezzled. Feli Rao alone, whose fortune twelve years ago was reckoned at 'only' fifty million, is 'worth' three and a half billion today. The Project itself has been terribly delayed. Nectar and Ambrosia should have been completed several yars ago, but in fact they will not be ready for another year and a half or two years. The situation is the same for the other canals. The Great Cause has been sabotaged by these marauders. They have sacrificed both it and the blood of the workers to their own boundless greed.

"The first conclusion to be drawn from all this seems obvious: include in your demands a stop to the thievery, the trial of the criminals, and the confiscation of everything they have stolen. At the same time that you issue your manifesto I will publish my book of disclosures, which will be buttressed by exact data and documents. On this point we can expect the support of broad segments of the bourgeoisie who have suffered at the hands of the syndicates and hate them and their billionaire swindlers. True, the struggle is going to be even more bitter than it is now, and our enemies are going to attack us with all the legal and illegal weapons at their disposal, but they will not make us back down. Do you agree with my first conclusion?"

"Yes! Yes! Of course!" resounded from all sides.

"Now let us review our demands and see what we have. We want the same wages, the same working day, and the same order and routines at the construction sites as we had before the first strike, that is, *during Menni's time*. We want to put an end to the stealing, the embezzlements, the incompetent technical supervision that risks the lives and health of the workers—in other words, all the things that have arisen *since* Menni. Need I tell you the second conclusion that follows from these facts? We must demand that *Menni be reinstated*."

A murmur of disapproval rose from the audience, mixed with exclamations: "Never!" "What's he saying!" "Impossible!" "He's laughing at us!"
"So that's what he was getting at!" The excitement increased, and several
of the delegates even jumped up from their seats. "Let him finish!"
shouted Arri. Netti stood motionless and waited while the chairman
called for silence. Gradually order was restored, though the atmosphere
remained one of bewilderment and suspicion. Netti continued:

"Brothers, it is no news to me that you hate Menni. But our feelings
are not important. What is important is the struggle and the victory. So let
us judge objectively. What do you have against Menni's return?"

There was a new outburst of stormy exclamations: "He is the enemy
of the unions!" "He murdered our brothers!" "You mean you don't know
that he was to blame for the strike and the bloodshed?" Netti made a sign
that he wished to go on. There was another uneasy silence.

"All right, you have said what you think, now hear me out and don't
interrupt me until I have finished. After all, the final decision is yours, not
mine. Let us look at the charges. Number one: Menni is the enemy of the
unions. Absolutely correct. But what of the present Project Administration? I suppose that it is not the enemy of the unions? Or that whoever
replaces today's leaders will be the friend of the unions? We are not
children who can be fooled into hoping for anything like that. We cannot
change this as long as the present order exists, as long as there is exploitation, as long as one class fears and rules over another. But there are
enemies and there are enemies. Menni did not recognize the unions and
refused to negotiate with them, but did he persecute them? Were workers dismissed for belonging to a union? Was our Federation forced to
operate underground? His outlook differed from ours, but he acted honestly and overtly, his enmity was ideological and based on principle. The
present directors sometimes tell you: 'Let the union send its delegates,
and we will discuss your demands with them.' And then what happens to
these delegates? Do you prefer the unions to be treated like this? No,
brothers, we seldom have the opportunity to choose our enemies, but
when it is possible we must learn to distinguish between them."

"That's not the point," a young worker interrupted. "What about the
blood of our brothers?"

"Indeed, that is the main point. And now I must tell you something
that you do not know. You have been deceived from the very beginning,
and your enemies have been concealing the truth from you all along. You
could not find it out on your own, and you had much more serious things
on your minds during those difficult years. The truth is this: Menni is
innocent, both of the deaths of those who succumbed to fever on the canal
and of the deaths of the men who were killed during the strike."

"Well then, who was it who sent the workers to the Rotten Bogs?"

"Brothers, it was not Menni who did that, but necessity. You were

taken in by the deceitful, traitorous brochure whose anonymous author—
Maro—knew he was lying to you and why he was lying to you. It was
impossible to chart any other course for the Ambrosia Canal, and I can tell
you why.

"You are probably all aware of the fact that our planet is a sphere
consisting of a fiery, molten mass covered with a crust that has cooled and
hardened. This crust is not as stationary or as solid as it appears to the
eye. It is made up of huge, tightly interlocking blocks or sheets rather in
the form of a giant mosaic. We do not yet know the laws governing the
movement within the molten ocean at the core of the planet, but such
movement takes place continuously—probably due to the gradual cooling
and contraction of this liquid mass—and, with imperceptible slowness
over the course of millennia, it raises the crust in certain spots and lowers
it in others. These movements, however, are not always quiet or even.
Sometimes they cause terrible, destructive shocks to the crust that can
either give birth to or eradicate whole canyons, mountains, lakes, or
islands, and this poses a serious and inescapable threat to all life in the
area.

"The cooling of the interior of our planet has proceeded quite far, so
that these phenomena occur only rarely, but they are all the more violent
when they do happen. It is obvious that the centers of such catastrophes,
the places where they are bound to be most destructive, lie along the
seams of the giant planetary mosaic. And it just so happens that the valley
through which the Ambrosia Canal supposedly could have been built lies
on one of these lines. The valley was in fact at one time formed as the
result of an earthquake of which no memory has been retained, but as
recently as some three hundred years ago its appearance was radically
altered by new subterranean disturbances. Several hundred people—not
more, since the area was sparsely populated—were killed. There are
other examples of earthquakes which have destroyed entire cities and
killed tens and hundreds of thousands of people.

"Now imagine that the canal with its irrigation system were to be
built through this valley. Huge cities would grow up along it, and millions
of people would cultivate the fields and meadows made fertile by its
waters. Fifty, a hundred, two hundred years would pass—science is as yet
unable to predict these events—and everything would be smashed and
perhaps destroyed completely in the space of a few minutes. Can you
honestly say that a few thousand lives today are worth more than millions
tomorrow? No, you would never think that way, for you are champions of
your cause and consider it just and sensible to sacrifice thousands of lives
today in order that millions may be freer in the future. Menni, a man of
science, reasoned the same way as you men of labor.

"You were deceived, provoked to fight, and lured into the firing line.
By whom? A gang of scoundrels led by Feli Rao and Maro. Why? To bring

down an incorruptible man who was blocking their way to billions. And they succeeded.

"I am not speaking of fairness, although it is best to be fair even to one's enemies. I am speaking about success, about victory. What better way to shatter the ranks of our enemies than to confront them with this unexpected and menacing demand? Public opinion will be on our side; it began to swing back toward Menni a long time ago, and people are indignant over the fact that prison seems to be the best place that can be found for so great a man. This cowardly and hypocritical opinion now declares that Menni has already paid for his crime. We do not feel that way, for we can understand that he acted as a man of conviction and that it was not he who was the criminal, but the capitalist lackeys who condemned him.

"Remember one other point: if Menni returns he will restore all previous conditions. Without him, on the other hand, our opponents will haggle with us, agreeing to one thing and rejecting another, and it is possible that the rank and file will be mollified by partial concessions.

"Finally, doesn't the mission we have set out to accomplish, the Great Project itself, mean a great deal to us? After all, it is for the good of all mankind. This means that the mission should be entrusted to the man whose genius conceived it and who is more competent than anyone else to lead it.

"As for the points about which we disagree, we will be able to give Menni a fight when we are standing face to face with him. And then, brothers, we shall try to show ourselves worthy of such an opponent!"

No one took the floor for several minutes after Netti had finished. Surprised and stunned, the audience sank into gloomy thought. Taking stock of the situation, Arri rose to speak.

"I can vouch for what Netti has just told you. I hated Menni more than any of you, and at first I was eager to fight him. Soon, however, certain facts raised doubts within me. I began to suspect that something was amiss when Maro came to me in secret. Evidently counting on my naïveté, he pretended he wanted to dampen the conflict and tried to arouse me to agitate against Menni personally. Then the anonymous brochure urging a strike appeared out of nowhere and was spread by the thousands among the workers. I tried to convince our comrades to stop and investigate the matter, I tried to tell them that someone was using us, and our chairman here backed me up. Unfortunately, the strike broke out spontaneously before we had managed to convince anyone. We and the entire Council of the Federation were arrested in order to enrage our brothers even more. To prevent me from testifying at Menni's trial, they treacherously arranged for me to be killed 'attempting to escape' from prison. It was sheer luck that my wound did not prove fatal. After this I decided to do everything in my power to find out the truth. Friends brought books to me in prison, I studied the relevant subjects, and I finally understood clearly the deceit and treachery that had been committed, who had needed it, and why. But I only had conjectures; it was Netti who found the proof, and it took him a long time. When I was released from prison two years ago I threw all my energy into resurrecting our Federation. I kept what I knew to myself in order not to forewarn our enemies or hamper Netti in his research. But now everything is ready and the time has come to act."

After Arri the young delegate who had most often interrupted Netti took the floor.

"All right," he said in a nervous voice quivering with emotion. "Netti and Arri have convinced me, and I will vote for their plan. But just look, brothers, what a terrible situation we are in. Today we have heard a lot of things we never even suspected, and yet our fate, our lives, our freedom depends on them! The traitors told our brothers that there was no reason for Menni to send them to the bogs, and they *believed* them. Arri spent ten years in prison, studied geology, and tells us now that this was a lie. Of course, we *believe* him. They made us work an extra two years in those same bogs on account of some rocks or other, and we knew nothing. Netti explains that this was unnecessary, that the engineers were lying, and we *believe* Netti. They make us work with defective explosives that can blow us to bits at any moment, and not until now, after the death of thousands of people, do we find this out. Netti is an engineer, he has made analyses, we have every reason to *believe* him. But what is this anyway—believing, believing, believing! If Netti hadn't left the ranks of the workers to become an engineer, or if Arri hadn't suffered for ten years in prison, we might never have learned any of this. We would have made other decisions and foolishly wasted our resources. Isn't this slavery, the worst form of slavery? Netti, Arri, brothers: how do we escape from this? What must we do so that we ourselves can *know and see,* and not just constantly believe? Or is that impossible? Is it always going to be like it is now? And if it is impossible, then what is the use of living and struggling if we are to remain slaves?"

Netti answered him:

"Brother, you have touched a sore spot. Thus far science is the weapon of our enemies. We will triumph when we have made it our weapon. Here before us is a great and difficult task. We will, of course, fight for and win the leisure time to study. We will gain knowledge wherever possible. But this is not enough. Scraps and crumbs of knowledge are not what is needed to arrive at an intelligent solution to the most important and complicated problems of life.

"Some of us will succeed as I have succeeded in approaching this alien science and properly learning some branch of it. Even this is very little. Nothing has been conquered for the proletariat until it has been won for everyone. And modern science is such that even the chosen few who have gained access to it master only a small part of it, a single specialty. There simply isn't time and energy for more. But no specialty can provide a grasp of man's labor as a whole.

"I have studied several disciplines; I have been able to do so because I happen to be more gifted than many other people. As I studied I came to the following conclusion. Modern science is just like the society that has created it: powerful but splintered, and extravagant with its resources. Because of this fragmentation the individual branches of science have developed separately and lost all vital connection with each other. This has given rise to all manner of deformities, sterile artificialities, and confusion. The same phenomena and notions have dozens of different names in the various disciplines and are studied in each branch as though they were something novel. Each branch has its special language which is the privilege of the initiated and serves to exclude everyone else. Many difficulties derive from the fact that science has become divorced from life and labor, forgotten its origin and lost sight of its purpose. For this reason it busies itself with pseudoproblems and often beats about the bush trying to answer simple questions.

"I have noticed all this, and my opinion of contemporary science is as follows. Such as it is today it is worthless to the working class, both because it is too difficult and because it is inadequate. The proletariat must master it by changing it. In the hands of the workers it must become much simpler, more harmonious and vital. Its fragmentation must be overcome, it must be brought closer to the labor that is its primary source. This is an enormous task. I have begun it, others will find the methods and means to continue it. As always, the first steps will be taken in isolation, but eventually men will join forces. The mission cannot be accomplished in a single generation, but each step on the way will contribute to liberation.

"The necessary task has been set. It is going to demand countless trials and strenuous exertion. The road to its fulfillment will be lined with setbacks and failures. But such is our struggle. Ours is a difficult battle and cannot be otherwise, because our ideals are lofty. But if it were easy, brothers, would it even be worth talking about?"

2. The Return

In prison Menni was afforded the possibility not only of pursuing scientific studies, which was permitted all prisoners, but also of following the course of current events. His enemies probably had a certain ulterior motive in this generosity; by letting him witness the destruction of the organization he had created, the dismissal of his best assistants and the treachery of others, they hoped to intensify his moral anguish so as to enable them to break his will once and for all. For the first few years Feli Rao still hoped to subdue him and win him over as an ally. On several occasions he communicated to him secretly through the warden that he could be granted a full pardon if he accepted the conditions mentioned by Maro in their last conversation. Menni did not respond to these proposals. He continued the whole while to work on his plan of the Project, keeping abreast of all the latest research. At the same time he managed to make a number of important inventions that were subsequently applied in the construction of the canals.

Feli Rao was uneasy. For various reasons public opinion kept turning its attention to the fate of Menni, and each time it did so, sympathy with him grew more persistent. Harsh speeches were delivered in Parliament, and the government and its loyal deputies found it increasingly difficult to maintain its previous position. Rao decided that he had to rid himself of his dangerous opponent at any price. As long as Menni was in prison, however, this was impossible. The Central House of Detention was so perfectly guarded that a murder attempt would require the participation of a great many bribed accomplices and was bound to be discovered. In the tenth year of his sentence Menni was officially offered a pardon by the President of the Republic. Menni declined, as he had the legal right to do, little knowing that this saved his life. Public opinion, however, was unpleasantly surprised at Menni's implacability, so that his refusal was at least a partial victory for Feli Rao.

But suddenly the storm broke. The manifesto of the Project Federation, declarations of solidarity by a number of other unions, and Netti's book, *The Great Project and the Great Crime,* were all published simultaneously. The workers gave the government and Parliament a month in which to answer, threatening to call a general strike. Netti's book was read at once by millions. His disclosures were amply confirmed, and new muckrakers appeared immediately. Demonstrations were held in the capital and other large cities. The ministry fell, and even the President of the Republic was forced to resign. Since the new government could not hope for a majority, it immediately dissolved Parliament and set new elections. It declared to the workers that it agreed in all essential respects with their demands, and organized an investigation of the crimes that had been disclosed. A great many dishonest financial and parliamentary leaders were brought to trial. The Minister of Justice even ordered the arrest of Feli Rao, but Feli would not surrender: realizing that all was lost, he put a bullet in his brain.

Menni was again offered a pardon, but once again he declined. The government did not know what to do with him, and was obliged to wait until Parliament had convened. By that time, the investigation had already uncovered huge quantities of materials, including many of the facts relating to what had gone on behind the scenes at Menni's trial. Finally the elections were over and the deputies assembled. The former minister who had supported Menni was elected President of the Republic. The government conferred with the leaders of his party and drew up new proposals to be presented to Menni.

Menni expressed no surprise whatever when the President of the Republic, the Prime Minister, and the Minister of Justice suddenly walked into his cell. He merely offered them his single chair with a touch of ironic hospitality and went himself to lean against the wall near the window. The President informed him officially that in view of newly discovered facts, the government intended to propose that the Supreme Tribunal review his case. Until the new verdict, Menni could be preliminarily released and rehabilitated. The government would like to know in advance whether he would be satisfied by such an arrangement and whether on these conditions he would agree to accept immediately the discharge of his former duties.

"On these conditions, no," replied Menni. "I will not accept preliminary release. If my case is reopened I will not participate in the trial, but will confine myself to the declaration that I consider the verdict of this court morally immaterial."

"But why?" exclaimed the Minister of Justice. "Why in heaven's name do you insist on rejecting the honorable solutions being offered you? If this is a protest against injustice, it is your personal protest, but you yourself are doing an injustice to all of mankind! The workers demand and the general public desires your return. The cause needs you, and you reject everything! What is it you want?"

Menni smiled and said:

"You have not quite understood me. I refuse to accept judgment by the Supreme Tribunal because I consider its first verdict unjust. Consequently, from my point of view, all a second verdict proves is that the judges are willing to work the will of the government, which fact I have no reason to doubt. I want my case to be reviewed by another, a higher court—the Court of Humanity. If that appeal is to remain in full inviolable force, I must refuse to make any compromise whatever and decline any open or disguised pardon. That is why I shall remain here to the end of my term. But I am not refusing to work. I have been following the Project all these years, and I can lead it regardless of where I am, much as you ministers do most of your governing from your offices. I know that this will involve inconveniences and difficulties, but if you want me to take charge of the matter you will have to reconcile yourselves to them."

"Do you have any idea how uncomfortable the position of the government will be all this time?" said the Prime Minister bitterly.

"Well, now, for over twelve years I have also been in a somewhat uncomfortable position," retorted Menni.

"We give up!" said the President.

3. Father!

The newspapers were dismayed for a while by Menni's refusal to accept a review of his case, but public opinion finally calmed down, deciding that he was evidently an eccentric, which as a great man he had a right to be. Several scholarly articles were written on the kinship between genius and madness. These were read and quoted a great deal, and society came to the conclusion that it had done all it could and had no reason to reproach itself. The "great man" looked upon all this with great indifference and threw all his energy into reorganizing the Great Project.

From among his former assistants he selected ten experienced and reliable people whom he dispatched as inspectors to the construction sites. They were empowered to dismiss dishonest officials of any rank, terminate disadvantageous contracts, discuss the workers' demands, and restore former labor conditions and work routines. Each inspector was instructed to pick his own assistants and take them with him, so that when necessary he could appoint them to fill the places of dismissed high-ranking executives. The inspectors plunged enthusiastically into their task and proved both incorruptible and merciless. The newspapers of the "liberals"—formerly Feli Rao's party—dubbed them "Duke Menni's Butchers."

The inspection and reform of the Central Project Administration was a particularly vital but also very difficult task. Menni had at first intended to take charge of it personally, but it soon became evident that being in prison presented considerable obstacles. The matter was of the utmost urgency, however, so Menni wrote a letter requesting the author of the exposé to come and see him. When Netti appeared, Menni invited him to be seated and asked him point-blank:

"Are you a socialist?"

"Yes," replied Netti.

Menni looked at him attentively; he was favorably impressed by the young man's clear, radiant eyes, candid face, high, intelligent forehead, and strong and well-proportioned figure. Menni shrugged his shoulders and, as he had taken to doing since coming to prison, murmured to himself:

"On the other hand the great Xarma was also a socialist."

He noticed his own involuntary bluntness, laughed, and said out loud:

"Actually, that is none of my business. If possible, I would like to know how you collected the proof for your exposures."

Netti briefly told him about the various connections he had exploited and the devices, some of them risky and not altogether legal, that he had employed to gain access to the documents; he also mentioned the cooperation of the workers and their organizations. Menni listened with interest and questioned him on details. Several times Netti happened to touch on important technical problems, and Menni was amazed at the enormous professional competence of his young visitor. He was especially impressed by Netti's profound and lucid understanding of the main ideas in all the basic plans of the Project system. Gradually their conversation shifted entirely to this topic.

Netti boldly proposed a number of radical changes in the previously published plans. Menni had to admit that he had already introduced certain of these changes into his latest revision and that the others at least merited consideration. Menni's eyes shone; it was difficult for him to conceal his pleasure at finding more than he had expected.

"I suppose that you have other materials besides those which you included in your book?"

"Yes," answered Netti, "I have a great deal more—everything which seemed suspicious and probable but could not be proved conclusively. If you wish I will put all these materials at your disposal."

"Very well," said Menni. "Now, would you be interested in taking charge of the inspection of the Central Project Administration under my immediate supervision?"

Thus began Netti's administrative career.

It was a colossal task. Twelve years of activity had to be investigated, hundreds of witnesses had to be questioned, and the suspects were both experienced and crafty. The job was made considerably easier, however, by the enthusiastic support of the lower-level employees. Netti's unswerving opposition to all attempts by the bosses to make scapegoats out of them quickly gained him their confidence. Thanks to these allies the business proceeded fairly rapidly. From time to time Netti would visit Menni and give him a report. They would hold a short conference in a large prison cell furnished with several chairs and shelves filled with books and papers. The two men understood each other intuitively, and in the space of a few minutes they had done their summing up and made the crucial decisions.

On one occasion Netti presented a detailed report on the "labor policy" of the Central Administration. Besides the means by which wages were embezzled, it described certain secret circulars addressed to local supervisors instructing them to offset the growing power of the unions by "tightening discipline so as to provoke the workers into overt action that would legally justify forceful countermeasures."

As Netti spoke his profound repressed indignation changed him entirely: his voice became muffled, the expression on his face became severe, his eyes darkened, and a deep crease appeared between his brows. An outside observer would have been struck by his resemblance to

Menni. When Netti had finished, Menni, who had been pacing from corner to corner, suddenly said:

"Strange! You remind me very much of someone. But who? Perhaps I have met your parents?"

"I don't think so . . . Anyway, I have never known my father personally, and no one has even wanted to tell me who he was. He was a rich man in a high position. He abandoned my mother, not even suspecting that I existed. She is a simple working woman from Libya. Her name is Nella."

"Nella!"

The name escaped Menni's lips like a moan. He blanched and leaned against the wall. Netti quickly asked him:

"Do you know her?"

"I am your father, Netti!"

"My father?"

There was only cold amazement in the word. The face of the young man became grim. Menni clutched at his chest. For a moment they were silent.

"Father . . ."

This time his voice betrayed a certain pensiveness, an effort to understand something. Netti's expression became softer and calmer.

"I don't know what to think of this. I shall ask my mother," he said slowly.

"I don't know what Nella will tell you, but I can tell you this much. When we parted she did not utter a single word of reproach. And when I was sentenced there was only one voice that protested, and that was her voice, Netti."

Netti's gaze cleared at once.

"That is true. I was there."

The young man sank into thought for another minute. Then he raised his head and took a step toward Menni.

"I know what Mama will say."

He offered Menni his hand, and now there was reserved affection in his voice as he repeated the word:

"Father!"

PART III

1. Two Kinds of Logic

The discovery of their kinship did not result in any externally observable intimacy between the two engineers. Menni was reticent by nature, and his long isolation had increased his outward coldness. Netti was reserved with him out of caution. In the presence of outsiders with whom they had occasion to work they maintained their former relationship of superior and subordinate. The new element of mutual interest and solicitude that had arisen between them was evident to them alone. Their conversations became longer, although they were just as businesslike as before. For a long time both men endeavored to avoid topics on which they sensed they had radically different views.

Their work progressed well. The reform of the Central Administration, now once again simply a bureau for the collection and further dissemination of information, had already come so far that Netti's services were no longer needed. More important, the task had ceased to represent any challenge to his knowledge and talents. Menni wanted him to begin working as the special agent of the Chief Inspector, in which capacity he would be in charge of on-the-spot checks at the various work sites, but there were a number of points that had to be negotiated first. They had no trouble coming to an agreement on technical and even administrative and financial questions, but labor conditions proved to be an entirely different matter.

"I assume," said Menni, "that you will want to introduce a number of improvements. I have no objections on principle and will probably agree to many of them, since experience has shown that both the vigor and the quality of labor are enhanced to a certain extent by better wages and a shorter working day. There is one preliminary condition I insist my representative accept, however: that he not be involved in official negotiations on such subjects with the labor unions."

"I cannot agree to that," Netti answered calmly.

Menni frowned.

"I do not quite understand you. You sympathize with the unions, and that is your self-evident right. One of their goals is to improve labor conditions, and now you would be in a position to help them a great deal. However, you hold an official post and are bound by certain instructions. You do not have to have the unions to tell you what the workers want and need. There is no reason why you yourself or anyone else should reproach you for avoiding violations of discipline in pursuing your goal. After all, we have no formal obligations whatsoever toward the unions."

"'Obligation' is an entirely inappropriate word where convictions are concerned," said Netti. "I am a socialist and a follower of Xarma. In his opinion, and mine, the workers' organizations are the only true representatives of the working class. I not only sympathize with them, I belong to them, and to disavow them, even for the sake of 'discipline,' is quite unthinkable."

"What you are saying seems strange to me. In all of our professional discussions I have become accustomed to your perfect, precise, stringent logic. Now it somehow appears to have failed you. You recognize the unions as the legitimate and even exclusive representatives of the workers. But it is patently obvious that this is not so. Looking at it concretely, the unions have only a minority—not the majority—of workers. And it is not the unions but rather the individual workers who formally conclude labor contracts. So why should the unions be granted the privilege of representing the workers? That would be like giving the vote to a minority in a country but making everyone bear full civic duties. Do you mean to say that you would recognize such a minority as the only legitimate representative of the people? Aren't you socialists democrats?"

"I could agree with you if the working class, like the modern state as reflected in its laws, were an adventitious, heterogeneous conglomerate of people who have nothing to do with each other. But the proletariat is not at all like that. What is the essence and basis of the worker's life? It is his labor, is it not? And does he in his labor exist separately, by himself? Not in the least. Removed from the great collective of millions of working people and from the chain of generations he immediately becomes a nonentity. The very purpose of his labor and his manpower also disappear. The goals which man is now pursuing presuppose cooperation on a gigantic scale. Building a railroad, a canal, a machine, manufacturing great quantities of yarn or cloth, or mining mountains of coal—what would be the sense in all this if everything were only a matter of the individual worker in isolation from all the others with whom he accomplishes such colossal tasks, in isolation from all those for whom they are accomplished? And what is his manpower worth without the tools, technical knowledge, and vital resources which support it? The tools are made by the hands of other workers; this is labor they have performed in the past which now enters into and increases enormously the might of the living stream of labor of the present. Knowledge has been accumulated by the lives of preceding generations; it is their labor experience which has now become a fundamental and necessary tool of any work. Food, clothes, and housing are created for the worker by others like him whom he does not even know. Take all this away and what is left of him? As a worker he exists and is real only when he is united in labor with countless human individuals of present and past generations."

"Very well. The division of labor and the exchange of services are real and important things. But, as facts show, they are quite possible without any workers' organizations. What logic has led you to your conclusion?"

"The logic of distinguishing the conscious from the unconscious. Do you think that the name 'man' in the true sense of the word should be given to a being who is unaware of himself, his relationship to others, and his place in nature? It is of no consequence that he looks like a man, for he still does not belong to humanity. Similarly, a worker who is unaware of his own essence as a worker, that is, who is not conscious of his indissoluble bond with those like him or of his place in the system of labor and in society is to my way of thinking not really a worker. If he understands or at least senses all this, then he will inevitably unite with other workers. If, on the other hand, he can and prefers to exist only for himself and live what he erroneously imagines to be a separate and independent life, then as an unconscious being he is not a member or a representative of his class, even if he and the likes of him constitute the overwhelming majority of workers."

"Isn't this mere sophistry? The worker is united with others in labor. Fine. But it so happens that the workers' organizations have nothing to do with that unity, which arises quite apart from them. The trade unions are mainly involved instead with terms of employment and lately also with politics. With regard to the labor contract and in his role of citizen, however, the worker is his own agent: he collects his wages for himself personally, and he votes according to his personal convictions. Where is the logical connection between the unity of labor and the significance which you attribute to the unions?"

"The connection is in the logic of life and in the logic of the consciousness that aspires to transform life into a harmonious whole. The unity of labor that is given to the workers from without and arranged for them by others is only a mechanical, unconscious unity, rather like that which joins together the parts of a complex machine. The discs and screws of a machine are not taken into account but merely counted. And such is the attitude of the ruling classes toward the worker; they are prepared to treat him fairly and according to the law as long as he lives for himself, because then he is powerless. A man's strength depends on how consistent and faithful he is to himself and on the correspondence that exists between the various spheres of his life—his labor, his thoughts, his relationship to others.

"If a worker stands united with his fellows in his labor but is divorced from them in his relationship to his employers, in his attitudes, or in his life-style generally, then he is not guided by any single principle, he is not conscious of reality. For he is quite mistaken in thinking that he is dealing with his employer only for himself or that he can make his own choice in politics. The labor conditions which he is offered and which he must accept depend entirely on such factors as the number of other workers competing with him, the standard to which they have become accustomed, their intelligence, and the vigor with which they struggle to protect their interests. The individual in isolation cannot understand politics, where the clash of collective forces gives rise to enormously complex relations. The worker who tries to do so apart from his fellows becomes the plaything of the agitation of the moment, of false promises, and of motives which are petty and often hostile to his own interests. He is not a conscious being, but simply material to be molded, a tool in the hands of others."

"Nevertheless, it does not at all follow from this that the trade-union minority should be the legitimate representative of the nonunion majority!"

"I have not said that. The conscious minority is the representative not of the unconscious majority, but of the *whole;* it is the representative of the class. Analogously, man in general is not the representative of the *other* organisms on our planet, but he is in full measure the representative of *life* here, because it is in him that this life has achieved self-consciousness."

"Applied to my own case," Menni said sarcastically, "your argument leads to a melancholy conclusion indeed. I would doubtless not have been able to accomplish anything without the millions of workers who turn my plans into reality. But I do not have the slightest desire to unite with them; on the contrary, I am more inclined to regard myself in opposition to them. Consequently, I must be the most unconscious being imaginable. How very flattering!"

Netti laughed.

"You have a *different* consciousness, which in its own way is very highly developed. It is the consciousness of the class which preceded the proletariat, which paved the way for it and continues with its own, admittedly not very gentle, methods to educate the workers. That class forged ahead through the struggle between man and man, through the war of all against all; it could not do otherwise, for its historical mission was to create a human *individual,* an active being inspired with self-confidence who would be distinct from the human herd of the feudal epoch. This mission has been accomplished, however, and now it is a different task that falls to the working class. What must be done now is to gather these active atoms, bind them together with a higher bond, introduce harmony and order into their uncoordinated collaboration, fuse them into a single intelligent human organism. This is the meaning of the new consciousness whose embryo is to be found in the workers' organizations."

"Be careful now, your argument borders on dangerous metaphysics. For you these classes and this future humanity have already become living beings with a special, fantastic life. . ."

"Why fantastic? It is real—much broader and more complex than the simple sum of individual lives of the chaos of isolated consciousness. Moreover, the notion of a living being changes from epoch to epoch. If our forefathers, even the most learned among them, had said a few hundred years ago that man is a colony of one to two hundred trillion invisibly small living beings, would it not have sounded like the strangest metaphysics?"

"So evidently you want to transform human individuals into beings which resemble cells?"

"No, that is not what we want. The cells of an organism are not conscious of the whole to which they belong. For that reason they instead resemble the present-day type of individual. We, on the other hand, are striving to make man fully aware of himself as an element of the great laboring whole."

Menni rose and paced the room in silence for a few moments. He stopped and said:

"Obviously this discussion is getting us nowhere. What should we do? Would you agree to share your authority with someone else in such a way that you would be responsible for the technical inspection and he would take charge of the administrative?"

He glanced somewhat uneasily at Netti.

"Very gladly," came the answer. "That would be the best solution."

"Thank you," said Menni. "I was afraid you would refuse."

"You had no reason to be," replied Netti. "Having administrative authority would put me in a difficult and delicate position. To be the official representative of one side and yet have all one's sympathies and interests with the other side would result in such divided loyalties that the proper balance would prove extremely difficult and perhaps even impossible to maintain. If one is to be true to oneself and preserve the lucid wholeness of one's consciousness, such contradictory roles must be avoided."

Menni paused to think for a moment, and after a brief silence remarked:

"You are consistent in your peculiar logic—I will grant you that much."

2. Arri

Upon returning home Netti reported as usual the entire conversation to Nella. Arri happened to be there at the time. When Netti left for a few moments to attend to something, Arri and Nella exchanged sober glances.

"What he says is very important," said Arri. "And of course it is only the beginning; there is more to come. We should think about it and talk it over."

"Yes," answered Nella. "Come to see me tomorrow morning. He won't be here then."

The following day Arri arrived tired and gloomy. It was as if he had aged during the night, but his eyes shone with a strange luster.

"I have been thinking a great deal, Nella. My thoughts have not been happy ones, but I am absolutely sure about the conclusion to which they have led me. Menni and Netti are natural enemies. Right now they are glad to avoid a struggle, but this will not last long. No matter how they try, life will bring them into conflict, violent conflict. They love and respect each other very much, but that will only make their clash the more painful. The first major strike on the Project and it will be impossible for them to remain at peace with each other. If it's not a strike, then it will be something else. Hostile forces are already gathering around them and will force them into a struggle which they do not want. I can see that it is painful for you to hear all of this, but it is the truth, Nella!"

"It is the truth," she said softly. "I was thinking the same thing myself."

"But how will it end, Nella? All the forces of the past, both the best and the worst, will rally around Menni, and the newborn forces of the future will close ranks around Netti. The old eagle will prove stronger than our young falcon and keep him from spreading his wings. Even if Netti does not perish in this struggle, his life and vigor will be sapped and our great cause will suffer an enormous loss. We must prevent this from happening, Nella!"

"But how? Is it even possible?" she asked. "I have been searching and searching, but I have not yet found a way."

"There is only one solution, Nella: Menni must withdraw, leave the field. He must be forced to step aside. That seems inconceivable, but there is only one way to do it: he must experience . . ."

He stopped short and hung his head, as if to brace himself. Troubled, Nella quickly walked over to him and took his hands in hers.

"What is it? Tell me! Don't you have the courage? It must be something very difficult. Tell me, for heaven's sake!"

"Yes, Nella, it is difficult. But listen to me carefully. I think that there is a force that can conquer Menni, deflect him from his path. That force is love. And there is a person who can evoke the force—you, Nella!"

She released his hands and took a step backward.

"What are you saying, Arri!"

"I have thought out very carefully what I am telling you, and you can believe me, Nella. You know that my feelings toward you have never been merely fraternal. Only the deep conviction that there is no other way is forcing me to suggest to you what I regard as the last possibility. You are still beautiful, Nella; time seems to be powerless against you. You still have your marvelous voice—that voice that no heart can resist.

Menni will be stunned when he sees you. To him you are the poetry of the past; more, you are Netti's mother and the person who inspired him in the struggle that gave Menni back his work and power. Menni is a man who did not know real love in his youth and who has spent many years in solitude. When he falls in love, it will prove stronger than he is."

Arri's voice was muffled and cracked. Nella sat down, bowed her head and hid her face in her hands.

"I don't know whether that is possible, but it is humiliating, Arri!"

"You are a mother. For a mother anything is possible and nothing is humiliating."

She raised her head.

"I do not really think so. And . . . we must wait, Arri. I have a feeling that something unexpected is going to happen."

At this very moment, Menni, alone, was pacing from corner to corner in his cell. Netti was about to leave on an inspection tour, and Menni was waiting for his son to come and get his final instructions. Menni was strangely agitated, and without noticing it himself, he began thinking aloud.

" . . . I won't be seeing him for several months . . . I've become quite attached to him . . . I have a pain in my heart . . . Childish sentimentality! I am going to miss him, it will be darker here . . . He has radiant eyes . . . Nella's eyes."

He stopped and sank into thought.

There were footsteps in the corridor and a knock on the door. Netti entered, and they began discussing business. When they had settled everything and Netti was getting ready to leave, Menni hesitated for a second and then stopped him.

"I wanted to ask you about something else. Do you have a picture of Nella?"

"Yes. As I matter of fact I have it on me. I took it because I am leaving this evening. Here it is."

Menni looked with amazement at the picture.

"Is this the latest one?" he asked.

"Yes, it was taken quite recently."

Netti thought for a moment and added: "You can keep it, if you like. I have another one."

3. Deeper and Deeper

Netti's trip turned out to be longer than expected. He left in early autumn and returned in spring, and was thus gone about a year, measured in our time. The mistakes and confusion that the dishonest administrators had allowed to creep into the technical organization of the Project proved more difficult to correct than the new leaders had imagined. Although throughout his trip Netti had sent brief, precise reports on his findings at the construction sites and the measures he had taken to rectify the situation, upon returning he was required to render a detailed oral report that took several days to discuss. These long conversations often digressed from purely factual matters to become exchanges of thoughts, opinions, and plans for the distant future. As often happens with persons who share a true inner kinship, the period of separation seemed to have brought father and son closer together and weakened their mutual reserve.

As a representative of Project Administration, toward the end of his trip Netti had attended the ceremonial opening of the newly completed Ambrosia Canal. The young engineer's impressions of the event were still fresh in his mind when he told Menni about it.

"I wish I were a poet so that I could do justice to all I experienced on that day. I stood together with the other engineers at the crest of the arched bridge that crosses the canal at the locks. On one side the steely mirror of the Mare Australe stretched into eternity, while below on the other side the gigantic excavated bed of the still unborn river ran off across a plain in a dark, broad band that narrowed as it approached the distant horizon. Hundreds of thousands of excited spectators dressed in their holiday best billowed in waves along the embankments. Farther on, the canal was lined on either side with the beautiful buildings and gardens of a city that did not exist fifteen years ago. Even farther off could be seen a forest of masts of ships that were anchored in two basins to protect them from the flood of water that would soon rush along the bed of the canal. The golden rays of the sun in the crystal-clear air mingled with a mood of joyous expectation, fusing everything together under an invisible blanket of delicate gossamer. For a moment it seemed as though this fabric would be rent asunder as a detachment of troops, their weapons flashing coldly and jangling harshly, cut through the brightly colored crowd. Dark, blood-stained memories flooded over everyone, threatening to drown the beauty of the moment. This time, however, the gray snake-like column was harmless, and the oppressive specters of the past dissolved into a fog and evaporated under the warm rays of the present.

"A signal shot was fired, and my hand gripped the lever of the electrically operated sluice gates. It seemed to me that everything had come to a complete standstill, but of course that was merely an illusion. The quiet surface of the sea was suddenly creased by a ravine whose walls plunged steeper and steeper as it approached the bridge. All sounds were immediately drowned in the deafening roar of the waterfall. Then the noise diminished somewhat, and the ecstatic shouts of thousands of people could be heard above it. Swirling and foaming, the turbid wall of water rushed northward at a terrifying speed along the bed of the canal. The great event had come to pass: the dawn of a new life was breaking. What a triumph for the united efforts of all mankind, for all-conquering labor!"

"Strange!" Menni remarked thoughtfully. "Everything undergoes such a peculiar transformation in your mind. Where I find it self-evident to speak of the triumph of an *idea,* you see the triumph of *labor.*"

"But it's all the same thing," said Netti.

"I do not understand," Menni continued in the same musing tone, as if he were thinking aloud. "I think that I know what an idea is and what exertion and labor are. I am not speaking of the united labor of the masses, which for some reason eclipses all else in your mind but which for me is merely a mechanical force that can expediently be replaced by the work of machines. But even the intellectual labor of a conscious individual . . . I have always served an idea, and I have always been the master of my exertions. Exertion is merely a means, while the idea is the highest goal. The idea is more than people and everything belonging to them. The idea does not depend on them—on the contrary, people are subordinate to the idea. I am as certain of this truth as I am of my own personal experiences.

"Several times in my life I have mastered an idea and uncovered the truth. It cost me a great deal of strenuous work and an intense struggle with the secret . . . And at these moments everything I had gone through was immediately blotted out by the radiant brilliance of my discovery. It was even as though I myself had ceased to exist. From behind the veil pierced by my thought and will emerged something so great and necessary that not even the entire collective energy of all mankind could change it. How could anyone make this idea cease to be the truth? If mankind refuses to recognize it and follow it, does the idea become any less true for that? Even if humanity disappears, the truth will remain the truth. No, we must not deprecate the idea! Effort is required to find the path to it, and crude labor is often needed to translate its greatness into reality, but such *means* are far removed from its higher essence."

"I do not at all wish to deprecate ideas, but I do have a different understanding of their essence and relation to labor. You are right when you say that the idea is higher than the individual and that it does not belong to him and rules over him. But look here, you have not defined its supreme essence, and there, I think, is the crux of the problem."

"I do not quite understand what you want. The supreme essence of an idea consists in its logical nature. Surely that is obvious to anyone who lives a life of ideas? Or is this still not enough for you? Do you want something else, something greater?"

"No, it is not enough, because your answer is sophistic. To say that the essence of an idea is logical is the same as saying that an idea is something ideational, or in other words, that an idea is an idea. One is no wiser after such an answer than before it. In your research you would not be satisfied with so little. It is not much use to you to know that air is air and water is water; you demand that they be analyzed."

"I do not find your comparison very apt. But in any case, if we could analyze ideas physically and chemically as we analyze air or water, I would be the first to welcome the possibility. But isn't that a dream?"

"Not as much as you seem to think. An idea cannot be analyzed chemically, of course, but an analysis based on life is quite possible. Xarma began but did not live to finish the task, and he has therefore remained incomprehensible. I have continued his work."

"And have you been successful?"

"Yes, I think I have."

"Then let me hear your findings . . . if you hope to make me understand you. I am not trying to be sarcastic; I have simply become convinced that in certain things we tend to follow different systems of logic. I will not presume to decide beforehand which of us is right."

"Very well, but in that case we will have to abandon the field of logical abstractions and approach ideas as they are found in life itself. For example, our forefathers struggled a thousand years for the idea of freedom, which is undeniably one of the great ideas of humanity. When I began studying history and tried to fathom the soul of those distant generations it became clear to me where the idea of freedom had come from and how it had developed. Millions of people lived within boundaries that they came to feel were increasingly constrictive. Each step of the way their labor, their efforts, their aspirations to develop their potential, and the creative work born in their minds ran into obstacles and encountered such overwhelming opposition that all this was reduced to impotence. Then the whole process would begin all over again and meet with the same fate. In such a way a myriad of isolated and uncoordinated human efforts perished; there was suffering, but there was no idea. This suffering gave birth to new efforts that were just as ill-defined but more intense and even more numerous. Little by little they began to merge and move in the same direction. As they flowed together they formed an ever mightier torrent beating against the old obstacles. And this was the *idea* of freedom—a unity of human efforts in a living struggle. The word 'freedom' was discovered. It was no better or worse than other words, but it became the banner of concerted effort, much as bits of ordinary cloth served to express the unity of combat forces in the armies of earlier times. Take away the word 'freedom' and the stream of efforts remains, but the awareness of their common direction and unity disappears. Remove these efforts and nothing will remain of the idea.

"And so it is with all ideas. The more grandiose the stream of united efforts—that is, the grander and loftier the idea—the weaker and more insignificant the individual in comparison with it, and the more natural it is for him to serve it and subjugate himself to it. It does not matter that people were themselves unaware of why they were happy to struggle and even die for the idea of freedom, for their feelings were clearer and deeper than their thoughts. Man knows no greater happiness than to feel himself a vital part of a mighty, all-encompassing impulse. The idea of freedom was such a universally sensed impulse."

"In other words, if not for despotism, oppression, and arbitrariness, there would not have been any idea of freedom, because there would have been no unified efforts to overcome these obstacles?"

"Precisely. It would have lacked all vital meaning. What sort of an idea would that have been?"

"I am not going to argue with you; I am only trying to understand you better. The idea of freedom served as a battle cry in history, and it is possible that it arose from the masses. But is your conclusion relevant to other ideas which have not had such a function? It seems to me that it was your choice of example which brought you to your conclusion, and that if you had selected something else instead, the result would have been quite different."

"All right then, let us take another example. Take your most cherished idea—the plan of the Great Project. It contains much more than is immediately apparent even to you, the author himself. On more than one occasion in the past humanity has felt cramped on the surface of our planet. This happened even when the population was still very small but lacked our present ability to take what nature had to offer; during the past few centuries it has become increasingly difficult to overcome this problem of overcrowding. In its constant striving to expand its field of operations the labor of man has repeatedly ground to a halt at the borders of the great deserts. Countless efforts to push on have been crushed there by the harsh might of the elements, leaving dissatisfaction and dreams in the wake of the struggle. A dream, after all, is merely an effort that has been frustrated in reality and retreated beyond it into the realm of fantasy. Not all attempts, however, were entirely fruitless: in these cases the unrewarded effort did not become a simple dream; rather, as it passed from men of labor to men of science, it assumed a new form as an aspiration to investigate. Daring explorers crossed the deserts from one end to the other, measuring and describing them, expending incalculable amounts of energy. They returned with theoretical knowledge about forever dead sands and plains which was seemingly irrelevant but which in actual fact represented the crystallized effort of these pioneer explorers: knowledge to be used in the future war against the Kingdom of the Inert.

"As time went on, such attempts multiplied, aspirations intensified, investigations became more complete and precise. The suppressed activity of centuries was seeking an outlet. And then a man appeared whose soul was so expansive and profound that it could instinctively unite and fuse within it all these different elements of human striving. As audacious as man's earlier dream, he was able to embrace the full immensity of the problem, bring all the energy of knowledge accumulated by past research to bear on its solution, and integrate it with all the methods that had been developed by the scientific technology of the Machine Age. Out of these theretofore disparate elements there arose a living, harmonious whole, and this synthesis was the idea of the Great Project. Its concentrated force united a new mass of labor around it, and the work of millions translated it into reality. And thus the goal toward which generation upon generation had been groping was attained."

"A vivid but strange picture," Menni remarked thoughtfully.

"It is a correct picture, believe me," Netti continued. "You probably do not know that about three hundred years ago, during a long and severe agricultural crisis, a certain long-forgotten dreamer envisaged something very similar to your plan in the form of a prophetic social utopia. His book was suggested to me by a young historian who was studying that epoch. Utopias are an expression of aspirations that cannot be realized, of efforts that are not equal to the resistance they encounter. Now these aspirations have grown and assumed the form of systematic labor, which is able to overcome such resistance; for this to happen it was necessary that they fuse into a single idea. This is why to me the victory of unified labor and the victory of the idea are one and the same thing. I could even say 'your victory' and not be wrong, for you did not discover or find your idea as you think you did. Rather, you created it out of something that was not yet an idea. Man is a creative being, Menni."

"Oh, is he? I thought that he was some sort of receptacle of universal exertion," Menni joked in order to conceal his emotion at hearing such an opinion coming from the ordinarily so reserved Netti.

Netti understood this and did not respond to the joke. There was a short silence which Menni again broke.

"What you are saying, even if it were true, could only apply to practical ideas. But there are also purely theoretical, contemplative ideas—in mathematics, for example, or logic. Your analysis is hardly relevant to them."

"There are no purely theoretical ideas. Those which seem to be are merely broader and more general than others. Engineering, for example, or even the machine-building industry as a whole, is based on mathematics, is it not? Would your plans and their realization have been possible without hundreds of thousands of mathematical calculations? As for logic, its only vital significance lies in the fact that it enables people to communicate with each other; that is, it allows them effectively to unite their efforts in labor or research."

"In that case, if every idea can be reduced to a unification of efforts, where is the difference between the truth and error?"

"The difference is in the results. The unification of efforts may be such that it leads to the accomplishment of the goal, in which case the idea is true. Or, it may also lead to waste and failure, in which case it is erroneous. The idea of freedom was true because it led mankind to victory, to an enrichment of life that is the ultimate goal of all labor. Mathematical formulas are true because they provide us with a reliable weapon in our battle with the natural elements. An error reveals itself to be an error when the effort behind it results in failure."

"Well, then, what happens to the truth once the goal has been fully attained? The efforts which were united by it have come to an end . . ."

"And so has the idea. Mankind moves on and sets itself new goals, and the particular truth dies. When crime has completely disappeared the idea of justice will also vanish. When the life and development of man are no longer restricted by oppression, the idea of freedom will also become obsolete. Ideas are born, struggle to live, and die. Often one idea kills another one; thus freedom nullifies authority, scientific thought kills religion, and new theories replace old ones.

"Three hundred years ago a great scientist discovered that matter is eternal. This was a truth, and one of the greatest. In order to master and exploit a given substance, human activity searches for that substance at the point where it disappears from sight and then traces it through all its transformations. This is the significance of this idea, which has yielded innumerable fruitful results in all areas of labor and thought. Yet now, as you know, a new idea is gaining currency according to which matter can be destroyed, meaning that it arises or at some time has arisen out of nothing. When this truth matures it will express the ultimate mastery and power of labor over the inner life of matter. At that time the old idea, having accomplished its task, will die out. And such is the fate of all other ideas, for humanity will never cease developing."

Menni closed his eyes and reclined against the back of his chair. He thought in silence for a few moments and then said:

"I know that you have studied what you are telling me more than I have, and it is clear to me that you have a good and lucid mind. Your words are all simple and clear, yet your thoughts remain strange and incomprehensible to me. It is as if I were separated from them by a dark veil. At moments—only at moments—there are rents in this veil through which I seem to catch a gleam of the distant truth. But then everything plunges back into darkness again. At other times I am suddenly seized by a hostile feeling that you are trying to destroy something that is sacred and dearer than all else to me, but then I quickly realize how unjust that feeling is. On the whole your views impress me as a kind of poetry of labor with which you want to supplement or perhaps even replace rigorous scientific thought. That, of course, is something which I can never accept. I have no desire to argue with you, however, for I realize that it would be useless. You have an answer for everything, although your explanations fail to convince me because they are based on what is to me an alien logic. At the same time, I am greatly interested in everything related to your life and thoughts. Tell me about your childhood, Netti."

4. Enemies and Allies

For a time Menni's position seemed unassailable. His enemies had been exposed, and their leader, in his own way a man of genius, had perished. Summoned to power by the workers and public opinion, rehabilitated by a unanimous resolution of Parliament, and supported by his former colleagues and Netti, Menni soon noted extraordinary successes. The gigantic project that had been on the verge of collapse was now resuscitated and running like clockwork. Several billion of the funds that had been embezzled under Feli Rao had already been recovered through confiscations, and the continuing series of investigations and trials would return another considerable share of the remainder. In this way an enormous fund was created for expanding and developing the Project.

All of this notwithstanding, however, there was something strange and vaguely oppressive in the air. It was especially noticeable in the popular democratic press. In the past, when Menni had achieved his first successes, it had enthusiastically welcomed and commented upon each of his victories with warm sympathy. Now, however, it was as if the newspapers had all entered a tacit conspiracy of silence. They reported—but only as much as was absolutely necessary—on events concerning the Great Project and its organization; however, they systematically refrained from offering opinions or even explanations, preferring instead to discuss other matters. Nor was this negligence merely the result of bribes or the influence of the old financiers. No, "public opinion" was in fact dissatisfied. It had no reason to complain about the new course things had taken, yet it did not feel the least inclined to voice approval of those who had brought about and were directing the development. There were important reasons for this.

In the first place, "society," which at the time meant the upper and middle classes taken together, could not reconcile itself to the role the proletariat had played in the upheaval. Not only had the workers taken the initiative—which society was willing to permit in cases where the conflict was dangerous and there was a risk of bloodshed—but even after the danger was over they refused to subordinate themselves for a single minute to the leadership of the old, established parties. On the contrary, they forced the other parties to acknowledge and satisfy their demands fully. This was something new in the history of the working class, which up until then had sometimes managed to assert itself economically, but had always been a convenient and obedient object of political manipulation.

Secondly, there was something incomprehensible and alarming

about Menni's stubborn refusal to allow a review of his case or accept an amnesty and about his alliance with the notorious revolutionary extremist Netti. The first circumstance was like a moral slap in the face of all of society's respected institutions, while the second represented a future threat. It was difficult to imagine what other surprises this puzzling alliance might hold, but that very vagueness made it seem all the more alarming to public opinion.

In addition, respectable society was unpleasantly impressed by the persistent and merciless prosecution of those who had participated in the budget swindles with Feli Rao and his accomplices, which resulted in the confiscation of the property of a number of them. It was reasoned that such penalties were excessive, for since the worst culprits had already been punished, nothing was to be gained by shifting the whole burden of reprisals onto the less guilty. Most of these were respected people, reputable leaders of industry and commerce, and in business it is not always so easy and simple to distinguish the boundaries of formal legality. Such arguments were influenced both by the innumerable subtle bonds uniting the members of "society" in their everyday life and by a natural lenience toward deeds whose motive—a drive for enrichment—was so close and understandable to all. Also, the defeat of the former bosses could not but affect the interests of a great many people involved in business with them. Feli Rao's suicide even came near to causing a stock-market crash. "Society," like its legitimate representative the stock exchange, values tranquillity and a predictable future above such abstractions as justice or the good of the common cause. Menni and everything around him were regarded as a kind of protest, as something restless, unknown, and menacingly powerful. All the crimes of the other side paled in comparison.

Menni's known former enemies, however, were hesitant to begin an offensive. Their reputations were too tainted and the motives behind such a move would have been too blatantly obvious, so they were forced to wait to avoid jeopardizing their prospects. The signal to attack would have to be given by someone authoritative and unsullied, someone who was above suspicion. For a long time no such figure could be found.

Absorbed by his work, new impressions, and memories, Menni did not notice the increasing tension in the air. Many people, and not just he alone, however, were stunned when Teo published a harshly critical article on him in the planet's largest newspaper. A veteran democrat and a universally respected publicist, Teo was one of the few men who had dared to oppose the Council of Syndicates after their victory, and he had even openly branded Menni's prison sentence "the work of lackeys." All this made his new move even more sensational. The article was entitled "It is Time to Think!" and was directed as a warning to the parties and to society at large.

"Is all well in our Republic?" he asked, and he answered that it was

not: little by little democracy was betraying itself, its principles were
being openly undermined, and all this was being tolerated. The way was
being paved for the worst sort of political reaction. "Is it permissible in a
democracy for one man to have dictatorial power over millions of people
and billions in public funds? Twenty years ago, when the plan of the Great
Project was first approved, such authority was created for the initiator.
That was an enormous mistake. It was forgivable in the beginning, before
its consequences had become obvious, but since then we have lived
through the epic of Feli Rao. What did Rao actually do? He simply
usurped Menni's power and used it in his own way. We all know what that
meant . . . Democracy overthrew Feli Rao—but then? The same dictatorship with the same total immunity was handed back to Menni. Have we
learned nothing?

"It will be objected that Menni is not a financier and not a politician,
but an honest engineer. He can be trusted, he wants nothing for himself,
he is devoted to the cause alone. Is this really so? Democracy must never
rely on a single individual; it does not have the right to do so, for it is
based on the principle of the majority. Even if Menni really were everything he is claimed to be by the naïve people who have been blinded by
the greatness of his services (which we by no means wish to belittle)—
even then a violation of the principle of democracy would pose a threat to
its future. But as a matter of fact, the danger is more imminent.

"Engineer Menni wants nothing for himself. Then why grant him a
dictatorship? Or did he not accept it for himself personally?. It will be
objected that people must be judged by their intentions and actions.
Fine. Let us consider Menni's actions in relation to democracy. Society,
the people, demanded that his case be reviewed. He declined. What is
this if not contempt for the will of the people and the institutions of the
Republic? He is justified in despising his former judges, who were the
instrument of a financial cabal. But not to respect republican justice as
such—who has given him that right? And just what is he trying to tell the
masses by such a gesture? No serious person is about to sacrifice several
years of freedom without some important practical reason. What is the
goal that compels him to don at any price the halo of a martyr?

"We all know Menni's former attitude toward the workers' organizations—it was undemocratic. Even today he has not explicitly refuted his
position. But consider the contradiction! Who do you suppose is his right-
hand man and chief assistant? A man who is, if not the acknowledged
leader of the trade unions, then certainly their political inspiration: the
socialist Netti. What do you make of this? Note that lately the unions have
displayed an incomprehensible and groundless distrust of our democratic
party, which has always defended their interests. The labor federations do
not want to restrict themselves to their professional concerns, but have
begun creating their own special political committees. A new workers'

party is turning its back on democracy before our very eyes. This disinte-
gration of the mass base of democracy is dangerous and may even prove
fatal to it. And it is proceeding under the direct influence, or more
precisely the leadership, of an entire school of revolutionary politicians
headed by Netti and his father, the mechanic Arri.

"These are all indisputable facts. When one knows them, is it so very
difficult to divine the purpose of the alliance between the engineer-
dictator and the socialists? Feli Rao was supported by the corporate syndicates; Menni looks to the workers' organizations. Feli Rao was satisfied
with wealth and economic power. He did not and could not challenge the
republican order, for he had the power of money but lacked the power of
the masses. Will Menni, who is backed by the working masses, be as
modest? He is indifferent to money, that is certain. Consequently, *he
wants something else.* Do you want to know why Menni keeps himself
hidden behind prison walls? It is to divert suspicion from himself until his
friends on the outside have had time to mobilize a gigantic army of
workers.

"I maintain that the alliance between the engineer's dictatorship and
the socialism of the workers can only be directed *against democracy,
against the Republic,* and that it cannot have any other purpose."

The article concluded with a fervent appeal to Parliament, the government, and all true republicans for immediate action to counter the
impending danger. Otherwise there would be no escaping it. The warning was published a few days before the beginning of the regular session
of Parliament. As always, the session was opened by a message from the
President of the Republic. Besides the conventional official phrases and a
list of bills contemplated by the government, this time it contained something unexpected.

". . . Although," it said, "the shock experienced not so very long ago
by the Republic ended in victory for the healthy elements of society and
although order has now been restored in accordance with the popular
will, the crisis has left traces which have not yet entirely disappeared.
During these past two years the sword of justice has tirelessly struck out
at those who have violated the interests of the State, and extensive
confiscations have repaired most of the damage done by them. We believe it appropriate to submit to Parliament the question of whether the
conscience of society and the interests of the State have not received
sufficient satisfaction; we must ask whether there is not an urgent need for
complete tranquillity and the definitive restoration of the social peace that
was temporarily disturbed. If Parliament considers that such is the case,
then the time has come to forgive and forget. . . ."

Reservations followed to the effect that the President and the administration had not committed themselves to any predetermined program in
this matter, that the sole right to analyze the situation belonged to Parlia-

ment, and so on, but in fact the document was proposing an amnesty and the suspension of confiscations.

This was the first blow aimed at Menni by official political circles, and it was a very heavy one. Netti was in the capital at the time on business which happened to concern an investigation prompted by the uncovering of new and significant facts. Menni, who had already become accustomed not to undertake anything important until he had conferred with his son, urgently recalled him.

They quickly drew up a plan of action. Menni would reply to the President's message in a written report to Parliament on the course of the investigations and trials connected with the Great Project. Netti provided figures from which it became apparent that less than half of the plunder had been recovered, and he also contributed a number of very important disclosures. The new facts unearthed by Netti and the other inspectors concerned not so much old crimes as subsequent attempts on the part of the criminals to keep their positions and their booty. Forgeries had been perpetrated in order to protect fortunes from confiscation: powerful financial bosses suddenly turned out to be paupers. Millions had been given to bribe investigative and judicial authorities to destroy important incriminating documents. The bribing of witnesses was still more common, and certain uncooperative persons had even been murdered. All in all, the report was bound to spoil the conciliatory mood of Parliament and delay the amnesty considerably. Only a few months remained until Menni's release, so it was of the essence to play for time.

Menni was unable to reply to Teo's attack (which in the meanwhile had been seized upon and supported by several large newspapers), for it would have ill befitted him to plead his innocence of such charges. The large unions in the capital, however, had already retorted with indignant declarations, and Netti was certain that the provincial organizations, especially the Project Federation, would voice similar reactions. The workers protested against the fact that the democratic party, on the pretext that the Republic was threatened by an impossible monarcho-proletarian conspiracy, was in effect attacking the nascent political unification of the proletariat. They argued that any "defense" of their interests by the official democrats had been inadequate and unsuccessful. "Did they save the working class from the oppressive dictatorship of the Council of Syndicates?" asked the Centropolis Federation of Mechanics. "No, in fact it was the other way round. And in the early days was it not above all the blood of the workers that paid for the founding of the Republic? So forget all these fables about conspiracies against the Republic, stop this pointless indignation over our distrust of your party, and reconcile yourselves to the fact that in the future we will defend our own political interests and perhaps even yours, should the two happen to coincide."

Netti concluded that the time was more propitious than ever for establishing a political federation of unions in the form of a regular work-ers' party. He resolved to throw all his energy into this project, and he was certain that his brother socialists would support him. The conflict, of course, was thereby inevitably aggravated, but the balance of forces had also altered considerably.

As Menni listened to these plans he caught himself involuntarily sympathizing with them. This disturbed his ideological conscience and evoked in him a vague sense of distrust of himself. Feeling compelled to justify himself in his own eyes he said:

"I do not at all share the basic ideas of the program you have drafted for your new party. However, I have always thought that the workers are free citizens and can unite in unions or parties as they see fit. If they choose to do so, it means that they have their reasons. I have refused to accept the demands of the unions, but I have never opposed their right to exist. I do not know what your party will bring in the future; at the moment I cannot deny that you need it. Perhaps it will serve as the threat that will halt the evident degeneration of the old parties. If it does that, I am prepared to sympathize with it."

5. The Legend of the Vampires

Their discussion of business matters being concluded, Menni turned to the thing that had particularly amazed and disturbed him about the latest events.

"I must admit that I am quite unable to understand the treachery of such persons as the President and Teo. I know them both, and they are incorruptible. Still . . . Do you think they are sincere?"

"I am sure they are," replied Netti. "Look at their arguments. Are they not based for the most part on what they have always maintained? Teo is a zealous defender of democracy and the Republic, while the President emphasizes social peace."

"You don't mean to say that they have remained true to themselves?"

"No, of course not. I am not saying that. The patterns are the same, but their relationship to life has become the opposite of what it was before. Recall what Teo once wrote apropos of insinuations by the moder-ate press about your 'dictatorship.' Democracy, he said, is too strong to be frightened by such specters. No matter how great the authority, if it is granted by the popular will and is subject to continuous review, there is nothing dictatorial about it. Under such conditions, the strength of the power determined by democracy merely reflects the strength of democ-racy itself: it selects the means best suited to ensure the common good, and it must not be restricted in that choice. In the present case, Teo added, the hostility of the enemies of democracy was in itself proof that the correct path had been chosen. At that time Teo was full of daring and

summoned the people forward to new conquests. Today he is full of fright
and calls for the preservation of the status quo. As for our President, in his
famous book he wrote: 'The workers' legitimate demands must be met; by
doing so we can put a stop to the growing enmity among classes. If we
encounter unreasonably stubborn resistance on the part of those who
without any effort or merit of their own have been blessed with everything and refuse to give anything to others, then we must not retreat in
the face of a violent struggle or hesitate to resort to vigorous measures;
social peace is more important than the egoism of the privileged.' And
now in his message to Parliament he is proposing, also in the interests of
social peace, to make concessions to these same privileged elements."

"That is correct," said Menni. "You have a very accurate memory.
But how can you speak of sincerity in a case where opposite conclusions
are drawn from the same premises? Is this not outright proof of hypoc-
risy?"

"No, it is not," replied Netti. "Formerly they reasoned with the logic
of living people. They wanted life to move ahead and improve, and this
led them to their earlier conclusions. Today, however, theirs is the logic of
dead men. They want peace and immobility, they want life around them
to come to a standstill. What has happened to them constantly happens to
people and to entire classes, to ideas and to institutions: they have quite
simply died and become vampires."

"Heaven alone knows what you are talking about," Menni exclaimed
in amazement. "I don't understand you at all."

Netti laughed.

"Are you familiar with the popular legend of the vampires?" he asked
instead of answering.

"Of course. It is an absurd fairy tale about corpses who rise from their
graves in order to drink the blood of the living."

"Taken literally it is indeed an absurd fairy tale. But the means by
which folk poetry expresses the truth differ from those of the exact sciences. In fact, the legend of the vampires embodies one of the most
profound, though also one of the most dismal, truths about life and death.
Dead life exists—history is full of it, it surrounds us on all sides and drinks
the blood of living life."

"I am aware that your workers often call the capitalists vampires, but
such language, after all, is merely abuse or at the very most agitational
rhetoric."

"That is not at all what I mean. Imagine a man who works in any
given field of labor or thought. He lives for himself as a physiological
organism and lives for society in his professional capacity. He pours his
energy into the common stream of life, strengthening it and contributing
to the conquest of that which is hostile to it. At the same time he doubtless costs society something, lives on the labor of others, subtracts something from the life around him. But as long as he gives more than he

takes, he increases the sum of life, and he is a plus, a positive quantity. Sometimes he remains such a plus right up until his physical death. His hands have grown weak, but his brain still functions well; the old man thinks, teaches, educates others, and communicates his experience to them. Later his brain may tire and his memory fade, but his heart continues to throb with tenderness and sympathy for young life, and this very purity and nobility contribute to life an invigorating harmony and spirit of unity.

"This happens very seldom, however. Much more often a man who lives too long sooner or later outlives himself. The time comes when he begins to take from life more than he gives it, and then his existence diminishes its total sum. Hostility arises between them: life rejects him, while he sinks his fangs into it and tries to turn it back to the past, to the time when he still sensed his bond with it. He is not only a parasite but an active enemy of life. He drinks its vital juices in order to live and tries in this way to prevent it from living and continuing its movement forward. He is not really a man, because the human and socially creative being in him has already died. He is but the body of such a being. An ordinary, physical corpse is also harmful—it must be removed and destroyed lest it contaminate the air and spread disease. But a vampire, a living corpse, is much more harmful and dangerous if he was a strong man during his lifetime."

"Is this how you regard the President and Teo?"

"Yes, and in fact they illustrate something even worse: the corpses of people contain the corpses of ideas. Ideas die just like people, but they cling to life even more stubbornly after their death. Recall the idea of religious authority; it became obsolete and incapable of leading mankind forward any longer, but think of the centuries that it continued to struggle for supremacy, think of the blood and tears that were shed and the resources that were wasted before it was buried once and for all. As for democracy, I think that this idea has not yet accomplished all that it can, but if it is to remain viable it must change and develop together with society. In Teo's case, however, it has stopped and stagnated in the past in which he actually lived. There was no workers' party then. That party is the beginning of something that is new and alien to him, and he opposes it in the name of his dead idea. At one time the slogan of 'social peace' may have been of some use as a protest against the furious war of each against all and the ruthless egoism of the victors. Today, however, when the class struggle has acquired a new meaning and has become a vehicle of the great future, such a slogan has been hopelessly exhausted, drained of the last drop of life."

"How strange to regard people you know as vampires!" said Menni thoughtfully.

"It is both strange and painful if you have thought of them earlier as noble and courageous fighters," Netti added.

Menni shook his head as if he were trying to rid himself of something.

"I do not even notice myself how I am charmed by your poetic imagery," he remarked with a smile. "But one more question. If I have understood you correctly, it is not only old people and other beings that can be vampires?"

"Of course not," said Netti. "According to popular superstition, still-born children also become vampires. When entire social classes become obsolete the dead give birth to corpses. The same is true of the world of ideas. After all, religious sects, including some new ones, arise even today."

"Yes, and this may be the weakest point in your theory. How does one determine the moment when a living being has become a vampire?"

"As a matter of fact, it is very difficult," replied Netti. "The metamorphosis does not usually become apparent until much later, when the damage is obvious and the vampire has already drunk a great deal of blood. Teo, of course, did not suddenly become an enemy of the future during the past few days. Earlier I was tormented by the riddle of when this moment occurs. I was very young when I first penetrated the meaning of the legend. I was very sensitive then, so my conclusions were rather extreme. Sometimes I would think: here I am, I meet different people, live with them, trust them, even love them, but do I always know *who they really are?* Perhaps, unbeknown to us both, at this very moment the person with whom I am having a friendly chat is crossing the fateful boundary. Something is changing, something is being destroyed within him—just a minute ago he was alive, but now . . . And I would become almost terrified. My attitude, of course, was childish."

"No, not entirely childish, if your theory can be believed," objected Menni. "And I am amazed how someone with your bright and joyous outlook on life could create such a gloomy fantasy."

"It was not I who created it, and it was history that suggested my interpretation to me," Netti said with a smile. "Also, to me it is not only gloomy. As a child I was very fond of fairy tales about heroes who fought with terrible monsters."

"Did you dream of becoming such a hero yourself, a vampire killer? Well, I suppose your dream has come true, and I understand that now you have no reason to fear any corpses."

"They are enemies, and why should one be afraid of one's enemies? Besides, sooner or later living life always triumphs over life that is dead."

6. The Vampire

The battle continued, and Menni's enemies fought with increasing ferocity. Much as it would have liked, however, the government was prevented from taking any effective measures against him by Netti's strategy, which skillfully exploited newly uncovered facts relating to the bribery of state officials. On the basis of old documents belonging to Feli Rao, Netti was able to reconstruct what had happened with the fifty deputies who had suddenly become millionaires and supporters of Rao. It turned out that certain of them, including some of Menni's bitter enemies, were still Members of Parliament. The parliamentary majority was paralyzed and unable to undertake any hostile actions for some time after this scandal. The government could inflict little more than pinpricks on Project Administration, harassing it with minor obstructions and nagging at it over trifles.

Oddly enough, Menni took little interest in the whole struggle. He listened to the reports of Netti and his other colleagues, approved most of their actions and ideas, and when occasionally necessary did what they advised. But it was obvious that his mind was almost constantly on something else. He became increasingly absentminded and even inconsistent in his relations to those around him, and he tried to cut his business meetings and discussions to a minimum, as if they greatly tired him. It seemed that his physical health, which had resisted the effects of prison life so many years, was also beginning to weaken now. His face often bore the marks of sleepless nights, and there was a feverish glitter in his eyes. Anyone who happened to mention this to him was crossly and coldly cut short.

He did not permit himself the least rudeness with Netti, although at times he did seem to be trying to avoid him somewhat. Much more often, however, he treated him with unusually affectionate attention, almost tenderness. He did not really discuss controversial subjects with him, but sometimes he would suddenly ask a question apropos of some extreme point in Netti's world-view, almost as if he were trying to measure the full extent of the disagreement between them. On such occasions he would then immediately change the subject. More than anything else he liked to ask him about his childhood, about everything that was directly or indirectly connected with Nella.

Netti noticed all this and even told his mother about it; absorbed as he was by the struggle and his plans, however, he did not give the matter any particular thought, but rested content with the easiest explanation. He simply concluded that Menni's behavior was due to the perfectly natural nervousness of a man who was approaching the day of his release after many long years in prison. Nella, whose heart was more sensitive, doubted that things were that simple, but she did not voice her fears for lack of any clear and definite conclusion. She had even thought of going to see Menni herself, but could not think of a proper excuse. In part she was held back by the memory of her conversation long before with Arri, who would attribute to her act a special significance that she found distasteful.

Each evening after his visitors had gone, Menni would remain alone for a long time in the enormous cell that served as his office. He would sit perfectly still leaning against the back of the chair, plunged in reflection. But the longer he mused the dimmer his thoughts became, and often Menni himself was unable to say with certainty what he had been thinking about. Two things, however, stood out more clearly than anything else and seemed to rise above this chaos: first, there were the thoughts and images connected with Netti's theory of the vampires, and secondly, there was the persistent feeling that soon he would be forced to make a very important decision.

Time passed. Late in the evening two days before his release Menni was alone as always in his gloomy office. He had done a great deal of work during the day, but he was not at all tired. On the contrary, he felt better than usual. His head was clear, though strangely empty. It seemed to him as if he was not thinking about anything at all, and the sensation was almost pleasant. The weak light from the shaded electric lamp was insufficient for the large room, and the corners were hidden in semidarkness.

Suddenly Menni had the feeling that someone was staring at him from behind. He turned his head. In the corner farthest from him the darkness grew denser and, vaguely at first, began to assume the contours of a human figure. The burning eyes, however, were already distinctly visible. The figure crept closer and became sharper. When it crossed into the space illuminated by the lamp, Menni, unsurprised yet abstractly aware of the incongruity of the fact, recognized it to be Engineer Maro.

The specter stopped a few paces from Menni, bowed derisively and sat down on the chair opposite him. He looked the same as during their last conversation, and wore the same cynical smile. But now his face was paler, his eyes brighter, and his lips redder than before, and on his neck there was an irregular bloody strip of ragged tissues.

"Greetings!" he said. "There is no need to introduce myself, for you know me well. You are not surprised, because you have actually been expecting me for some time. Yes, I am the Vampire. Not particularly your friend Maro, but the Vampire in general, lord of the dead life. I have taken this form today as being best suited to our little chat, and indeed it is one of my best guises. But I have any number of them, and very soon I will assume another which is much better."

The specter stopped and gave a soft, smug chuckle. It continued:

"We have some important things to talk about. You and I shall come to an understanding. Yes, indeed! Taking everything in order, let us first consider your situation. It is quite simple, but absolutely absurd. You will honestly have to agree. For three years now Menni Aldo, the great engineer, has been playing a strange role, one which is entirely unbecoming to him: the role of a tool in the hands of others. Such is the melancholy truth. You have always thought that the truth does not depend on the person who utters it. If what you hear from me seems unpleasant, that is just too bad for you, for it becomes no less true for that. Recall the course of events and consider them dispassionately.

"Take your return to power—who willed that? Alas! It was the trade unions, the old enemies you treated so nonchalantly before. Yes! If you are honest you cannot deny it. You were quite unable to do anything yourself at the time—everything came from the outside. Netti's disclosures, of course, were very important, but whose interests did he have at heart? Those of the unions. The plan of his secret investigation, you know, came from none other than Arri, who managed to figure out a great deal during his ten years in prison. Also, Feli Rao was a master at silencing scandals; what would have come of the revelations of an unknown young man without the manifesto of the Federation to lend them real force? The unions demanded you as they would demand a wage increase of five kopecks. Perhaps this is flattering—they got you as they would have got a corresponding number of kopecks. But you, who have always refused to give in to them or even negotiate with them—you played the role of an object that was conceded to them . . ."

Mildly irritated by this mockery, Menni interrupted.

"Well, so what? Do you mean that I should have refused?" he asked coldly. "Did I not have any *other* right to lead the Project? Was it not *my* creation?"

"I am not suggesting anything of the kind," the Vampire answered with his former sarcastic smile. "Naturally, it would have been stupid to decline the power, but the question of rights was quite immaterial at the time. It was a question of force that was at issue, and it was decided for you by others. It would have still been possible to reconcile yourself to that, however, if it had been a case of your using the crude strength of the masses to gain your own ends. But that is not at all what happened. Were you from that moment on really the master of the situation? No, and again, no! The likeable figure of a former worker, the engineer Netti, appeared in your entourage. I shall not permit myself to speak disrespectfully of him, for he is your son. But I will permit myself to speak the truth about him: for someone like yourself who serves an idea, kinship does not carry a vote in important matters, does it now? He is a worthy young man, and his hand is as heavy as yours, as well I know."

Menni smiled and nodded his head in assent. He had almost forgotten already how fantastic the situation was and was attentively following the arguments of his guest, just as he would have done in a discussion with a real enemy. The Vampire continued:

"That does not prevent him from being a hopeless utopian. You yourself, at any rate, were of that opinion recently. He is a harmful utopian, because he distorts the very principles of rigorous science and replaces them, as you aptly put it on one occasion, with a strange 'poetry of labor.' He denies the pure eternal truth and wants to cast it down to be trampled beneath the feet of the masses. This is all the more dangerous because it is done in a form that is attractive and in its own way logical and which, though it cannot of course influence you and me, appeals to very many people. That is Engineer Netti. And what is his position? Why, he is considered your chief assistant. That in itself is a great deal, but in actual fact he is much more. He has shut you off from everything: you see with his eyes and think with his head. It is he who is the real leader and master.

"You will try to deny this. You will say that you did not give in to Netti on the question of the unions, that you in fact limited his power by appointing a second assistant. Those are all lame excuses unworthy of you. It was Netti who suggested appointing another assistant. He did not want to demand too much all at once, you see, he could wait: 'all in due course.' Most importantly, concrete results meant more to him than an empty gesture, and he expected to benefit from his noble renunciation. Recall the instructions you gave your other assistant concerning concessions to the workers—Netti himself could hardly have wished for more. And now, when your directors are involved in negotiations with the workers, who is it they have in mind, who is it they take into account? Who do you think—you, or Netti? Finally what could be more typical than the present campaign? *You and your work* are under attack, but who is in charge of the defense? Who is leading the counterattack? You hardly even bother to approve Netti's proposals. Teo is so naïve! He has the whole thing backwards. True, people like you and Netti are beyond his understanding, but Teo is not the only one who would have trouble guessing that the great Menni, as if prison were not enough for him, is also the captive of the socialists."

Menni shrugged his shoulders.

"It is fairly easy to reply to all this. It is of no consequence to me whether or not what you are saying is true: it is not for me to become involved in your thoroughly petty arguments. *The cause* has not suffered; on the contrary, it is going well, and its defense is assured. That is all that matters to me."

"But in that case why call it *your* cause? You should frankly recognize reality and simply come out and say: 'this cause is no longer mine.' Besides, it remains to be seen whether it has suffered or not—we must await the outcome of the present situation. In the meanwhile, you are already indebted to Netti for his help in the conflict with the democrats. Let us see what happens when Netti and his unions make their next move. But the main point is that all guarantees for the future are disappearing. There was such a guarantee in you, in your strength and fidelity to yourself. But little by little you are *ceasing to be yourself.* That is the danger, and that is what I was getting at with my 'petty arguments.' Worse yet, you do not notice and do not *want* to notice it. Yes, you are intentionally closing your eyes, for otherwise you would be astonished by how much you have changed. Once the greatest triumphs and the ecstatic celebration of your victories by millions of people left you as calm and cold as the eternal snows of the high mountain peaks. But now the most timid, reserved expression of approval from Netti sets your heart throbbing as if you were a schoolboy being praised by his teachers. Even worse: remember when the Council of Unions recently declared in reply to the democrats that the bourgeoisie only knows how to persecute and slander its great men, whereas the proletariat is able to defend them as it does the cause of humanity which they serve . . . Yes, the prison walls can be proud that they have seen tears in the eyes of the great Menni!"

Menni angrily leapt up from his seat; in a moment he had regained his self-control, however, and he remarked contemptuously as he sat down again:

"It is best not to talk of things which you will never understand, Vampire."

"Really?" the Vampire laughed with complacent cynicism. "You are right. Certain things are hard to understand. For example, when Menni listens sympathetically to Netti's revolutionary plans and at the same time rejects them in principle and regards them as harmful utopias. Or when he spends hours on end gazing at the picture of a woman—Menni, who once with a proud effort of will conquered and cast aside love as an obstacle on the path to his great goals. No, there is no use trying to evade the facts, for they are obvious: you are betraying yourself, you are tangled in a net from which you cannot bring yourself to break free."

The Vampire paused for a moment, and the grin disappeared from his face. He fixed Menni with his burning eyes and, changing his tone completely, said seriously, almost solemnly:

"You know what you must do. *You must once again become yourself.* You simply must—your dignity and your honor demand it. And it is difficult, perhaps the most difficult thing you have ever done. You will need heroism to conquer at one blow everything that is driving you to betray yourself: love, friendship, paternal feelings, sympathy, gratitude. No other man in the whole world would be able to do this, but you can. It will not be the first time you have achieved the impossible. The moment will soon be at hand: life itself will demand of you a firm answer. The idyll with the unions will not last much longer. They have not yet raised the standard of their battle for official recognition, because they are too busy with other things, such as the structure and defense of their new political organization. But that organization will make them even stronger, and for them might is right. When you are released from prison your very first trip to the construction sites will cause the old question to be raised again. And then? Will Engineer Menni allow external force and his personal feelings to get the better of his convictions? If you do not, then it will mean breaking with Netti and Nella, a bitter struggle, a great sacrifice.

Yes, but also a great victory! I do not wish to insult you by doubting your choice."

"Are you so sure that I will follow *your* advice?" said Menni, ironically stressing the person of his visitor.

"That is a very weak argument against the truth," replied the Vampire. "People resort to such arguments when they have nothing else to say. I expected you to use it, so that I could ask you what has happened to your faith in the pure truth. Does the fact that it is presented to you in a disagreeable wrapping suffice to compromise it in your eyes? I am saying the opposite of what Maro once told you. He suggested: 'betray yourself.' I, on the other hand, am reminding you: 'be true to yourself!' "

"Like Teo and the President," Menni added sarcastically.

"No, not like them. Be true to yourself, not like the weak, but like the strong. Not like those who become confused trying to bring back the past, but like those who follow the same road to the very end. You have surrendered to Netti's theory and been deceived by it. I am not death and not a return to the past. I am life that wants to live by remaining true to itself. Only such life is true. Life which changes demonstrates by that very fact that it is a lie, because the truth is forever the same. If you were one man yesterday and have become another today, then you died overnight and a new man was born whose life will be just as ephemeral. Everything dies: you, mankind, the world. Everything will be submerged in eternity. Only the truth will remain, because it alone is eternal. And it is eternal because it is immutable. Prove that you belong to truth and eternity: be as unchanging as they!"

Menni rose, his eyes flashing.

"You are lying, Vampire, and you cannot deceive me with your naïve sophisms. You, as always, are urging treason. I know the road I have traveled. Each step was a blow to the past. And you dream of making me an enemy of the future! I know my path. My struggle with the elements . . . only Netti is worthy of continuing it as my successor. My struggle with you, Feli Rao, and the likes of you . . . Netti and his friends are the best, the truest allies in that battle. I do not know whether they are right to believe in their socialism—I tend to think that they are not. But I am sure that if they are wrong they will realize their mistake sooner than anyone else. The truth will triumph, but it will not triumph *against* that which is full of strength and purity and nobility, but *together with it!*"

The Vampire also drew himself up to his full height. His red lips were twisted in an expression of malicious certainty in his victory.

"So, you do not want to listen to some friendly advice," he hissed. "Very well then, you shall hear the voice of a sovereign!" And he stretched his hand toward Menni, his fingers convulsively crooked like claws trying to seize their prey. "Know that your fate is sealed—you will not escape me! For fifteen years you have been living in my kingdom, for fifteen years I have been drinking your blood, little by little. There are still a few drops of living blood left, and that is why you are rebelling. But this will pass, it will pass! I am Necessity and therefore I am the truth. You are mine, you are mine, you are mine!"

Menni's eyes darkened, and he haughtily tossed back his head.

"You are a lie, a dead lie!" he said with icy contempt. "Thank you, at any rate, for casting off your mask and putting an end to my vacillation. Your triumph is a delusion. You will not take the last drops of my living blood! The tone of a sovereign little befits you, least of all with me. I killed you once when you crossed my path, and now I will kill you again!"

He turned and went to the door connecting his office with the cell in which he slept. He glanced back on the threshold as he closed the door. The Vampire had vanished.

PART IV

1. The Heart of Nella

The following morning Menni urgently summoned an old comrade of his, a prominent chemist. They rarely saw each other, but their relationship was such that the chemist could never refuse Menni anything. Long ago they had gone on a number of expeditions together through the desert, and Menni, whose physical strength and stamina far exceeded that of his friend, had saved the chemist's life on several occasions. When he arrived, they conferred alone for over an hour behind locked doors. The chemist seemed very upset when he left, and there were tears in his eyes. Smiling as he accompanied him down the corridor, Menni shook his hand affectionately and thanked him warmly as they parted. Two hours later a sealed parcel addressed to Menni arrived from the chemist's laboratory.

Menni spent most of the day going through his papers and putting them in order. Netti came to see him in the evening. He was surprised by the considerable change he noticed in his father's manner and even in his appearance. The nervousness of the past few months, his absentmindedness, the feverish glitter in his eyes, and his abrupt movements had all disappeared without a trace. Calm and attentive, he discussed their business matters with the greatest lucidity, outlining several important technical and administrative improvements. When they were finished with these questions he said:

"By the way, I wanted to ask you a great favor. I am thinking of taking a vacation for . . ."—he hesitated for a moment and then went on—"for a while. I think it is a legitimate wish. Could you take my place for the time being and take over tomorrow? I have made the necessary preparations."

"Of course, I'd be glad to," replied Netti. "I have thought for some time now that you need a rest. I have been worried about your health lately."

"Well, that is all over now," said Menni with a smile. "You can see that I am all right today, aren't I?"

He then began talking about Netti's scientific revolutionary ideas and plans, questioning him in detail on a number of points. He did not object or make any sarcastic comments, and even refrained from his usual habit of registering his disagreement. On the contrary, at some moments it seemed as though he quite shared Netti's thoughts and that his remarks and amplifications were intended to develop them more fully. Netti was thoroughly enchanted; they became so absorbed in their lively conversation that neither of them noticed that they had talked far into the night. As they said goodbye Menni remarked:

"Still, there is only one of your theories I can accept wholeheartedly. On the other hand, I think I have learned it well."

"Which one is that?" Netti quickly asked.

"The theory of the vampires," replied Menni.

The young engineer returned home deeply engrossed in thought. Nella was there waiting up for him. He told her in detail about his conversation with Menni and about his own impressions. Apropos of Menni's final remark Nella had her son repeat word for word the earlier discussion to which it referred. Then she made him promise to come to see her the next day immediately after his meeting with Menni.

Nella spent the whole night in thought.

When Netti went to pick up his assignments the following morning, Menni announced to him:

"Officially I am turning over my responsibilities for a month. But bear in mind that I may be gone even longer. I want to have a real vacation."

The work took several hours. As Netti was leaving, Menni detained him for a moment and said:

"Tomorrow we will probably not be seeing each other. According to law, criminals who have served their sentences are released at dawn, and I have decided to set off on a trip immediately. Well, then, good luck."

He embraced and kissed Netti, the first time ever, and added:

"Give my best to Nella."

Nella was waiting impatiently for her son. When he had described the meeting in detail she turned very pale. Summing up his impressions Netti said:

"Still, there is something strange about him, but I can't put my finger on it. I'm afraid that he is not as healthy as he appears. What do you think—would it be meddlesome of me if I were to drop in on him uninvited this evening?"

"You don't have to, Netti," she replied. "I shall go myself."

2. The Faces of Death

Several hours passed. Menni had fallen asleep in Nella's arms. She carefully freed herself from his embrace and sat up next to him on the bed so that she could look at his face. Perhaps he sensed in his sleep that she had moved away from him. He was overpowered by oppressive visions.

. . . .

Cold within; darkness all around; stone everywhere—below, on all sides, above. So tiring to walk down the narrow, stuffy corridor. But must go. So very long!

Ah! Faint, almost phosphorescent light flickering ahead . . . Closer, clearer . . . Walls and an arch begin to emerge dully from the gloom. Corridor narrower and narrower.

Of course! Can't go any farther. Blank wall like the others, end of the corridor. White figure leaning motionless against it. Incomprehensible feeling of alarm deep within. Have to, must see it . . .

The sheet slides off and falls to the floor. The face of a corpse . . . strangely familiar features. The clouded eyes are immobile, but from its gray lips escapes a noiseless whisper: "I am you!"

Greenish patches appear on the dead face, grow larger, merge together. The eyes sink in their sockets and ooze a dirty liquid; decaying chunks of flesh slide from the bones . . . Now it has all fallen off, leaving only a bony mask with its stereotyped grin.

Phosphorescent fires dance all around, flare up brighter and die out. The empty grin changes in the flickering light, the dusty yellow features of the mask become animated. It seems to Menni that he can clearly read their strange, mute speech.

"This is you, and this is everything," says the sneering mask. "And even this is still too much. Man thinks to himself: it is so sad and dreary to be rotting away like this among will-o'-the-wisps in a dark pit. But no! It is actually much worse. The sad thing is not even that these little bubbles of false light produced by the decaying remnants of your own body will also soon disappear. Darkness would not be so bad. But there is not even that!

"Yes, if there were darkness, dreariness, dull yearning . . . Darkness which you once had seen, dreariness which you felt, yearning which you cursed. You loved the bright sun and the countless forms that bask in its rays; the solid inky darkness, of course, is not the same thing—but still, it is something like a reminder of them. Here you are even robbed of that. The changing impressions of an intense life were your joy; but even the most hopeless dreariness contains a dull reflection of them, a vague faith in them. Here there is not a trace of that. Struggle and victory were the meaning of your existence. When they were insufficient the venomous voice of yearning reminded you of them. Now even it has fallen silent forever . . . Understand this final reckoning as your thought enters its death throes . . . understand and accept it!

"I am you. Even my appearance and my speech are flashes of your life, the life that is now departing. Well, that is something anyway, and it is infinitely better than what is left from now on, better than that unfathomable something called *nothing*."

By an agonizing effort Menni overcomes the pain clutching at his heart.

"I do not believe you," he says. "I know who you are, there is no use in trying to disguise yourself. You are a lie through and through, and only lies can come from you."

But the smile of the skull becomes sad. "Let's see you disprove them!" it seems to say. "Alas, it is impossible . . ."

The lights die out, the contours fade. The darkness thickens. Cold deep within.

But what's this? A soft breeze, like someone's gentle breathing, brushed his face. How strange! In it there is a dim ray of hope that warms the heart. And now the darkness is also beginning to lift. The air is gradually suffused with a wan, pale light. His eyes drink it in greedily . . . Where are the walls?

An endless rocky plain. Above it, the dark leaden vault of the sky. No sign of life. Only a gray valley ahead.

Menni turns around and shudders. Before him stands a motionless black figure muffled up from head to toe; not even its face is visible. The twilight seems to gather around it, and in this halo the severe lines of a silhouette stand out as in an engraving. Menni senses in them something familiar . . . close . . . dear . . . He tries to remember but cannot. He cautiously stretches out his hands and shudders again as he touches the cold, very cold cloth. He pulls it off in anxious expectation . . . Nella!

It is she, and yet not she . . . What is it about her that has changed so strangely? Yes—her eyes are not the same. They are just as huge, but now they are not blue green like the waves of the southern seas, but black, completely black, deep, bottomless. There is a solemn and gentle expression on her lusterless pale face; her breathing is so quiet that her breast does not rise or fall beneath the still folds of her clothing. Everything about her is suffused with a serenity that is inaccessible to a mortal man.

She spoke softly, so softly that it seemed to Menni that he was listening to thoughts rather than sounds.

"It is I, Menni, the one who has always been your destiny. You know that it will all come to an end for you in my caresses. You are a man and you are in pain—unnecessary pain.

"What are you losing? The radiance of the sun, the joy of struggle, Nella's love? You are wrong, my friend. You are not losing them, they are losing you. How can someone who does not exist lose anything? For you will be no more, but they will remain. The sun will go on shining for millions of years; the struggle of life will continue forever. The soul of Nella will be repeated an infinite number of times and become ever more beautiful and harmonious in the women of the future.

"No, you will be no more. Your name and your body and your chain of memories will all disappear. But look here. Suppose you were offered eternity, and with it light, joy, love, but on the condition that they existed for you alone and no one else. Suppose it were all as vivid and palpable as reality even though it was only your dream. With what contempt would you not reject this false happiness, this wretched eternity! You would say that it is better to have lived the shortest and most difficult life, if only it was a real life . . . And you can see that all real life remains and goes on. All that is dying is the single gleam and particle of it that is you.

"In the infinity of mighty, living Being, what you loved more than yourself—your work—will survive. It will lose you, and that is indeed a loss. But the idea lives on after the man disappears, and you have come to understand the main thing: the creativity that found one of its incarnations in you has no end."

She fell silent. Still was her figure amid the stillness of the desert, and still were the tranquil features of her lusterless wan face.

Menni took a step toward her, and seizing her in his powerful embrace he pressed his lips to her cold lips. His gaze plunged into her bottomless dark eyes; a joyous pain pierced his heart—and everything was lost in confusion.

. . . .

"Is that you, Nella? The other one, or as you used to be?" murmured Menni, who had not yet fully emerged from his delirium. "Ah, yes! Perhaps you do not know . . . I have just seen death, Nella . . . There were two of them. One was repulsive and empty; there is no use even talking about it. The other one was beautiful and kind. It was you, Nella . . . I kissed her, like this . . ."

3. The Legacy

Again caresses in the night . . . and once again reality dissolves and recedes from consciousness . . . and new visions overwhelm Menni's soul.

. . . .

A bloody red sphere high in the dark sky. It is not the sun—it is not painful to look at it, and its brilliance is not strong enough to blot out the bright, quietly twinkling stars. A third moon? No, it is too bright for that. What is it? The dying sun would look like that . . . Yes, that is what it is: the sun, and it is dying. Impossible! That is not to happen for millions of years yet. But then, what of it? To a man for whom time does not exist millions of years are but a moment.

But in that case—it is the end of everything: humanity, life, the struggle! Everything that is born of the sun, everything that has absorbed the energy of its rays. The end of the brilliance of human thought, the end of the will, the end of joy and love! Here it is, then—the inevitable, the inescapable, after which there is nothing, nothing remains . . .

Cold within and cold without. Menni looks around him. A smooth, level road crosses a desert plain which may once have been a field or meadow. In the distance there are strange, beautiful buildings. The air is still, all nature is still. Not a single human being, or animal, or plant. Only a deep, bottomless silence that drowns the feeble rays of the dying luminary.

Is it really all over? Has the kingdom of silence already come to claim its due? On the other hand, what difference does it make? Even if there are some remnants of life smoldering somewhere in those buildings or beneath the earth . . . they are already in their death throes—not really alive . . .

The final judgment and the ultimate verdict has come, and it cannot be appealed. Everything that was an end or a means to an end is being reckoned up, everything that had any meaning or significance. The skeleton was right: the sum of this reckoning is zero. Millions of years of striving and learning . . . Myriads of lives, wretched and splendid ones, insignificant and mighty . . . But what is the difference if they are longer or shorter, better or worse, when they are no more and have no other heir than the mute, eternal, indifferent ether? They were, they took from life what was due them. They were an illusion! "They were": *now* that means only one thing—that they are no more. And whatever they took from life has disappeared along with them.

But after all, life is not coming to an end everywhere in the universe. It dies out in some worlds, but thrives on in others and is being born in yet others. Humbug! Comforting words masking the bitter truth! What does life here care about life somewhere else that knows nothing about it and derives nothing from it? And if each of these manifestations of life is exhausted in the same way in a sterile cycle, what do they add, separately or together, to that inevitable sum total? What is the good of such incoherent fantasies of the universe scattered across time and space? Why did the sun weave this false fabric of life from its chimerical rays? What mockery!

What is this? One of the giant, graceful buildings resembling a temple of the feudal era is brightly illuminated. Have to go and see. It is not far, and the going is easy on the level road. A door opens.

An enormous hall with a high ceiling, flooded in light; thousands of people. But are they people? How casual their poses, how serene and bright their faces, how their bodies breathe strength. And these are the doomed?

What has brought them here? What idea, what feeling has united them here in this universal silence? A man enters the hall and ascends a raised platform in the middle of the room. This is evidently the one they have been waiting for. The gazes of the crowd are fixed on him. Is it Netti? Yes, Netti, but he is different. He looks like a god, he is surrounded by an aura of superhuman beauty. His voice breaks the deep, solemn silence:

"Brothers, on behalf of those who have attempted to solve the last problem, I hereby announce that our mission is accomplished.

"You know that the fate of our world became fully clear to us thousands of years ago. The rays of the dying sun have long been unable to nourish the growth of our life, our great common labor. We have kept its flame burning as long as possible. We have exploded and cast into the sun all of our planets in turn, except the one upon which we stand at this moment. The energy released by these collisions gave us an additional hundred thousand years. We have spent most of that time trying to find the means to resettle in other solar systems. Here we have failed utterly. We could not completely conquer time and space. Because of the enormous distances between the stars, we would be forced to travel for tens of thousands of years through the hostile ether. It would be impossible to preserve the life of a single living being to the end of such a journey. It became necessary to reformulate the problem. We have incontrovertible proof that there are intelligent beings in other stellar systems. We shall base our new plan on this fact.

"What we want to save from the inevitable destruction of our world is not at all our own lives, the life of our humanity. The death of the last generation is in itself no more significant than the death of the preceding ones, if only our *cause* can remain and be continued. What is dear to us instead is all that has been accomplished by our united efforts through thousands of centuries: our power over the elements, our understanding of nature, the beauty of life that we have created. This is what we must preserve in the universe at any price, this is what we must pass on to other intelligent beings as our legacy. Then our life will be reincarnated in their work, and our creation will transform other worlds.

"How are we to accomplish this task? The problem was difficult, but we already know how to solve it. The cold vacuum of the ethereal wastes, while it is fatal to life, is powerless against inert matter. Thus we can commit to such matter the signs and symbols expressing the meaning and content of our history, our labor, our entire struggle and all our victories. Cast into space with sufficient force, it will passively and obediently transport our cherished idea, our last act of will, across immeasurable distances.

"What could be more natural than this thought? Was it not the ether itself that created our first bond with those worlds, bringing us the rays of their suns like vague tidings from a distant life?

"I can announce to you that our efforts have been successful. Out of the most durable material provided by nature we have prepared millions of giant projectiles. Each is a faithful copy of our testament, consisting of thin, rolled sheets covered with artistic images and simple signs that can easily be deciphered by any intelligent being. These projectiles have been positioned at different places on our planet, and for each of them we have calculated the direction and velocity that it will be given by the initial detonation. These calculations are very rigorous and have been checked hundreds of times. The missiles are bound to reach their destinations.

"As for the initial thrust, brothers, it will come in a few minutes. In the bowels of our planet we have collected an enormous mass of unstable matter whose atoms are destroyed in a split second as they explode, generating the most powerful of all natural forces. In a few minutes our planet will be no more, and its fragments will be cast out into infinite space along with our dead bodies and our living cause.

"Brothers, let us joyfully welcome this moment, when the greatness of death will fuse with the greatest act of creation, the moment which will conclude our life only to pass its soul on to our brothers, whoever they may be!"

The cry incarnating the single thought and feeling of all echoed through the hall:

"To our brothers, whoever they may be!"

A moment later Menni's vision was sucked after everything else into a hurricane of fire and light, leaving only this same thought resounding within him:

"To our brothers, whoever they may be!"

. . . .

4. Sunrise

When Menni awoke less than an hour remained until sunrise.

"Haven't you slept at all, Nella? Now I must get dressed and write a few more words to the President and the government . . ."

The dawn was burning in the sky, and its rays shone through the bars on the window. Menni had dressed and lay again on the bed. Nella sat beside him, looking at him attentively, greedily. She had been able to see him so little.

"Sing me a song, Nella dearest."

"This will be a song for you alone. It is also about you, Menni."

The walls of the prison had heard many songs of anguish and hope through the years, but it is doubtful whether they had ever echoed such a pure, beautiful voice full of such emotion . . .

While yet a youth of lusty passion,
You gave your love all to the cause;
Where fate once ruled and blindly fashioned,
Your will and thought now wrote the laws.

Creator, leader, man of honor,
You found new worlds yet unexplored;
Through toil and strife you led us onward
O'er paths no man had tread before.

But triumph cost you untold anguish,
For with your freedom forced to part
You lay alone for years and languished,
And pain and sorrow pierced your heart.

You waited; and though still his captive,
The craven foe shrank back in fear.
The New Life dawned, in joy and rapture
Its mighty song rang loud and clear.

Life gave you love both warm and tender,
In triumph proved your ally true.
Your proud heart softened and surrendered—
Embracing life, you loved it too.

Alas! You could not break the power
Of iron will and logic cold;
You could not be life's chosen lover—
And then the fateful bell did toll.

And so, lest life be stayed or hampered,
You leave the ranks; your struggle ends.
The warrior's blade for battle tempered
Can sometimes break, but never bend.

You bore your burdens gladly, lightly;
You shoulder this one now as well.
Like life itself your cause was mighty—
In death your love proves greater still!

The last words were broken by sobs; the tears gushed in torrents from Nella's eyes, and she could not see Menni make a single swift movement . . .

Peacefully, joyfully, amid the kisses of the woman he loved, by sunrise he had fallen asleep, murmuring the words: "Nella . . . Netti . . . Victory!"

Epilogue

Menni's death untied many knots. It dealt a heavy blow to his enemies, disproving their cries about his monarchistic ambitions and immediately putting them in the position of slanderers who had been exposed by the facts. The question of the "Project dictatorship" fell away at the same time, as Netti was not at all interested in such power for himself. A Central Project Board was organized from among Menni's former colleagues. Netti, its chairman, took complete charge of technical matters. He wielded considerable influence; thanks to him, relations between the Central Board and the unions were peaceful for almost ten years. Netti himself understood very well, however, that such a situation was only temporary, and he used these years to elaborate in detail on the plan of the Great Project so that it could continue when the time had come for him to go.

Little by little the staff of Project Administration changed. Some died, others retired, still others transferred to other posts. Finally Netti found himself in the minority. An industrial crisis broke out, and, encouraged by the ruling party, the Administration decided to take advantage of it to worsen labor conditions. Netti immediately resigned and threw himself into organizing the struggle against this encroachment. The crisis was considerably aggravated by a gigantic strike that stopped the Great Project, the energetic offensive of the workers' party against the government, and uprisings in several different places. In view of such enormous difficulties, the ruling circles decided to retreat for the time being. But from this moment on there were no longer any ambiguities in class ideologies, and the rupture of the proletariat with the entire existing social order became definitive.

At about that time Nella died. It was almost as if she had been waiting to do so until another young and beautiful woman with clear radiant eyes had replaced her at Netti's side. The workers loved Nella, calling her simply "Mother." Hundreds of thousands marched in her funeral procession and strewed flowers over her grave. On the evening of the day of her burial Arri also passed away.

Leaving his work as an engineer, Netti directed all his scientific research toward fulfilling his old plan of transforming science so as to make it accessible to the working class. An entire school of cultural revolutionaries formed around him. A number of his pupils—some of them were from working-class backgrounds while others had abandoned the opposing camp of young scholars—worked together with him on the famous *Encyclopedia of Labor*, from which the proletariat drew both guidance and inspiration in its later struggle for ideological unity.

It was while working on this project that Netti made his greatest discovery and laid the foundations of Universal Organizational Science.* He sought to simplify and unify scientific methods, and to this end he studied and compared the most disparate approaches applied by man in his learning and labor. Netti found that the two spheres were very intimately related, that theoretical methods derived entirely from practical ones, and that all of them could be reduced to a few simple schemes. When he then compared these schemes with various organic combinations in nature and with the means by which nature creates her stable and developing systems, he was once again struck by a number of similarities and coincidences. Finally he arrived at the following conclusion: no matter how different the various elements of the Universe—electrons, atoms, things, people, ideas, planets, stars—and regardless of the considerable differences in their combinations, it is possible to establish a small number of general methods by which any of these elements joins with another, both in spontaneous natural processes and in human activity. Netti clearly defined three basic "universal organizational methods." His pupils continued his work, scrutinizing and developing his conclusions in more detail. Thus was born Universal Science, which soon embraced the entire organizational experience of mankind. The philosophy of former times was nothing but a vague presentiment of this science, while the laws governing nature, social life, and thought that had been discovered by the different disciplines turned out to be individual manifestations of its principles.

From this time on the solution of the most complicated organizational questions became the task not of a talented individual or genius, but of a scientific analysis that resembled the mathematical calculations used to solve problems of practical mechanics. Thanks to this, when the time came for the radical reformation of the entire social order, even the most serious difficulties of the new organization could be overcome relatively easily and quite systematically. Just as natural science had earlier served as a tool of scientific technique, now Universal Science became a tool in the scientific construction of social life as a whole. Even before this period, however, it had found widespread application in developing the

---

*This refers to Bogdanov's own system of Tectology.

organizations of the working class and preparing them for the final, decisive struggle.

Although he lived to be an old man, Netti witnessed only the first battles of this struggle, which continued for half a century. His children were not outstanding people, but neither were they a disgrace to the memory of their great forebears. They fought just as honestly and bravely for the cause of humanity.

A MARTIAN
STRANDED ON EARTH

Published as a supplement to the second (sixth) edition of *Red Star* in 1924, the poem outlines the content of a third novel which Bogdanov planned but never completed. A Martian has reached Earth but is unable to return to his native planet, where mankind has attained a superior level of communist civilization.

A MARTIAN
STRANDED ON EARTH

Our ship plunged and crashed against Earth's solid face.
My comrades are all dead and gone.
There is no return from this damnable place,
This cruel planet is my home from now on.

In the bottomless night, glowing brightly out there
Is Mars, my native red star.
But the pull of Earth is heavy to bear
And its atmosphere weighs on my heart.

The choice is a grave one—from this life depart
Where all but outrages my view,
Taking with me a dream of my own native Mars
Where reason and brotherhood rule?

Or bear this deep anguish and tormenting pain
For a life that is alien to me,
For a life that wretchedly gropes on in vain
Toward happiness, seeking to be free?

Yes, people—it may seem that the difference is small
Between them and my own Martian race,
But their hearts and their souls are not ours at all,
And I am no friend of their ways.

The harmony of life is outside their ken.
Though their souls swarm with hazy ideas,
The inherited past is the lord of these men;
It has ruled them for so many years.

Their infantile babble and rapacious desires
Veil all but a rare flash or spark

Of other dreams and passions that vaguely aspire
To a culture that glimmers afar.

But then once again, like a barrier of steel
—Invisible, but most surely there—
The difference in nature between them and me
Springs up, and I'm plunged in despair.

I yearn for a union with life proud and free,
For fraternity sacred and pure,
But this shadowy world chills my heart as I see
The tragedy I'm doomed to endure.

But then I hear Science, whose voice sounds on high
From my home in the sky far away:
"They too are the children of almighty Life,
Your younger blood brothers are they.

"You are older than they, but you scaled the same stairs
Toward consciousness, knowledge, and light.
Your path was as brutal and wretched as theirs
And as often was lost in the night.

"It was violent and raw and drenched through in gore,
And by vileness and greed was it stained,
But such are the roads to ideals, and what's more,
They are paved with illusions and pain."

My poor weary heart listens meekly and feels:
Yes—this, then, is the fate sealed for me—
To labor and struggle in this bleak rocky field
For the future that one day will be.

For the bright day when man will grope blindly no more
But will see how his task must be done;
If he chooses the path that leads straight to the core
He and life can then fuse into one.

When space, yes, and time have been conquered by man
And the elements and death are but words,
Our two races will merge into one mighty clan
Of builders of brilliant new worlds.

So this is the mission for which I've been spared;
I must banish despair from my breast
And serenely press on to life's border, and there
Leave behind me this one last behest:

Take a word of farewell when the victory is won
To my loved ones on the star of my birth—
Tell them their brother is glad to have come
To this wondrous young planet called Earth!

BOGDANOV'S INNER MESSAGE

Loren R. Graham

Alexander Bogdanov's novels *Red Star* and *Engineer Menni* were popular illustrations of his theories of politics and philosophy.[1] *Red Star* portrayed developed socialism on the planet Mars and it opposed socialist humanity and cooperation to capitalist cruelty and individualism. The hero, Leonid, held out the hope that socialism could soon be created in Russia. Published almost ten years before the Russian Revolution of 1917, the book was popular among Russian radicals both before and after that date. *Engineer Menni*, published five years later, in 1913, was based on the success of the earlier work and portrayed the history of Mars during the period of capitalism that preceded the events narrated in *Red Star*. Let us look more closely at these novels, first *Red Star* and then *Engineer Menni*, in an attempt to understand more fully Bogdanov's intentions.

The primary ideological goal of *Red Star*, the encouragement of revolution, is clear. However, the novel contains a secondary message which has not been noticed, yet which is striking and prescient. Indeed, the novel is an example of how the readers of a utopia may consider it a success yet not understand what the author meant when he wrote it.

Was *Red Star* merely an effort by Bogdanov to present the Russian workers with a visible model for their revolutionary strivings? At first glance Mars *does* appear to serve this role, to be a socialist utopia, pure and simple. Many of the goals of European socialists have been realized there: all means of production are common property; class conflict has disappeared; money is no longer used; education is based on collectivist principles; the economy is scientifically and centrally planned, a task accomplished with the help of a computer center; artistic life has been reorganized around the needs of the society as a whole rather than around great individuals; political hierarchy and authoritarianism have disappeared (interestingly, there is no mention of a ruling communist party, nor of any political parties); violence, wars, and racism are similarly absent; medical science has advanced to such a degree that people live indefinitely long lives; the workers of Mars have escaped the stultifying effects of the division of labor by switching occupations voluntarily whenever they wish; furthermore, they have become inherently fair-minded and altruistic, they have dropped all the superfluous conventions of bourgeois society, and they treat each other honestly and sincerely. In sum, Martian society seems to be an inspiring model of socialism, one particularly instructive for Earthlings still struggling with the last phases of exploitative capitalism.

And yet if one penetrates beyond this obvious message of social well-being on Mars, one finds that Bogdanov has given Mars another whole set of surprising characteristics that introduce elements of dystopia into his picture of socialism. When the Earthling Leonid remarks to one of his Martian friends that Mars seems so happy and peaceful, the reply is, "Happy? Peaceful? Where did you get that impression?" And the Martian then tells Leonid of the multitude of problems facing socialist Mars. Many of the industries are so dangerous that they must be kept underground; the population is growing so rapidly that food shortages and even famines are predicted within several decades; natural resources are rapidly being exhausted, as is the radioactive matter that is the main source of energy; in order to continue to utilize their diminishing minerals the Martians have been forced to destroy their beloved forests and degrade their environment; the prolongation of life by advanced medicine has resulted in the problem of forcing people to decide when to end their own lives, and suicide clinics are provided for that purpose.

The favorite form of drama on Mars is tragedy. Even some of the blessings of socialism have brought their unfortunate reverse sides: the elimination of the division of labor has increased the accident rate in Martian factories, as workers shift from one workplace to another, constantly using machines with which they are not familiar. And nervous disorders have not disappeared, but instead are one of the two most common forms of illness. Most surprising of all, instead of colonialism being merely one of the last stages of decadent capitalism, as Marxists usually believed, socialist Mars has created a Colonial Group in its government and is preparing to create colonies on either Earth or Venus, or both.

Why does this pessimism show up so clearly in Bogdanov's writings? Was he secretly out of sympathy with the Marxism to which he professed allegiance? Was he an early apostle of the dangers of socialism, an antecedent of such writers as Orwell?

A careful study of Bogdanov's life and writings shows that, contrary to the implication of these questions, he was a sincere, albeit idiosyncratic, Marxist who was committed to the construction of socialism. But he believed that even after socialism had been successfully created, civilization would be plagued by a whole series of problems, which we would now probably recognize as problems of "postindustrial societies." Bogdanov was brilliantly prescient in sketching out issues that would face all industrialized nations two generations after he first conceived them: the dangers of atomic energy, the problems of preserving the environment, the dilemmas of biomedical ethics, and the shortages of natural resources and food. Indeed, Bogdanov believed that nature was a far more implacable foe than the class enemy. The capitalists would eventually be defeated, but nature never would be; as one of his Martian heroes observed, "the tighter our humanity closes ranks to conquer nature, the tighter the elements close theirs to avenge the victory."

We begin to see, then, that a proper appreciation of Bogdanov's importance requires that he be regarded as much more than a Russian revolutionary trying to rally the spirits of a discouraged proletariat. He was a deeply original thinker about the relationship of science and society. He would have fitted well into one of the university programs formed in the United States and Europe in the late seventies on "Science, Technology and Society."

In one of the most interesting passages in *Red Star* a Martian tries to explain to Leonid why the problems which plague Mars are so incomprehensible to Earthlings. The Martian observes that the reason these issues are "beyond your understanding is because in your world they are eclipsed by others which are more direct and obvious." These more obvious problems are the struggles between classes, groups, and individuals. Thus, Bogdanov believed that only after the proletarian revolution had been successful and had eliminated struggles among human beings would they see that a more daunting battle still lay ahead: the struggle of united humanity to avoid being overwhelmed by the by-products of its own technological successes. No wonder that Lenin had his doubts about whether Bogdanov's writings were adequately inspiring!

The utopian novels *Red Star* and *Engineer Menni* were based on philosophical principles which Bogdanov worked out in detail in technical articles and books. Understanding Bogdanov, then, requires looking at these other works and then returning to his novels about the Red Planet. We will find in his technical treatises two basic ideas that influenced all of Bogdanov's work and life: the first was an explanation of why people disagree on so many topics, the second, an effort to show how, despite these disagreements, understanding is still possible. These two ideas—the one pessimistic, the other optimistic—were imbedded in Bogdanov's personality, driving him alternately to revolutionary hopefulness and individualistic despair.

Bogdanov's two major theoretical works were *Empiriomonizm* (1904–1907) and *Tektologiia* (1913–1929). The first was in process at the time of the writing of *Red Star,* and the second was similarly underway at the moment of the writing of the sequel, *Engineer Menni;* the underlying principles of both show up clearly in the novels. In *Empiriomonizm* Bogdanov maintained that the key to knowledge lay in the principles of its organization, not in a search for "reality" or "essence." Neither materialism nor idealism, therefore, was an appropriate or useful epistemological position. Bogdanov preferred to follow the path of Ernst Mach and Richard Avenarius in denying the dualism of sense perceptions and physical objects, but he believed that they had not gone far enough in explaining the existence of two different realms of experience, the subjective (e.g., emotions and impulses) and the objective (e.g., sight, sound, smell). Bogdanov attempted to unite these realms in a new philosophical system, empiriomonism, by deriving the physical world from "socially organized experience" and the mental world from "individually organized experience." The two worlds revealed two different "biological-organizational tendencies."

Why, asked Bogdanov, do people differ so radically about the second realm, the sphere of individually organized values? The answer, he thought, was that people are torn apart by conflicts that derive from differences in class, race, sex, language, or nationality, by specialization arising from technical knowledge, and by relations of dominance and subordination of all kinds. If these conflicts could be overcome, he continued, a new consciousness would emerge, as a result of which people would be in much greater agreement about values than ever before.

Bogdanov believed that, in fastening upon class conflict as the key to explaining social strife, Marxism was a great liberating force, but that class difference was only one of several sources of social struggle. He wished to generalize Marxism, to show that the framework of Marxism could be widened to include the other sources of social disruption as well. He paid particular attention to male-female relationships, noticing that women and men on Mars were much more physically similar than on Earth, and concluded that on earth "it is the enslavement of women in the home and the feverish struggle for survival on the part of the men which ultimately account for the physical discrepancies between them." But to Bogdanov male-female differences were just one of many possible sources of social conflict. To him, any relationship of domination and subordination, whether based on sex, race, class, nationality, or possession of technical knowledge, was also appropriate for criticism within a broader Marxism.

So much for the sources of strife among people. How did Bogdanov believe that these differences could be overcome? In developing his concept of "tectology" Bogdanov tried to find through structural analogies and models the organizational principles that would unite under one conceptual scheme "the most disparate phenomena" in the organic and inorganic worlds. Tectology to Bogdanov was a potential metascience both of nature and of society, a unifying concept that would allow human beings torn apart by strife to find a common language. Since the sources of strife were larger than the merely economic, the common language must be larger than traditional Marxism, although it would include Marxism as a special case.

All objects which exist, he wrote, can be distinguished in terms of the degree of their organization. According to Bogdanov the key to understanding the world is organizational analysis. As Netti explained in the epilogue to *Engineer Menni*, "no matter how different the various elements of the universe—electrons, atoms, things, people, ideas, planets, stars—and regardless of the considerable differences in their combinations, it is possible to establish a small number of general methods by which any of these elements joins with another." Entities on higher levels of organization possess properties that are greater than the sum of their parts. Living beings and automatic machines are dynamically structured complexes in which "bi-regulators" provide for the maintenance of order. Recent commentators on Bogdanov have pointed repeatedly to the apparent prefiguring here of the concept of cybernetic feedback.[2] Bogdanov called for the application of concepts of bi-regulation and a degree of organization in his "universal organizational science" that would embrace the biological and social worlds in the way in which mathematics had described classical mechanics. When Bogdanov called his system "universal" he meant not only that it was equally applicable to all complicated systems, natural and social; he meant also that it was the common language that might unite individuals torn apart by their "individually organized experience."

Although Bogdanov struggled manfully to complete his universal philosophical system of tectology, eventually writing a three-volume treatise on the subject, one senses that he realized that it was never complete. He was more successful at describing the issues that divided human beings than he was in developing an intellectual scheme that would allow them to unite again with a common language. Hence, Bogdanov's optimistic struggle to find universal understanding is periodically disrupted by his pessimistic realization that it will never quite happen, that the divisive forces are too strong, that history—on Earth at least—will continue its bloody, barbaric path.

When Bogdanov wrote *Red Star* he was trying to explain to himself why his task was so difficult, why he so often despaired of its completion. He took the path of maintaining that Earth was an incredibly unfortunate place to live if one dreamed of creating a new socialist civilization in which strife would disappear. Compared to Mars, Earth was violent, fratricidal, divided. In explaining this unfortunate uniqueness of Earth, Bogdanov analytically followed the evolutionary naturalism that was so popular among many Russian revolutionaries. Science and nature lay behind the social brutality of the residents of Earth. The planet Earth was closer to the sun and larger in size than Mars, and therefore life on Earth differed from life on Mars in several important ways. First of all, the warm rays of the sun infused life on Earth with more energy and a faster rate of metabolism. Second, the large size of Earth, compared to Mars, meant that the force of gravity on Earth was stronger, causing Earthlings by necessity to evolve with greater physical strength to counter this binding force.

As a result of their rapid metabolism and physical force, Earthlings, compared to Martians, were irascible, even violent. They loved more deeply and they fought harder. At one point Netti turned to Leonid and remarked, "Your love is like murder." And Leonid learned that even during the period of the socialist revolution on Mars the struggles between the socialists and the capitalists had never been very violent; the Martian capitalists, unlike their brethren on Earth, gave up rather easily. Martians and Earthlings were simply very different in terms of their basic constitutions; a physician of the seventeenth century, classifying humans in terms of the Galenic humors, would have observed that Earthlings were choleric, Martians phlegmatic. And behind these differences lay natural forces.

But the physical violence of Earthlings was just the beginning of their misfortunes. They were hopelessly divided among themselves linguistically and nationally. In explaining this linguistic diversity Bogdanov employed science to the same effect that Earthlings used the Old Testament story of the Tower of Babel. Genesis tell us that God punished the builders of the Tower for their presumption by confusing their tongues. Bogdanov writes that because the planet Earth was much larger than Mars, and because it was divided by great oceans, the humans who inhabited it split into groups that could not physically stay in contact. The various groups and tribes developed instead into separate language communities, and, eventually, nations. When socialism arrived on the historical scene and tried to unite the inhabitants of Earth under a common banner, the effort often foundered on the nationalistic wars that the Earthlings continued to support against each other. In this regard, as in so many others, Mars was different. Easily bound together by communication and transportation even in its early history, Mars had remained an organic whole and had never been plagued by great wars.

All of this seems to add up to a heavy condemnation of Earthlings in comparison to Martians. Yet Bogdanov was too subtle to leave the situation so one-sidedly in favor of the Martians. (Or was even he infected by a bit of patriotic loyalty to his home planet?) The highlight of *Red Star* is the debate between Sterni and Netti over whether the Martians should exterminate the Earthlings in their struggle to find more natural resources. Sterni takes the position that Earthlings are so hopelessly malformed by their evolutionary past, and so irrevocably prejudiced by nationalism, that even the Earth's socialist minority would never be able to find a way to work together amicably with their fellow socialists on Mars. If the

Martians try to utilize the natural resources of Earth in place of their own exhausted resources, the Earthlings will rise up in rebellion, refusing to recognize that Martian civilization is vastly superior to their own. The Martians will get involved in a hopeless guerrilla war waged against them by the ferocious Earthlings. The superior technology of the Martians will mean that the Earthlings cannot win this struggle, but the militant spirit of the Earthlings will guarantee an indefinite and costly war. The only way to avoid this ordeal, said Sterni, is to wipe them out in advance with death rays, and then use the riches of Earth to build a more humane socialism on Mars.

The speech of Leonid's lover Netti in reply to Sterni is the most moving section of the entire novel. Netti's argument even reminds one of recent ecological treatises on the importance of diversity in nature; Netti's sympathy for Earthlings resembles contemporary ecologists' arguments for preservation of dolphins or whales. She reprimands Sterni for proposing to eliminate "an entire individual type of life, a type which we can never resurrect or replace." Sterni, she says, "would drain forever this stormy but beautiful ocean of life." He does not recognize, she continues, that "the Earthlings are not the same as we. They and their civilization are not simply lower and weaker than ours—they are *different*." There may even be some advantages in the differences; although the presence of many languages on Earth enforces national prejudices and splinters understanding, this diversity of means of expression also has "liberated notions from the tyranny of the words by which they are expressed."

One should remember that Mars and Earth in this story are not simply two different planets; they also represent, in accordance with Marxism, the two successive historical epochs of capitalism and socialism. Within the orthodox Marxist framework, there is no doubt that socialism is viewed as superior. But when we see the tolerance and love of heterogeneity that Bogdanov expresses through Netti, can we wonder about how he will react after the Russian Revolution to the campaign to wipe out "the vestiges of capitalism"? Leonid learns from the Martians that they have retained, because of inherent esthetic attraction, forms of literature that originated before the arrival of socialism; one Martian comments that "if rhyme really is of feudal provenance, then the same may be said of many other good and beautiful things." Bogdanov's intellectual colleague Lunacharsky wept when he heard that the victorious Bolshevik forces were shelling the architectural and artistic treasures in the tsarist Kremlin.[3] Bogdanov was similarly tortured by his simultaneous commitments to the new age of socialism and his respect and admiration for human creation in the diversity of all its forms, including that of capitalism.

But it is not only communication between historical epochs that concerns Bogdanov; he is also deeply interested in how individuals communicate. If, as Marx believed, social being determines consciousness, how can two humans with completely different backgrounds (for example, capitalism and socialism) ever communicate with each other in mutually understandable terms?

Leonid serves as Bogdanov's example of how difficult it is for an individual to live in two dramatically different epochs. The Martians who landed on Earth searched everywhere for a person who could "serve as a living link between the human races of Earth and Mars." At first they despaired, but finally they found Leonid, a Russian revolutionary. They considered him to be the most advanced Earthling, in terms of social views, whom they had seen. Yet when Leonid arrived in Mars he had great psychological difficulties in adjusting to life there. When he studied Martian literature he found that "its images seemed simple and clear, yet somehow they remained alien to me." When he learned that his lover Netti had been married to several men at the same time, Leonid, despite his belief in free love, reacts with the cry, "Why then this agitated bewilderment, this incomprehensible pain that made me want to scream and laugh at the same time? Was it that I did not know how to *feel* as I *thought?*" When Leonid tried to learn the principles of Martian science his response was: "Their scientific methods bewildered me. I learned them mechanically . . . [but] I did not really understand them. . . . I was like those mathematicians of the seventeenth century whose static thought was organically incapable of comprehending the living dynamism of infinitely small quantities." When Leonid tried to work alongside Martians in a clothing factory he found that he lacked "the *culture of concentration*" and could not keep up with their work tempo. He was humiliated when they constantly had to help him, even with simple tasks.

The difficulty of communicating across this chasm provides much of the tension in both *Red Star* and its sequel, *Engineer Menni*. It explains Leonid's nervous breakdown while living on Mars; his murder of Sterni; the difficulties he, as an Earthling, has in loving the Martian Netti; and the painfulness of his recovery while in the hospital back on Earth. It also underlies the "wrecking" activities of some engineers trained before the Martian revolution, people who are constitutionally incapable of adjusting to the new socialist order. (The "wrecker" phenomenon was an uncanny prediction of later Soviet attitudes toward bourgeois engineers, including their prosecution.)[4]

The incommensurability of language in different epochs is a particularly strong element in the novel *Engineer Menni*. Here in one family, the ancient ducal house of Aldo, three successive generations of strong men—Ormen, Menni, and Netti—fall into three completely different historical epochs—feudalism, capitalism, socialism—and are incapable of understanding each other. Old Duke Ormen Aldo was a convinced feudalist who could not adjust to the successful republican revolution that swept

Mars. At first he pretended to go along with the new order, but at the first opportunity he rose up in rebellion and tried to reestablish the old aristocracy, just as Henri La Rochejacquelein of the Vendée in France had done after the French Revolution. And of course Ormen failed to turn back the clock. Ormen's son, Menni, received a republican education in isolation from his father and became Mars's greatest engineer. In politics, Menni was equally opposed to the surviving feudal elements in Mars and to the rising proletariat. At first Menni was a great success, but gradually he, too, was overtaken by events. The workers turned against him because of his antipathy to the unions. Menni's son, Netti, raised in isolation as a worker, was a convinced defender of socialism, a viewpoint that Menni never could understand. As Netti said to his father, "You have a *different* consciousness. . . . It is the consciousness of the class which preceded the proletariat."

The poignant relationship between Menni and Netti reveals Bogdanov's ambiguity about the harsh judgments inherent in class conflict. It is obvious that Menni and Netti love each other deeply, but the labor leader Arri correctly observes that "Menni and Netti are natural enemies. . . . No matter how they try, life will bring them into conflict, violent conflict. They love and respect each other very much, but that will only make their clash the more painful." Bogdanov entitled one of the chapters describing Menni's and Netti's conversations "Two Kinds of Logic," illustrating the unbridgeable gap between these representatives of different classes, and Menni tells his son "Your words are all simple and clear, yet your thoughts remain strange and incomprehensible to me."

Toward the end of this second novel, Menni is called by history to perform the reactionary role of his father, Duke Ormen, to revolt against developing socialism just as his father revolted against capitalism. The Vampire who comes to him in a vision urges "You know what you must do. *You must once again become yourself.* . . . The idyll with the unions will not last much longer. . . . It will mean breaking with Netti and Nella, a bitter struggle, a great sacrifice. Yes, but also a great victory!"

Menni knows that the Vampire is correct in his assertion that Menni cannot become a true socialist; he irretrievably belongs to the previous order. The Vampire exults in this knowledge, crying: "Hear the voice of a sovereign! . . . You are mine, you are mine, you are mine!" Menni also knows that cooperation with his socialist son Netti has now gone beyond the breaking point. But in a desperate act inspired by love for Netti and Nella, Menni refuses to play the role of his father, and defeats the iron logic of history in the only way it can be defeated, by committing suicide. His lover Nella sings to him at his death, "Lest life be stayed or hampered/You leave the ranks; your struggle ends."

Russian radical readers of Bogdanov recognized the best elements of the prerevolutionary Russian technical intelligentsia in *Engineer Menni.*

And they saw other familiar elements in the novel. The great economist "Xarma" is unmistakably Marx. The debate between Menni and Netti over whether a minority of workers belonging to radical unions should be recognized as the sole representatives of the working class was a raging discussion in Russian left-wing circles. The suspicion of engineers by workers was a current in prerevolutionary Russia that would continue after the Revolution, and would be cruelly manipulated by Stalin. And Netti's opinion that a person's political beliefs were often hidden from view was endemic among Russian revolutionaries, always suspicious of counterrevolutionary conspiracies. As Netti observed, "Here I am, I meet different people, live with them, trust them, even love them, but do I always know *who they really are?*"

In *Engineer Menni* Bogdanov illustrated more fully than in *Red Star* his concern about the role that science would play during a revolution. Does knowledge lead to freedom, or is it just one more weapon in the hands of the upper-class oppressors, who have the advantage of better education? The workers who are trying to figure out whether a canal must be dug through the dangerous Rotten Bogs or along another path are confused and frustrated by the differing arguments on the subject given by the "specialists," many of whom they do not trust politically. A young worker asks why workers always have to *believe* specialists. "Isn't this slavery, the worst form of slavery? What must we do so that we ourselves can *know and see,* and not just constantly believe?"

This suspicion of bourgeois specialists would come out strongly after the Russian Revolution. Perhaps it was expressed most graphically by Alexandra Kollontai, a leader of the Workers' Opposition, who asserted that the technical specialists were "remnants of the past, by their entire nature closely, unalterably bound to the bourgeois system that we aim to destroy."[5]

Bogdanov was committed both to revolution and to science, and he struggled to find a way to have the first without throwing out the second. In *Engineer Menni* the proletarian engineer Netti explained, "Thus far science is the weapon of our enemies. We will triumph when we have made it our weapon. . . . The proletariat must master it by changing it." The new science transformed by the workers would be "Universal Organizational Science," in other words Bogdanov's favorite intellectual creation, tectology.

Bogdanov's novels tell us much about Russia at the time of their composition, the last decade of tsarism, but they also may tell us something about the strange story of Bogdanov's death. In a 1928 obituary entitled "The Tragedy of a Great Mind," his old friend and fellow revolutionary P. N. Lepeshinsky wrote that Leonid in the utopian novels was the "alter ego," even the "twin," of Bogdanov himself, and that the clue to Bogdanov's life and death could be found in his literary creations.

Lepeshinsky also remarked that the "walls of the institute" where Bog-danov spent his last days may have been "the witness of a secret Bogdanov drama," the last chapter of a life that united reality and literature.[6]

Bogdanov in the years of Soviet power stood aside from politics and immersed himself in scientific and literary activities. One of his major concerns was blood transfusion, a technique that became popular in World War I. To Bogdanov, blood transfusion acquired almost metaphys-ical overtones: it was a way to rejuvenate the exhausted human organism, and it was a symbol of the future of medicine in which the replacement of parts of the body would become routine. He created an institute for blood transfusion, and devoted himself to a series of experiments aimed at improving the technique.[7]

While Bogdanov, after the Russian Revolution, turned more and more toward science, he did not give up his literary aspirations. Indeed, he was planning a third book in the series of utopian novels that began with *Red Star.* A few years after the Revolution he wrote a poem, included in this volume, giving the outlines of the third book. The third novel would be, in a sense, the mirror image of *Red Star;* instead of revolving around an Earthling's attempt to adjust to life on Mars, it would concern the difficulties encountered by a Martian who tries to live on Earth.

In the poem, a Martian space ship crashes on Earth while attempting to land, and only one Martian survives. With his means of transportation destroyed, the Martian has no alternative but to adjust to terrestrial life. Yet he finds life on Earth to be so cruel and predatory that it is, for him, the same as hell. His faith that eventually the inhabitants of Earth will find the path to humane socialism such as that which exists on his native Mars is not enough to sustain him. Just as Leonid had fallen into melan-choly as he tried to comprehend life on Mars, so the shipwrecked Martian plunges into despair on Earth. The chasm separating incompatible modes of cognition that so preoccupied Bogdanov as a philosopher once again emerges in his literary work.

It seems likely that, metaphorically speaking, Bogdanov considered himself to be a shipwrecked Martian looking upon the crudities of Earthly life. He believed that his philosophical systems of empiriomonism and tectology gave him the sort of understanding that the members of an advanced socialist society like his fictional Mars possessed. In an intellec-tual sense, Bogdanov believed that he had already lived on Mars, but reality condemned him bodily to live on Earth before socialism was suc-cessfully created there. Early Soviet Russia was to him not socialism but that life "that wretchedly gropes on in vain / Toward happiness, seeking to be free."

In the late twenties, as Stalin gradually tightened his control over the Soviet Union, it became more and more difficult for a sensitive intellec-tual like Bogdanov to retain his faith that Russian socialism would ever find its way. He must have been haunted by the words he had put in the mouth of Sterni years earlier; Sterni had maintained that even if socialism begins to develop on Earth it will be "perverted deeply" and turn toward militarism because of its unfortunate environment.

Bogdanov must have felt like his hero Leonid in *Red Star* after he returned to Earth; Leonid found life there almost unbearable. He commented, "The new life is inaccessible to me, while I do not want the old one, to which I no longer belong either intellectually or emotionally." Leonid decided to join the revolutionary struggle, and Dr. Werner wrote that "by exposing himself to the dangers there he is evidently indirectly trying to commit suicide."

In real life in early 1928 some of the events described in the utopian novels seemed to be coming true in Stalinist Russia, but in a way that shocked Bogdanov. The secret police announced that it had discovered a counterrevolutionary conspiracy among the engineers of the coal mines in the Ukraine. Fifty-three engineers and technicians were to be brought to court under accusations punishable by death. Bogdanov must have seen in the looming Shakhty trial the grotesque perversion of the ideas in his novels.

On April 7, 1928, the day after a special plenum of the Central Committee of the Communist Party had been called by Stalin to consider the Shakhty conspiracy, Bogdanov conducted an experiment on himself that, as a physician, he well understood was likely to be fatal. He exchanged his own blood with that of a young student who was suffering from both malaria and tuberculosis. He continued making detailed observations on his own condition until the last minutes of his life. His colleagues were amazed by the nonchalance with which he approached death, loyal to the attitude of the Martian physician attending the "room for the dying" who remarked that death "was only death, and no more." (The student with whom Bogdanov exchanged blood, a man named Koldomasov, lives on in the Soviet Union to the present day.)[8]

Thus, Bogdanov's death bears a striking resemblance to that of Engineer Menni in Bogdanov's novel, who dreamed about the meaning of death just before his act of suicide. Menni's hope was that "the greatness of death will fuse with the greatest act of creation, the moment which will conclude our life only to pass its soul on to our brothers, whoever they may be!"

NOTES

1. No definitive intellectual biography of Bogdanov exists, and there is not even a complete bibliography of his voluminous works. Major works on him are listed here in the selected bibliography: see especially Grille 1966 and Jensen 1978; see also Jensen 1982, Haupt 1974, Vucinich 1976, Ballestrem 1969, Shcheglov 1937, and Utechin 1962. For an article emphasizing Bogdanov's importance in the history of science, see Graham 1977. Bogdanov wrote a short autobiography in *Entsiklopedicheskii slovar'*, XLI (1926).

2. Susiluoto 1982, Iakhot 1982, and Setrov 1967. I am grateful to Zenovia Sochor for drawing the Iakhot reference to my attention.

3. Not only did he weep, but, upon hearing of the destruction of St. Basil's and the Uspensky Cathedral, he resigned from the Bolshevik government. When he learned that the reports were false, he withdrew his resignation. See Fitzpatrick 1970, pp. 13–14.

4. Boris Souvarine wrote that the novel had a great influence on Bolshevik leaders, including Stalin. One cannot help but wonder if Stalin derived part of his suspicions of engineers as "bourgeois wreckers" from the novel. See Souvarine 1939, p. 504.

5. Kollontai 1968, p. 6.

6. Lepeshinsky 1928, p. 265.

7. Bogdanov 1927.

8. Interview with Bogdanov's son, A. A. Malinovsky, Moscow, 20 January 1983.

Selected Bibliography

Bogdanov and Related Matters

Bailes, Kendall. 1977. "Alexei Gastev and the Soviet Controversy over Taylorism," *Soviet Studies* 29/3 (July 1977).

Ballestrem, Karl. 1969. "Lenin and Bogdanov," *Studies in Soviet Thought* 9 (December 1969).

Bogdanov, A. A. (Aleksandr Aleksandrovich Malinovsky). 1904–07. *Empiriomonizm*, 3 vols. Moscow and St. Petersburg.

———. 1908. *Krasnaya zvezda*. St. Petersburg.

———. 1913. *Inzhener Menni*. Moscow.

———. 1913–1929. *Vseobshchaya organizatsionnaya nauka (Tektologiya)*, Parts 1–3. Moscow and St. Petersburg.

———. 1926. "Avtobiografiya," *Entsiklopedicheskii slovar'*, XLI, 29–34. 1926.

———. 1927. *God raboty Instituta perelivaniya krovi (1926–1927)*. Moscow.

Britikov, A. F. 1970. *Russkii Sovetskii nauchno-fantasticheskii roman*. Leningrad.

Brooks, Jeffrey. 1978. "Readers and Reading at the End of Tsarist Russia," in William M. Todd, ed., *Literature and Society in Imperial Russia*. Stanford: Stanford University Press.

Fetzer, Leland, ed. and tr. 1982. *Pre-Revolutionary Russian Science Fiction: An Anthology (Seven Utopias and a Dream)*. Ann Arbor, MI.: Ardis Publishers.

Fitzpatrick, Sheila. 1970. *The Commissariat of Enlightenment*. Cambridge: Cambridge University Press.

Graham, Loren R. 1977. "Alexander Bogdanov," *Dictionary of Scientific Biography*, Supplementary Volume. New York: Charles Scribner's Sons.

Gregg, Percy. 1880. *Across the Zodiac*. 2 vols. London.

Grille, Dietrich. 1966. *Lenins Rivale: Bogdanov und seine Philosophie*. Cologne: Verlag Wissenschaft und Politik.

Haupt, Georges. 1974. "Aleksandr Aleksandrovich Bogdanov (Malinovsky)," pp. 289–292 in G. Haupt and Jean-Jacques Marie, *Makers of the Russian Revolution*. Ithaca: Cornell University Press.

Iakhot, Iegoshua. 1982. "Gibel' tektologii Bogdanova—predshestvennitsy kibernetiki i sistemnoi teorii," in *SSSR: Vnutrennye protivorechiya* (No. 3, 1982), 227–273.

Ingold, Felix Philipp. 1978. *Literatur und Aviatik: europäische Flugdichtung 1909–27*. Basel.

Jensen, Kenneth. 1978. *Beyond Marx and Mach: Aleksandr Bogdanov's Philosophy of Living Experience*. Dordrecht: D. Reidel.

———. 1982. "Red Star: Bogdanov Builds a Utopia," *Studies in Soviet Thought* 23/1 (January 1982), 1–34.

Joravsky, David. 1961. *Soviet Marxism and Natural Science* (1917–1932). London: Routledge and Kegan Paul.

Khazanova, V. E. 1980. *Sovetskaya arkhitektura pervoi pyatiletki: problemy goroda budushchego.* Moscow.

Kline, George. 1969. "Nietzschean Marxism in Russia," pp. 166–183 in F. J. Adelmann, ed., *Demythologizing Marxism.* The Hague: Martinus Nijhoff.

Kollontai, Alexandra. 1969. "The Roots of the Workers' Opposition," *Solidarity Pamphlet.* London.

Lasswitz, Kurd. 1971. *Two Planets.* H. Rudnik, tr. Carbondale: Southern Illinois University Press. Translation of *Auf zwei Planeten.*

Lepeshinsky, P. 1928. "Tragediya krupnogo uma," *Ogonëk* 17 (22 April 1928), 265.

Lowell, Percival. 1906. *Mars and its Canals.* London.

McGuire, Patrick. 1977. *Red Stars: Political Aspects of Soviet Science Fiction.* Ph.D. dissertation, Princeton University.

Omelchenko, A. P. 1908. *Svobodnaya lyubov i semya.* St. Petersburg.

Scherrer, Jutta. 1978. "Les écoles du Parti de Capri et de Bologna," *Cahiers du monde russe et soviétique,* 3/19 (1978), 258–284.

Setrov, M. I. 1967. "Ob obshchikh elementakh tektologii A. Bogdanova, kibernetiki i teorii sistem," *Uchënye zapiski kafedr obshchestvennykh nauk vuzov goroda Leningrada* (No. 8, 1967), 49–60.

Shcheglov, A. V. 1937. *Borba lenina protiv bogdanovskoi revizii marksizma.* Moscow.

Souvarine, Boris. 1939. *Stalin: A Critical Survey of Bolshevism.* New York: Longmans, Green and Company.

Susiluoto, Ilmari. 1982. *The Origins and Development of Systems Thinking in the Soviet Union: Political and Philosophical Controversies from Bogdanov and Bukharin to Present-Day Reevaluations.* Helsinki.

Suvin, Darko. 1971. "The Utopian Tradition in Russian Science Fiction," *Modern Language Review* 66/1 (1971), 139–159.

———. 1979. *Metamorphoses of Science Fiction.* New Haven: Yale University Press.

Utechin, S. V. 1962. "Philosophy and Society: Alexander Bogdanov," pp. 117–125 in L. Labedz, ed., *Revisionism.* New York: Praeger.

Vechnoe solntse: russkaya sotsialnaya utopiya i nauchnaya fantastika (vtoraya polovina XIX veka-nachalo XX veka), pp. 248–379. Moscow. (Bogdanov, *Krasnaya zvezda.*)

Von Braun, Werner, and Frederick Ordway. 1969. *History of Rocketry and Space Travel,* rev. ed. New York.

Vucinich, Alexander. 1976. *Social Thought in Tsarist Russia: The Quest for a General Science of Society, 1861–1917.* Chicago: University of Chicago Press.

Williams, Robert C. 1980. "Collective Immortality: The Syndicalist Origins of Proletarian Culture, 1905–1910," *Slavic Review* 3/39 (September 1980), 389–402.

Utopias and Works of Science Fiction in Russian 1895–1915 (in chronological order)

V. N. Chikolev. 1895. *Ne byl, no i ne vydumka—elektricheskii raskaz* (Fiction but not Fantasy—an Electric Tale). St. Petersburg.

SELECTED BIBLIOGRAPHY 257

K. E. Tsiolkovsky. 1896. *Vne zemli: nauchno-fantasticheskaya povest* (Beyond the Earth: A Science Fiction Story). Moscow, 1958.
A. I. Krasnitsky. 1900. *Za pripodnyatoyu zavesoi: fantasticheskaya povest o delakh budushchago (XX vek)*. (Behind Upraised Curtains: A Fantastic Story about Things in the Future (the 20th Century)). St. Petersburg.
L. B. Afanasev. 1901. "Puteshestvie na Mars" (Journey to Mars). *Niva* 1 (January 1901), 275–330, and *Niva* 3 (March 1901), 483–534.
August Bebel. (1905). *Budushchee obshchestvo* (The Society of the Future). Translated from German (1905). Moscow. 1918.
Atlanticus (pseud. of Karl Ballod). 1906. *Gosudarstvo budushchago* (The Future State). Translated from German. Preface by Karl Kautsky. Moscow.
N. Fëdorov. 1906 *Vecher v 2217 godu* (An Evening in the Year 2217). St. Petersburg.
I. Morskoi. 1907 *Anarkhisty budushchago—(Moskva cherez 20 let: fantasticheskii roman)* (Anarchists of the Future—Moscow in 20 Years: A Novel of Fantasy). Moscow.
Jack London. 1908. *Zheleznaya pyata* (The Iron Heel). Moscow, 1918.
V. Semënov. 1908. *Tsaritsa mira: roman-fantaziya* (Empress of the World: A Fantasy Novel). St. Petersburg.
N. A. Morozov. 1910. *Na granitse nevedomago* (On the Verge of the Unknown). Moscow.
V. Ya. Bryusov. 1910 *Zemnaya os* (Axis of the Equator). 2nd. ed. Stories, 1901–1907. Moscow.
A. Ossendovsky. 1915. *Zhenshchiny, vostavshiya i pobezhdënnyya: fantasticheskaya povest* (Women Insurgent and Repressed: A Fantastic Story). Moscow.